COGNITIVE BEHAVIOUR THERAPY WITH OLDER PEOPLE

Ken Laidlaw
Department of Psychiatry, University of Edinburgh, UK

Larry W. Thompson
Pacific Graduate School of Psychology and Stanford
University School of Medicine, USA

Leah Dick-Siskin
Psychological Services & Geriatric Psychiatry Division,
Hillside Hospital, North Shore–Long Island Jewish
Health System, USA

Dolores Gallagher-Thompson
Department of Psychiatry and Behavioral Sciences,
Stanford University School of Medicine, USA

WILEY

Other Wiley Editorial Offices

John Wiley & Sons Inc., 111 River Street, Hoboken, NJ 07030, USA

Jossey-Bass, 989 Market Street, San Francisco, CA 94103-1741, USA

Wiley-VCH Verlag GmbH, Boschstr. 12, D-69469 Weinheim, Germany

John Wiley & Sons Australia Ltd, 33 Park Road, Milton, Queensland 4064, Australia

John Wiley & Sons (Asia) Pte Ltd, 2 Clementi Loop #02-01, Jin Xing Distripark, Singapore 129809

John Wiley & Sons (Canada) Ltd, 22 Worcester Road, Etobicoke, Ontario M9W 1L1

Wiley also publishes its books in a variety of electronic formats. Some content that appears in print
may not be available in electronic books.

Library of Congress Cataloging-in-Publication Data

Cognitive behaviour therapy with older people / Ken Laidlaw . . . [et
al.].
 p. m.
Includes bibliograhical references and index.
 ISBN 0–471–48710–4 (alk. paper) — ISBN 0–471–48711–2 (pbk. : alk.
paper)
 1. Cognitive therapy. 2. Psychotherapy for the aged. I. Laidlaw,
Kent, 1961–
 RC489.C63 C6426 2003
 616.89′142—dc21   2002152209

British Library Cataloguing in Publication Data

A catalogue record for this book is available from the British Library

ISBN 0–471–48710–4 (hbk)
ISBN 0–471–48711–2 (pbk)

Typeset in 10/12pt Palatino by Dobbie Typesetting Limited, Tavistock, Devon
Printed and bound in Great Britain by Biddles Ltd, King's Lynn, Norfolk
This book is printed on acid-free paper responsibly manufactured from sustainable forestation,
for which at least two trees are planted for each one used for paper production.

CONTENTS

ABOUT THE AUTHORS

Ken Laidlaw has a specialist interest in mental health problems in older adults. He is a Consultant Clinical Psychologist working with older people and a Lecturer in Clinical Psychology at the University of Edinburgh. Over recent years, Ken has developed specialist skills in psychological treatment methods, particularly cognitive therapy, for depression in older people. In 1999 he was awarded a Winston Churchill Travelling Fellowship to visit the USA and share with research colleagues ideas on cognitive therapy with older people. In 2000–2001 he spent a year as a visiting scholar with Dr Aaron T. Beck at the Center for Psychopathology Research at the University of Pennsylvania in Philadelphia. Ken has been invited to present colloquia on psychotherapy with older people in the UK, the USA and Europe. He has an interest in evaluating CBT and was the principal investigator in the first UK evaluation of individual CBT for late-life depression. He is developing research looking at the efficacy of CBT as a treatment for late-life depression comorbid with physical conditions, and is currently involved in research looking at quality of life in older people. Ken has also authored book chapters and articles in the area of psychological treatment for older people.

Larry W. Thompson earned his PhD degree from the Florida State University in 1961 and since then has had an illustrious career, spanning many aspects of clinical psychology in a variety of academic institutions. Larry began working in the areas of electrophysiology and neuropsychology—researching cognitive function in older adults and how it was affected by dementia and other brain insults. He was on the faculty of the medical school at Duke University for a number of years, followed by a professorship at the University of Southern California in Los Angeles, where he directed the first clinical-ageing psychology doctoral programme in the country at the time. There his interest in conducting empirical studies relevant to the field of clinical psychology was re-awakened; Larry conducted a series of funded studies there on the efficacy of a variety of psychotherapeutic modalities of the treatment of late-life depression. He also took specialized training in cognitive and behaviour therapy with Dr Aaron T. Beck and has since become a founding member of the Academy of Cognitive Therapy. About 20 years ago he moved to Stanford University and took a position as professor of research in the School of Medicine there. Larry continued his research into empirically supported methods of psychotherapy to use with older adults, and completed one of the only studies in the United States in which CBT was directly compared to antidepressant medication in a randomized-controlled clinical trial. He has since retired from Stanford, but that did not last long! Larry has been awarded the Goldman Family Chair of Psychology at the Pacific Graduate School of Psychology in Palo Alto, CA, where he continues to teach, do research, mentor graduate students, and collaborate with others in the field who are committed to advancing knowledge about how to improve the mental health of older adults.

Leah Dick-Siskin received her doctorate from Washington University in St Louis, Missouri, where she specialized in geropsychology. She completed her internship and fellowship at the Palo Alto Veterans Affairs Health Care System where she continued her specialization in clinical geropsychology and cognitive behaviour therapy. Leah worked for four years as the Clinical Coordinator at the Older Adult and Family Center at the Palo Alto Veterans Affairs Health Care System where she focused on the teaching and training of pre-doctoral psychology interns, post-doctoral clinical psychology fellows, and psychiatry residents in using CBT with older adults. She worked extensively with Larry Thompson, PhD, and Dolores Gallagher-Thompson, PhD, to refine and adapt CBT interventions to treat late-life depression and anxiety. Leah is currently the Admissions Coordinator and Staff Psychologist at the Geriatric Partial Hospital in the Geriatric Psychiatry Division of the Hillside Hospital, North Shore–Long Island Jewish Health System. In this position, she is a member of a multidisciplinary team treating acute psychiatric symptoms in older adults who are at risk for psychiatric hospitalization. Leah is also an active member of Hillside Hospital's clinical faculty where she teaches CBT seminars to train interns in the treatment of depression and anxiety. She also ran a year-long seminar for staff members interested in refining their skills in administering CBT. For two years, Leah held the position of Chair of the Ad Hoc Continuing Education Committee for the Behavioral and Social Sciences Section for the Gerontological Society of America and, in this role, organized and presented day-long workshops held at the society's national meeting focusing on (1) treating personality disorders in late-life and (2) the use of CBT in treating late-life depression, anxiety, and dementia. At many national meetings, she has presented on the efficacy of CBT in treating various disorders in an elderly population, managing a chronic illness, and stress and coping in family caregivers. Leah is currently working on methods to adapt CBT to the treatment of the acutely psychiatric older patient. She authored and co-authored numerous published articles on

UNIVERSITY OF WOLVERHAMPTON
Harrison Learning Centre

ITEMS ISSUED:

Customer ID: WPP62892940

Title: Cognitive behaviour therapy with older
people
ID: 762442188X
Due: 16/11/2017 23:59

Total items: 1
Total fines: £1.20
09/11/2017 13:49
Issued: 1
Overdue: 0

Thank you for using Self Service.
Please keep your receipt.

Overdue books are fined at 40p per day for
1 week loans, 10p per day for long loans.

these topics as well as co-authored a treatment manual and a therapist guide outlining the treatment to older adults with such problems as depression and anxiety using cognitive behaviour therapy.

Dolores Gallagher-Thompson earned her PhD degree in both clinical psychology and adult development and ageing from the University of Southern California in 1979 where she trained at the Andrus Gerontology Center, then under the direction of Dr James Birren. Dolores' interest was always in clinical research: her doctoral dissertation was an empirical study of several methods of group therapy to treat late-life depression. She joined the staff of the Veterans Administration Medical Center in Palo Alto, CA, in 1981 as the first director of interdisciplinary team training programmes in geriatrics and gerontology. Since then she has held many significant positions in the VA system, including associate director for geriatric education in several different settings, while at the same time actively serving on the faculty at Stanford University. She has been a funded researcher for about 20 years, focusing her career at first on treatment of late-life depression (working collaboratively with her husband Larry on several projects) and then on interventions to reduce psychological distress in family caregivers of older relatives with Alzheimer's disease or other forms of dementia. In the past decade she has become increasingly interested in the unique problems and concerns of the major ethnic minority groups in the USA as they undertake family caregiving, and is now very well regarded in the field of ethnogerontology. She was, in fact, one of the original core faculty of the Stanford Geriatric Education Center, which has as its mission the development of this field as it pertains to physical and mental health issues of older adults. In 1996 she became an Associate Professor of Research in the Department of Psychiatry and Behavioral Sciences at the University of Stanford, California. In 2002 she was promoted to full Professor of Research in the same department. She is still very active in training psychiatry residents, psychology interns and post-doctoral fellows, and conducting her research. She is Director of the Older Adult and Family Center, which provides the administrative structure for her work to continue.

PREFACE

The main aim of this book is to fill what is perceived to be a need among psychotherapists working with older people; that is, for a comprehensive guide to applying cognitive behaviour therapy (CBT) with older people. Given the very real increase in longevity evident in the developed and developing world, psychotherapists and other health-care workers will increasingly come into contact with older people. It is our view that older people will be better served when their practitioners have access to up-to-date and clear information on psychological treatment options. We sincerely believe that we have reached our goal in this respect. Anyone with the most basic understanding of CBT will be able to use the information contained in this text to tailor high-quality and effective therapy for older people. This book provides therapists with a clear rationale for treatment interventions, not just the 'what to' and 'how to do' but the 'why' of interventions. To that end our book is strong on formulation and conceptualization. In the numerous training sessions and workshops with which we have collectively been involved over the years, there have been numerous instances where people gave us examples of difficulties in applying CBT with older people, and other numerous instances where people would tell us how de-skilled they had felt as therapists when working with older people with multiple physical and psychological comorbidities. This book is written to share our knowledge and experiences with therapists, and to transfer our optimism about treating older people in distress.

- In our experience of applying CBT with older people, we know that old dogs *can* learn new tricks.
- In our experience, CBT *is* effective, adaptable and very popular with older people.
- In our experience, CBT with older people *can* make such a difference to people's lives.

This book is, in part, motivated to provide evidence to show how much can be achieved. In working with older people our experience tells us that we should always retain an open mind on what can be achieved. In writing this book we wanted to provide a resource that therapists at all levels of experience and expertise would find helpful. When applying cognitive therapy with older people, the question is often asked: 'What adaptations are necessary to make CBT effective and applicable?' In the broad literature there are many answers to this question. In this book we have provided a model for CBT with older people that retains the main identity of the therapy but reflects an honest account of the types of issues that need to be addressed if CBT is to be maximally effective. It was our intention that the reader should see this book as a resource that extends beyond cognitive behaviour therapy, and we have therefore provided up-to-date information on gerontology to enable the readers to be better equipped to help their patients identify and challenge age-related myths and stereotypes.

STRUCTURE OF THE BOOK

The book is divided into four sections. Section One (Chapters 1–3) outlines the basic information that therapists would need to work effectively with older people. Chapter 1 provides basic background information on growing older and up-to-date demographic projections. Chapter 2 provides therapists with essential efficacy evidence for CBT that they may wish to share with their patients. In this chapter a number of myths associated with psychotherapy and older people are debunked. In Chapter 3 a model for working with older people is introduced and fully described. This model provides a unifying structure for interventions described throughout the subsequent chapters of this book.

In Section Two (Chapters 4–7) cognitive behaviour therapy for late-life depression is described in great detail. Chapter 4 provides basic information on planning treatment and also deals with the issues of assessment and diagnosis. Chapter 5 provides a thorough explanation of the use of behavioural techniques in the treatment of depression. Chapter 6 provides a description of cognitive interventions, and challenges many misconceptions about the use of these techniques with older people. This chapter shows how to introduce and use thought diaries successfully with older people. Chapter 7 provides a perspective on dealing with more in-depth schema issues in CBT with older people. This chapter is one of the very few published accounts of this type of work with older people.

In Section Three CBT is applied with other disorders apart from depression. Chapter 8 gives an account of the assessment and treatment of late-life anxiety, while Chapter 9 deals with insomnia. Chapters 10–12 deal with important developments in the use of CBT with medically ill populations. Innovative accounts of treatment are published in these chapters and the accounts of treatment here place this book at the cutting edge of CBT for older people.

Section Four, the final section, provides an overview of the many common challenges experienced in applying CBT with older people and offers a look towards the future.

It is our sincerest hope that the material contained in this book will be helpful to our readers and, hence, to older people. We are aware, however, that a book such as this can only take someone so far, therefore we recommend appropriate training and continued supervision in cognitive therapy to anyone wishing to use these techniques. Good luck to all our readers.

Ken Laidlaw

FOREWORD

A book looking at the application of cognitive therapy (CT) with older people is long overdue, especially as the first empirical evaluation of this approach with older people took place almost 20 years ago, and was conducted by two of the four authors. This book is the first non-edited book on the use of CT with older people. The authors have all been involved in the clinical evaluation of CT with older people and remain at the forefront in the development of this approach's application in a number of settings and with a broad range of older client groups. An innovative aspect of this book is that information from the field of gerontology is provided in the introductory section so that therapists less experienced in working with older people are less affected by age-related biases in terms of treatment options and treatment outcomes. In many previous works researchers have stated that therapists ought to know about normal ageing and normal age-related changes when working with older people, but have stopped short of stating what that knowledge should be, and its relevance. This book corrects that omission.

The book is firmly within the tradition of CT and helps therapists to remain empirical in their approach to working with older people. The model of CT is clearly stated and real case examples of CT in action are provided throughout. In many ways Chapter 3 is the most important as it outlines the integration of gerontology and CT when working with older people. At the centre of this new approach is the cognitive model and the authors are explicit in their desire to keep this as the basis for treatment. The cognitive model of psychopathology is supplemented with important additional areas of enquiry in conceptualizing work with older people such as the importance of cohort beliefs, intergenerational biases, role status, health status and the sociocultural context. All of these elements are combined into a formulation that retains a strong cognitive theory identity. This model directly addresses the common misconception that CT needs to be adapted before it can be effective with older people. In that sense this book makes an important contribution to the CT literature, and I am happy to have been the mentor of the first author and also a long-term colleague of two other authors of this book.

The book covers the issue of anxiety, discusses the research and treatment gaps in this area, and provides an up-to-date review of treatment options for late-life anxiety. The important issue of medical comorbidity is given extensive coverage as there are chapters on post-stroke depression in addition to depression in Parkinson's disease and depression in dementia. This is another important contribution to the CT treatment programme. While many of the techniques are familiar, the application of these techniques with stroke victims and people with chronic degenerative diseases such as PD and Alzheimer's disease is innovative. The authors carefully show how effective CT can be in dealing with depression and medical comorbidity. Case examples provide novice therapists with models of working and applying CT that show the power of CT as a treatment intervention.

At its core the book never wavers from its strong empirical basis and each chapter provides a review of evidence for the application of CT before giving clinical guidance on treatment issues. The book provides an in-depth and cutting edge guide to the use of CT with older people and, in reality, there is no other text with this depth of coverage on the market.

This text reflects the collective experience of four geriatric mental health practitioners/researchers working in a variety of settings for over a decade developing and evaluating innovative clinical solutions for improving the mental health care needs of older people. The authors are known for their commitment to the betterment of treatments for older people and this remains the main aim of their book.

Aaron T. Beck, M.D.

University Professor of Psychiatry
University of Pennsylvania
Department of Psychiatry
26 September 2002

Section One

WORKING EFFECTIVELY WITH OLDER PEOPLE: KNOWLEDGE AND SKILLS

Chapter 1

BASIC GERONTOLOGY FOR COGNITIVE THERAPISTS

INTRODUCTION

Working with older people presents many challenges, but to what extent should one expect older people to change their lifestyles as a result of therapy? With what changes in society do therapists need to acquaint themselves in order to have realistic expectations of this patient group? Before embarking upon therapy with older people, many considerations need to be taken into account, not least of which is an understanding of the realities facing the individuals with whom the therapist may be working. Many authoritative articles have been written about the process of working therapeutically with older people and it is often stated that knowledge of normal ageing is necessary for working with that age group. However, it is rare for guidance to be given on the aspects of knowledge of the ageing process that would be helpful to the psychotherapeutic process. This chapter aims to orient the therapist to aspects of ageing that are important and to provide affirmation of existing knowledge of good practice for the experienced clinician.

UNDERSTANDING DEMOGRAPHIC CHANGES IN SOCIETY

In the developed and developing world, people are living longer, and increasing longevity across societies is a major societal achievement, *and a*

Cognitive Behaviour Therapy with Older People.
Ken Laidlaw, Larry W. Thompson, Leah Dick-Siskin & Dolores Gallagher-Thompson.
© 2003 John Wiley & Sons Ltd.

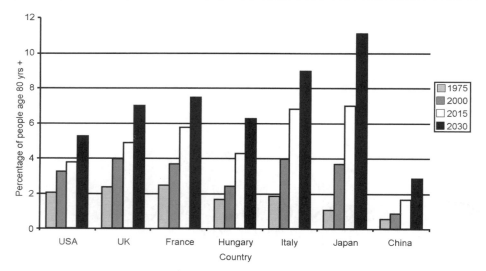

Figure 1.1 Percentage of oldest-old 1975, 2000, 2015, 2030 across countries (*source:* Kinsella & Velkoff, 2001)

challenge (WHO, 2002). A combination of low fertility rates and increased life expectancy has resulted in the relative ageing of societies world wide. According to recent statistics (UN, 2001), the world's older adult population is estimated to show a three-fold increase over the next 50 years, from the present population of 606 million people to 2 billion in 2050. In fact, given the increase in lifespan that is occurring world wide, this may require people to modify their notions of when old age is considered to have started (OECD, 2001). It is the oldest-old section of society (people aged 80 years plus) that shows the most dramatic increase with an almost five-fold increase from 69 million in 2000 to 379 million older people in 2050 (see Figure 1.1). It is estimated that, over the next 50 years, the numbers of people aged 90 and above will show an eight-fold increase, but the number of centenarians will show the greatest increase in numbers as the number of people aged 100 and above in 2050 will be 18 times greater than the numbers in 2000. Interestingly the growth of the oldest-old section of society is also a feature in developing countries and the absolute numbers of older people in developing countries is increasing markedly (WHO, 2002).

The ageing index and the dependency ratios are important indicators of how societies are ageing. The ageing index is calculated by comparing the number of people aged 65 years and over per 100 young people aged 15 years and younger. According to the latest figures, in the UK in 2000 the ageing index was 82, meaning that for every 100 youths there were 82 people aged at least 65 years. This figure is set to rise to 152 by the year 2030. In the USA, the ageing index is currently 59, but is set to rise to 102 by the year 2030. By the year 2030, Italy, Bulgaria, the Czech Republic, Greece and Japan will all have age indices above 200, indicating that there will be two older people for every one young person in these societies (Kinsella & Velkoff, 2001; WHO, 2001a; OECD, 2001). The dependency ratio is also of interest to psychotherapists working with older adults as it may give a guide to the number of psychotherapists specializing in working with older people that will be needed in the future. The dependency ratio is calculated by dividing the total population over the age of 60 and of retirement age (the effective age of retirement in European Union countries is now 58; Anderson, 2002) by the total population aged 15–60, of working age. In 2002 in North America the dependency ratio was 0.26, and for the countries of the European Union, the ratio was 0.36. In 2025 it is estimated that the ratio will rise to 0.44 in the USA and to 0.56 in Europe. In effect, by the year 2025, there will be 56 people aged 60 years and over for every 100 people aged 15–60.

In the UK in 2000, older people accounted for nearly one-sixth of the population (16 per cent). It is estimated that by 2020 there will be twice as many people aged 60 and above living in the European community than there were in 1960. The recent US national census (Kinsella & Velkoff, 2001) revealed that people over the age of 65 years accounted for almost 13 per cent of the total population and it is estimated that by 2030 older people will account for about one-fifth of the total population. Since 1900, the percentage of Americans aged 65 years and above has increased more than three-fold and the increase in the numbers and percentages of older people living in the USA is higher than for any other age group (Administration on Aging, 2000).

Data published by the UK Office of National Statistics (ONS, 2001) for 1997 suggest that a man aged 60 years could expect to live for another 18.9 years and a woman aged 60 years could expect to live for another 22.7 years. In the UK in 1931, the life expectancy at birth for men was 58 years and for women it was 62 years (Help the Aged, 2000). In 2000 in the UK, life expectancy at birth increased to 75 years for men and 80 years for women. Over the period 1900–1990, the average gain in life expectancy at birth in developed countries was 66 per cent for men and 71 per cent for women (Kinsella & Velkoff, 2001). Accordingly there will be a greater need for psychotherapists to develop knowledge and expertise in dealing with older clients.

There is a gender gap in life expectancy resulting in large numbers of older women than older men in many parts of the world (WHO, 2002, 2001a, 1999). The gender gap is important for therapists to take note of, as women tend to report higher levels of depression than men and are more likely to come to the attention of the psychiatric services (Crawford et al., 1998). Men on average tend to die before women (WHO, 2002; Wood & Bain, 2001). The reality of this statement is brought out by the fact that in the UK in 1997 there were 5523 centenarians and only 580 of these were men (ONS, 2001). In 2000 in the USA, one in every eight American is over the age of 65 and three out of five of these individuals are women (Kinsella & Velkoff, 2001). The mortality age gap between the sexes, however, has fallen over recent years and is now on average between 5 and 7 years. Nonetheless, as women on average tend to marry men older than themselves, older women are more likely to be widows, to live alone and to experience chronic ill-health. The likelihood of living alone increases with age; 19 per cent of men and 31 per cent of women aged between 65 and 69 years live alone, while 43 per cent of men and 72 per cent of women aged 85 years and above live alone (ONS, 2000).

The mental health needs of older people have often been neglected in the past. As people are living longer, pressures on services will increase to deliver the types of interventions that are required to meet the emotional as well as the physical health needs of older people. Greater numbers of older people will result in greater potential sociopolitical power and may influence the ways in which health services, particularly mental health services, are organized and resources allocated. The need for effective psychological treatments for older adults will become more important rather than less (Laidlaw, 2003).

WHO IS AN OLDER PERSON? WHEN DOES AGEING START?

In Europe and the USA, older people are most commonly defined by chronological age. For legal and occupational purposes an older person is generally defined as someone aged 65 years and older. It has become popular to characterize people as young-old (65–75 years), old-old (75–85 years), and oldest-old (85 years plus). In working with older adults, it is important to understand the individuality of each person you see. The age of an individual is more complex than chronological age (years since birth). In a sense, chronological age confuses the picture more than it clarifies it. To understand the individual capabilities of an older adult it may be more important to take into account biological, psychological and social factors rather than age.

An important concept, functional ageing, refers to the ability of people to perform activities relative to their life experience. Two exemplary individuals, one from the UK and one from the USA, are cited here as evidence that ageing does not automatically mean loss of abilities or poor functioning. In the UK, the late Sir Stanley Matthews continued to play professional football (soccer) at a high level until he was 50 years of age. When he was 41, Sir Stanley Matthews won the first-ever European Player of the Year award, an immensely impressive achievement since this is an age when most athletes have long since retired from any active sport. As Matthews grew older during his professional soccer career, his pace diminished but his skills remained and were augmented with years of life experience. Matthews had an American counterpart in the baseball player Satchel Paige who defied chronological age to continue his career until his retirement from sport at the age of 59 years.

When Paige was once asked by a reporter about his age, he replied, 'How old would you be if you did not know what age you was?' This is an important point to keep in mind when working with older people. Do not assume that older age necessarily means decrepitude (Midwinter, 1992) and do not assume that chronological age will tell you everything you need to know about an individual. Many people have a mental age that is years younger than their chronological age. Ask yourself, 'How old do I feel?'

Older adults are *the least* homogeneous of all age groups, and often have many more dissimilarities than similarities (Steuer & Hammen, 1983; Futterman et al., 1995). As Zeiss and Steffen (1996a) point out, at least two generations are contained within this age grouping. With the increase in longevity there can be four decades separating the youngest-old from the oldest-old.

The therapist also ought to bear in mind the importance of cohort (Knight, 1996a; Thompson, 1996). Cohort refers to the set of cultural norms, historical events, and personal events that occurred during a specific generation. For example, today's older people would be affected by great social upheavals such as the economic depression of the 1920s and 1930s. Tom Brokaw (1998) provides an insight into the cohort experience of the generation of adults who lived through World War II. Understanding older people in terms of their generational cohort allows therapists a way of gaining insight into the societal norms and rules that may influence an individual's behaviour. The therapist may need to take account of the different cultural expectations regarding health-seeking behaviour among older adults as compared to younger adults, especially with regard to views on the care and treatment of conditions such as depression and anxiety. Understanding cohort experiences and taking these into account when working psychotherapeutically with older people is no more difficult, and no less important, than when working with cohorts such as ethnic minority groups.

NORMAL AGEING, DISABILITY AND DEPRESSION

Old age is often characterized as a time of loss: loss of health, loss of income and loss of companionship through bereavement. While for many older people, bereavement and ill-health are unfortunately more common with advancing years, this is only part of the current picture of growing old in Britain, Europe or the USA.

Old Age as a Time of Loss of Income and Loss of Companionship

Today's older people face more challenges and opportunities from the increase in leisure time, as a result of increased life expectancy, than any previous generation. The change in number of lifetime hours devoted to paid work has declined, but has not been replaced by an increase in time devoted to unpaid work or voluntary activities; unfortunately older people currently spend a lot of their retirement time in passive activities (Gauthier & Smeeding, 2001). In a report on attitudes of older people towards ageing, Midwinter (1992) provides evidence that many older people see retirement as a time of new challenge. Midwinter reports that 27 per cent of older people enjoy life more now, whereas 30 per cent enjoy life less. Thus while at least a third of older people find increasing age to be a time of great challenge, the majority of older people enjoy life as much as, or even more than, at any other time. Working therapeutically with older people means having to keep an open mind about the individual response to the stages of life. Of those enjoying life less there is an association between poor health, living alone and low income. Midwinter (1992) states that to characterize older age as a time of loneliness is overstating things. Even although 82 per cent of retired people sampled believed that loneliness was a common problem in older age, only 22 per cent of the sample stated this was a problem for them personally. Midwinter (1992) makes the point that, overall, one-fifth of the general population report loneliness as a problem, therefore, older people are not especially worse off on this issue than other sections of society.

In the UK General Household Survey in 1998 (ONS, 2000), four out of five older people reported having contact with relatives on a weekly basis. Indeed one out of four older people reported having daily or near daily contact with family. Of course, one ought to bear in mind that the quality of relationships and interactions are often more important than quantity. When working with older people it can be very important to enquire about the pre-morbid nature of familial relationships in order to determine the true nature of the supports available to the person you may be working with.

For many older people financial worries can make later life a time of stress. Older people's income comes from four main sources: social security benefits (state pension, income support, disability benefits), occupational pension, savings and investments, and employment earnings. Since 1974, the proportion of income gained from occupational pensions has almost doubled, from 15 per cent to 26 per cent, while at the same time the proportion of income from employment activities has halved, from 17 per cent in 1974 to 8 per cent in 2000 (Help the Aged, 2000). This trend indicates that many people are retiring earlier. In the late 1970s and 1980s, political pressures due to the reduction of employment opportunities in heavy industries contributed to large numbers of men and women taking early retirement.

Given the increase in longevity across developed societies this is likely to result in a reversal of the trend to retirement at an earlier age (OECD, 2001), and, consequently, there are calls to legislate against compulsory retirement in many countries. Many proponents of this approach point out that insurance schemes to support retirement at the age of 65 years were first set by the

Prussian leader Earl von Bismark between 1883 and 1889 shortly after the unification of Germany. The age was set at 65 purely for politically expedient reasons; in the late nineteenth century very few men or women were able to take advantage of State benefits as many people did not reach this age.

In the UK in 1997, 70 per cent of pensioner households were dependent upon State benefits for at least 50 per cent of their income, and 13 per cent received all their income from State benefits. In the UK, the current (2002) basic pension is £72.50 per week for a single person's pension, and £115.90 per week for a married couple's pension (ONS, 2002). Financially, increasing age results in increasing levels of relative poverty. Older people in the age bracket of 65 to 74 years are often more financially secure than older people in the age bracket 85 years plus. Many older people aged 85 years and above, particularly women, will be living alone and may have had to live on limited means for a number of years. The financial gap between the youngest-old and oldest-old sections of society gives the lie to the homogeneity suggested by the term 'older' people. However, when working with older people, a mindset expecting older people to be financially and interpersonally impoverished may be inaccurate for the majority, especially the youngest-old.

Old Age as a Time of Loss of Health

While older people are living longer they are generally remaining healthier with an increase in percentage of life lived with good health (Baltes & Smith, 2002; WHO, 2002). There has also been a change in the leading causes of death, with death occurring after chronic rather than acute disease. The three major causes of death are listed as heart disease, cancer and stroke (Sahyoun et al., 2001). Thus it is probable that when working with older adults they are likely to have at least one chronic medical condition and many will have multiple conditions such as arthritis, hypertension, heart disease, cataracts or diabetes.

Older people are more likely than younger people to have visited their family doctor within the previous three months, and are more likely to have received care at home by their doctor (ONS, 2000). Older people were also most likely to have attended an outpatient or casualty department of a hospital and to have required an inpatient stay in hospital (ONS, 2001). Despite the increased likelihood of chronic disease in later life, this does not equate with ill-health per se (WHO, 2002, 1999). An important point to bear in mind is that the majority of older persons report good health compared with others of their age (Midwinter, 1992). In the General Household Survey carried out in 1998 (ONS, 2000) in the UK, 60 per cent of men aged 65 years and over described their health as 'good' or very good, and 61 per cent of women aged 65 years and over described their health as 'good' or very good. Overall, 77 per cent of older people stated that their health was good or fairly good and only 12 per cent described their health as bad or very bad. Many chronic medical conditions will have developed gradually over a number of years and therefore the person may have had time to adapt or compensate for the disability.

As the age of a person increases, so does the likelihood of developing a chronic medical condition. In 1998 in the UK, 20 per cent of people aged 44 years or less reported a longstanding illness, whereas 50 per cent of people aged 45 years and above reported a longstanding illness. In the General Household Survey carried out in 1998 in the UK, 59 per cent of people aged between 65 and 74 years and 66 per cent of people aged 75 years and above reported experiencing a longstanding illness and disability; 42 per cent of older people stated that their mobility was limited by their longstanding illness and 20 per cent reported no limitations. The most common longstanding conditions were either musculoskeletal conditions or conditions of the heart and circulatory system. The rate for developing medical conditions increases with age. Increasing age is also associated with larger numbers of people experiencing heart or circulatory system problems; 19 men and 13 women per 1000 aged 16 to 44 years of age, compared to 310 men and 299 women per 1000 aged 75 years and above, experienced cardiac problems. The UK has one of the worst rates for heart disease in Europe (TWG, 1999). While it is evident that with increasing age there are higher rates of physical ill-health, it is important to remember that the rates still indicate that *not every older person has a debilitating medical condition*. The rates for heart disease in men aged 75 years and above indicate that two-thirds are free from significant heart or circulatory problems.

Older people appear to accept longstanding illness as a normal part of ageing since a number of older people assessed as having a longstanding illness did not report any disability associated with their medically diagnosed conditions (ONS, 2000). Although poor physical health may be an important risk factor for the development of psychological distress (Kramer et al., 1992), symptoms of mental disorders are often undetected by health professionals treating older people for physical complaints. While it may be true that depression increases the risk of developing a disability, and that disability may increase the risk of depression (Gurland et al., 1988), the association between depression and disability is more complex than a single one-to-one correspondence.

Depression and Disability

In understanding the impact of longstanding illnesses in the context of ageing, psychotherapists working with older adults need to look beyond the medical model. The World Health Organization (WHO) in 1980 developed a disease classification[1] for differentiating between impairment, disability and handicap

---

[1]The World Health Organization has recently published an update and revision of this classification system. The updated classification system is discussed in more detail in Chapter 10. However, as the original classification provides a useful way of understanding disease in a psychological context it is retained for descriptive purposes in this chapter.

that is very helpful for identifying initiatives for the development of psychotherapy in the presence of physical conditions such as a stroke or Parkinson's disease. *Impairment* refers to the disease process itself, e.g. brain infarctions in a stroke; *disability* is the impact that disease has on the individual's ability to carry out activities such as dressing, walking or talking, e.g. following a stroke an individual may no longer be able to continue with previously pleasurable activities such as ballroom dancing; and *handicap* is the socialization of disability or impairment, e.g. following a stroke, an individual with left-sided paralysis may not be able to access social clubs or other places where social events were enjoyed previously.

Consistent with the WHO (1980) disease classification system is the concept of excess disability, i.e. the proportion of a person's disability that is not determined by the physical impairments of the condition. Excess disability, for example, is evident when a person surviving a stroke withdraws from activities prematurely because of embarrassment at the consequences of a stroke (e.g. a hemiparetic limb). In this instance, the cognitive therapist does not aim to reverse cognitive deterioration or to provide physical rehabilitation for the individual, but to target the psychological consequences of a physical condition as they impact upon the individual. In the case of embarrassment at a hemiparetic limb, the therapist works with the individual to understand the reasons for embarrassment and aims to develop interventions to enable the individual to maintain maximal levels of independence, given the circumstances. The self-imposed isolation given in the example above is not a direct consequence of the physical symptoms of a stroke, but is determined by the thoughts and feelings experienced by the individual concerning his or her body image. In other words, embarrassment rather than the stroke prevents the individual from socializing with friends. It is at the level of the excess disability that cognitive therapy can be very effective in tackling depression and improving the quality of life of individuals. Bearing this in mind allows clinicians to step back from fears about the applicability of psychotherapy when a patient presents with so-called 'realistic depression'.

PREVALENCE AND PROGNOSIS OF DEPRESSION IN OLDER ADULTS

Depression is generally considered to be the most common psychiatric disorder among older adults (Blazer, 2002; Ames & Allen, 1991), although recent evidence suggests that anxiety disorders may actually be more common (Blazer, 1997). Data from the Epidemiological Catchment Area Study (Regier et al., 1988) suggested that rates of major depressive disorder among older adults are lower than rates for younger adults (for a review see Futterman et al., 1995). A recent systematic review of community-based studies assessing the prevalence of late-life depression carried out by Beekman et al. (1999) calculated an average prevalence rate of 13.5 per cent for clinically relevant depression symptoms.

Data from the UK suggests that major depressive disorder affects only a minority of older people, with Livingston et al. (1990) identifying an overall prevalence rate of 16 per cent for depression symptoms in their inner London sample. Consistent with other prevalence studies of depression in older adults, Livingstone and colleagues found that depressed older adults were more likely to be living alone and were more likely to have been in recent contact with GPs and hospital services. Lindesay, Brigs and Murphy (1989) report similar rates of depression in older adults living in the community, with 13.5 per cent of their sample identified with mild to moderate depressive symptoms and 4.3 per cent identified with severe depressive symptoms.

Katona et al. (1997) state that in younger people the comorbidity of depression with other psychiatric conditions has received a lot of attention and yet, in older adults, depression comorbidity has received relatively little attention. This would appear to be surprising as Katona et al. (1997) found very high rates of comorbid generalized anxiety in older adults diagnosed with depression. The association between depression and heightened levels of generalized anxiety was so great in their sample that they suggest that depression should be looked for whenever anxiety is present in older people. These findings correspond to reports by Flint (1999) that late-life generalized anxiety disorder is usually associated with depression. Lenze et al. (2001) comment that older adults with depression and comorbid anxiety are more likely to present with greater severity levels and are more likely to experience poorer treatment response.

Rates of depression in older people vary, depending upon the sample considered. For example, Katz et al. (1989) identified a prevalence rate of major depressive disorder among nursing home residents of 18 to 20 per cent, and up to 27 to 44 per cent overall for other dysphoric mood states. Likewise, Abrams et al. (1992) describe depression as being widespread in nursing home residents. Unfortunately, although nurses are good at detecting depression in nursing home residents, levels of treatment are low (Katz et al., 1989).

SUICIDE AND OLDER PEOPLE: ASSESSING FOR SUICIDAL INTENT

Older people are more likely to complete suicide than any other age group, resulting in relatively lower levels of suicide attempts in comparisons to younger age groups (Gallagher-Thompson & Osgood, 1997; Conwell et al., 1996). Suicide attempts by older people are more likely to result in a fatal outcome compared with younger age groups (Hepple & Quinton, 1997). While depression does not necessarily result in suicide, the majority of older people who attempt suicide are depressed. Among older people who make suicide attempts, depression is the most frequent diagnosis (Conwell et al., 1996). Suicide rates for persons aged 65 years and older are higher than for any other age group, and the suicide rate for persons 85 plus is the highest of all—nearly twice the overall national rate. In the USA the suicide rate for older people is almost six times the rate of the age-adjusted suicide for all races and for both sexes (Center for Disease Control, 2001). Nonetheless the suicide rate of older people in the USA is average when compared with many countries in the developed world (see Table 1.1). Suicide rates for men and women tend to rise with age, but are highest for men aged 75 years and above (WHO, 2002; Kinsella & Velkoff, 2001).

The high suicide rate among older people, especially older men living on their own, may be partly explained by the fact that older people are more likely to use higher lethality methods of suicide and much less likely to communicate their intention beforehand. Sadly, however, although most older people who complete a suicide act visit their family doctor within one month of their act, this does not always result in recognition and treatment. For example, Caine, Lyness and Conwell (1996) carried out a review of the cases of 97 older people who had completed suicide and discovered that while 51 had visited their GP within one month prior to the suicide act, 47 had been diagnosed with a psychiatric problem, but only 19 had received treatment. Caine et al. (1996) reviewed the treatment received by these individuals and

Table 1.1 Suicide rates[1] among older men and women compared to suicide rates in young people (*source:* Kinsella & Velkoff, 2001)

Country	Men aged 15–24	Men aged 75+	Women aged 15–24	Women aged 75+
Australia	23	27	6	5
Bulgaria	15	116	6	50
Canada	22	27	5	4
Denmark	13	71	2	20
France	13	87	4	20
Germany	13	71	3	21
Hungary	18	131	4	50
Ireland (Eire)	25	22	5	2
Israel	9	41	2	15
Italy	7	43	2	8
Japan	11	53	6	33
Netherlands	11	34	4	12
Norway	23	24	6	5
Poland	17	31	3	6
Portugal	4	39	1	9
Russia	53	97	9	33
Switzerland	25	80	6	24
UK	10	17	2	4
USA	19	45	4	5

[1]*Note:* Rate per 100 000 in each age group. Data collected by different countries all within the last seven years.

concluded that only two had received appropriate treatment. The reality is that suicide rates for older people are probably underestimates as the true cause of death may not always be recorded on the death certificate either due to a reticence on the part of the family doctor to cause a family distress or because the means of death is uncertain (O'Carroll, 1989). There are two paradoxes when thinking about suicide in later life; older people are living longer and yet those surviving longer (especially older men) are more likely than ever to die by their own hand. The second paradox is that it is older women, especially those aged 85 years and above, who are faced with the greatest challenges of ageing and yet they have much lower rates of suicide than men of the same ages.

In the UK, drug overdose was the most frequent method of suicide among older people (Draper, 1996). For anyone working with depressed older adults a thorough evaluation of their suicide risk should be taken into account during treatment.

SUMMARY

Old age is certainly a time of challenge. Many older people will develop illnesses that may threaten their independence and quality of life; diseases such as stroke, Parkinson's disease, the dementias and arthritis are primarily diseases of old age. Nonetheless, to see older age as a time of decrepitude and melancholy is to miss the point completely. Even in circumstances where illness is present, this does not automatically lead to the development of depression and loss of independence. For many people, an adjustment to the reduction in their physical capacity may take place over many decades. To view old age from the perspective of younger age and as something to dread is to forget that in all stages of life we are faced with challenges that we may need to overcome (Knight, 1996b). In working with older people, a knowledge of normal age-related changes is necessary, but so too is an open-minded perspective that seeks to understand the individual's response to increasing age. While it may be a mistake to adopt a perspective on ageing that is too positive, a negative perspective is much more harmful and unhelpful, closing, as it does, one's mind to the possibility of change and learning at all ages.

Chapter 2

PSYCHOTHERAPY WITH OLDER PEOPLE

INTRODUCTION

When first working with older people it is very easy to develop anxiety about whether psychological approaches are going to be helpful to your patient, especially when physical conditions may be present. It can be very challenging to use psychotherapy to treat depression when disability appears to be an important 'causal' factor in the person's depression. Consequently it is very easy to feel de-skilled and hopeless about possible interventions and outcomes. This chapter will tackle some of the issues that may present themselves when working with older adults. Many myths have also arisen over the years with regard to psychotherapy and older people. These myths are explored and challenged in the second part of this chapter.

WORKING WITH OLDER PEOPLE

In the case of depression or anxiety comorbid with physical conditions, psychological treatments such as cognitive behaviour therapy are very flexible. Morris and Morris (1991) state there are a number of reasons why cognitive-behavioural interventions can be particularly effective with older people as they are:

Cognitive Behaviour Therapy with Older People.
Ken Laidlaw, Larry W. Thompson, Leah Dick-Siskin & Dolores Gallagher-Thompson.
© 2003 John Wiley & Sons Ltd.

- *Focused on the 'here and now'*. The individual's current needs are identified and interventions are developed to target specific stressors.
- *Skills enhancing and practical*. The individual is taught specific ways to manage their individual stressors.
- *Structured*. The organized nature of therapy can help to keep the person oriented to tasks within and across sessions. Homework is used to keep the individual focused on managing problems.
- *Self-monitoring*. The individual is taught to recognize mood fluctuations and emotional vulnerabilities and to develop strategies that enhance coping ability.
- *Educative*. The connection between thoughts, mood and behaviour is explained. The model explains the impact of negative cycles of depression upon the person's activity level and vice versa.
- *Goal oriented*. Interventions are developed to challenge stereotyped beliefs, i.e. 'You can't teach an old dog new tricks.'

Despite suggestions that adaptations are necessary to cognitive therapy to make it relevant for working with older people (Wilkinson, 1997; Koder, Brodaty & Anstey, 1996; Steuer & Hammen, 1986; Yost et al., 1986; Church, 1983), it is the types of age specific issues that older people bring into therapy that makes the application of CBT potentially challenging, rather than any questions about the validity of the CBT interventions themselves. This book aims to guide therapists in considering what modifications of approach may be necessary when working with older adults within the context of a cognitive-behavioural approach. Within our definition, modifications are intended to enhance treatment outcome within therapeutic approach (i.e. CBT), whereas adaptations suggest to clinicians that the treatment model they have chosen may be inadequate in some important respect for the patient they intend to treat.

While modification of therapy may be indicated and may be required to take account of normal age-related changes (Laidlaw, 2001; Knight, 1999; Knight & Satre, 1999; Knight & McCallum, 1998; Thompson, 1996; Gallagher-Thompson & Thompson, 1996; Grant & Casey, 1995), there is a great deal of individual variation in this section of the population. The problems that older adults bring into therapy may not be unique to old age but may be more likely (Knight, 1996b). Cognitive therapy is idiosyncratically based and is always modified to take account of an individual's particular circumstances. As Aaron Beck suggests (personal communication), cognitive therapy is based upon a constantly evolving formulation of the person and, in a sense, there is no such thing as a 'standard' or 'traditional' type of cognitive therapy.

EFFICACY OF CBT WITH OLDER PEOPLE

Powers et al. (2002) and Blazer (2002) have provided comprehensive and timely reviews of both psychosocial and somatic treatments for late-life depression. Perhaps the most noteworthy feature of research in this area is that there simply is not enough of it to draw firm conclusions about the differential effectiveness of various psychosocial and pharmacotherapy treatments when used alone. What little data that are available suggest that, as has been found with young adults with depression, psychotherapy is equally effective or perhaps even more effective than medication alone in some instances, but the combination of the two is clearly superior to either one alone. Table 2.1 summarizes the findings of meta-analytic reviews of the efficacy of cognitive therapy for late-life depression.

Scogin and McElreath (1994) produced the first meta-analysis of the efficacy of psychosocial treatments for late-life depression mainly in response to the NIH consensus statement (NIH, 1991), suggesting limited supporting evidence for psychotherapy for late-life depression. In 1997, the consensus statement was updated (Lebowitz et al., 1997) to take account of important new information in a range of areas pertinent to late-life depression. Lebowitz et al. (1997) concluded that cognitive-behavioural and interpersonal approaches had established evidence for treatment efficacy and that psychological treatments deserved greater emphasis as a treatment alternative to anti-depressant medications and ECT.

Reviewing evidence for psychosocial treatments for late-life depression, Scogin and McElreath (1994) note that effect sizes for treatment versus no treatment or placebo were substantial. In the most specific review of outcome research into strictly defined cognitive therapy (CT) for the treatment of depression in older adults, Koder, Brodaty and Anstey (1996) state that CT is undoubtedly an effective treatment procedure for late-life depression. In later analyses, Engels and Verney (1997) report that those receiving treatment were better off than 74 per cent of people not receiving treatment. Cognitive therapy and behaviour therapy were considered to be the most effective psychological treatments. Cuijpers (1998) noted that overall effect sizes of psychological treatments for late-life depression were large and similar to effect sizes quoted by Robinson, Berman and Neimeyer (1990) for age ranges. Thus, psychological treatments would appear equally efficacious for young or for older adults.

In a departure from meta-analyses that looked only at pharmacological or only psychosocial treatments for late-life depression, Gerson et al. (1999) investigated the effectiveness of pharmacological and psychological treatments for depression in older people, and report that pharmacological and psychological treatments for major depressive disorder in late-life appear equally efficacious. Analyses also revealed no difference in attrition rates between pharmacological and psychological treatments. Gerson and colleagues conclude: 'Effective psychological interventions constitute a much-needed addition to antidepressant medication for depressed older patients.'

Table 2.1 Summary of meta-analyses studies

Authors	Years reviewed	No. of studies in analyses	Effect sizes	Conclusions
Scogin & McElreath (1994)	1970–88	17 broad categorization of treatments	Overall effect size for treatment versus no treatment or placebo is 0.78	No clear superiority for any system of psychotherapy in the treatment of geriatric depression
Koder, Brodaty & Anstey (1996)	1981–94	7 all CT studies	CT vs BT mean effect size is 0.26; CT vs PP mean effect size is 0.41; CT to WL mean effect size is 1.22	Too few studies of sufficient scientific and methodological merit upon which a definitive conclusion can be reached about the relative efficacy of CT over other treatments but CT is undoubtedly an effective treatment option for late-life depression
Engels & Verney (1997)	1974–92	17 studies—all patients carry diagnosis of MDD	Mean effect size of 0.63 (i.e. client was on average 74% better off than non-treated controls)	Individual treatment more effective than group methods of treatment for depression in older people. Cognitive and behavioural treatments produce largest effects
Cuijpers (1998)	1981–94	14 psychological treatments	Effect size of 0.77 comparable to that found in younger samples	'Effects of interventions in which the depressed elderly are actively recruited from the community are large. These effects are comparable to the effects of psychotherapy of depression in younger age groups'
Gerson et al. (1999)	1974–98	45 (4 non-drug) 28 (2 non-drug)	Drug and non-drug treatments appear equally efficacious. No difference in results if use stricter criteria for studies	'Effective psychological interventions constitute a much-needed addition to antidepressant medication for depressed older patients'
Robinson, Berman & Neimeyer (1990)*	1976–86	58 studies	Overall effect size for treatment versus no treatment is 0.73	All forms of psychotherapy more effective than no treatment. Differences in efficacy of psychotherapies disappear when therapist allegiance taken into account

CT = cognitive therapy; BT = behaviour therapy; PP = psychodynamic psychotherapy. *N.B.* Cohen (1992) recommends that for the behavioural sciences, effect size of 0.8 is large, 0.5 is moderate, 0.2 is small.
* = For comparison of outcome between age groups.
Source: Laidlaw (2001); reproduced by permission of John Wiley & Sons, Ltd.

Table 2.2 Features of outcome studies using CBT for late-life depression

Authors	Treatment conditions	N	Age	Sessions (weeks)	Drop out (%)	Format	Summary
Gallagher & Thompson (1982, 1983)	Cognitive Behavioural Insight-oriented	10 10 10	68.3 66.0 69.0	16 sessions	10[1] 50[1] 20[1]	Individual	Non-endogenous depressed patients do better in psychotherapy
Fry (1984)	Cog-behav.	35	65.1	36 sessions	20	Individual	Treatment effective at end of treatment and at follow-up
Jarvik et al. (1982); Steuer et al. (1984)	Cognitive Psychodynamic	16 17	66 66	46 sessions	39 39	Group	CT and psychodynamic therapy equally efficacious. CT superior on BDI scores
Beutler et al. (1987)	CT+medic.[+] CT+placebo Medication[+] Placebo	13 16 12 15	71.2 (F) 70.2(M)	20 weeks	31 CBT 67 medic.	Group	No differences between any treatment groups although CT+placebo generates largest effect sizes (also lowest attrition)
Thompson, Gallagher & Breckenridge (1987)	Cognitive Behavioural Brief Psychodynamic Delayed control	27 25 24 19	66.1 66.9 66.7 67.6	16 to 20 weekly sessions	27 14 14 n/a	Individual	No difference evident between psychotherapies despite good adherence to protocols
Leung & Orrell (1992)	Cognitive	27	70.4	7 weekly sessions	0.0	Group	Very brief intervention yet efficacious even for MDD
Kemp, Corgiat & Gill (1992)	Cognitive	51	74.2	12 weekly sessions	20	Group	Both non-disabled and disabled groups improved over treatment, disabled group maintained gains but no further gains at follow-up
Arean et al. (1993)	Problem solving Reminiscence Wait list	19 28 20	67.0 66.7 65.5	12 weekly sessions	33 20 n/a	Group	Problem-solving Tx more effective than psychoed. or no treatment
Gallagher-Thompson & Steffen (1994)	Cognitive Brief Psychodynamic	36 30	62.0[2]	20 sessions	14 30	Individual	No differences in efficacy between treatments. CT better for longer caregiver time
Rokke, Tomhave & Jocic (2000)	Self-mgmt[++] Education Wait List	9 9 16	67.2[3]	10 weekly sessions	25 10 11	Group	No difference in efficacy although small numbers hampers analysis
Thompson et al. (2001)	CBT alone CBT+medic.[+++] Medic. alone[+++]	31 36 33	66.5 67.2 66.8	16–20 weekly sessions	23 33 34	Individual	All Txs result in improvement. CBT alone and CBT+medic. similar improve. CBT+medic.= CBT alone > medic. alone

[1] In total 8 patients dropped out of treatment within the first 4 weeks and were replaced. [2] Median only reported for both groups as a whole. [3] Mean for sample as whole reported. [+] = Alprazolam. [++] = Self-management is based upon the cognitive therapy model of Rehm. [+++] = Desipramine.

OUTCOME STUDIES IN CBT FOR LATE LIFE DEPRESSION

Thompson, Gallagher-Thompson and colleagues have carried out the most systematic investigations of the effectiveness of CBT for the treatment of late-life depression (Thompson et al., 2002; Kaplan & Gallagher-Thompson, 1995; Dick & Gallagher-Thompson, 1995; Gallagher & Steffen, 1994; Gallagher-Thompson et al., 1990; Thompson, Gallagher & Breckenridge, 1987; Gallagher & Thompson, 1982, 1983). Gallagher and Thompson (1981) produced one of the first treatment manuals for applying cognitive and behavioural techniques with older people. Subsequently periodical updates of their cognitive therapy treatment manuals for the treatment of depression in older people have been produced (Thompson et al., 2000; Thompson, Gallagher-Thompson & Dick, 1995). All of the manuals are available on request by writing to the addresses listed in Appendix 2.

Using criteria accepted by the American Psychological Association to determine treatment efficacy, Chambless et al. (1996) concluded that CT and CBT were well-established, empirically validated treatments for depression in both young and older adults. Gatz et al. (1998, p. 13) consider CBT to have met the APA category of probable efficaciousness 'for depressed community-dwelling residents who are intact, have minimal comorbid psychopathology, and are not suicidal'. Analysis of the literature, combined with the clinical experience of the current authors in working with depressed older adult patients across a range of clinical settings, leads to the conclusion that the conservatism expressed by Gatz et al. (1998) is neither entirely accurate nor fair.

CBT is an effective treatment for depressive disorders in a wide variety of older adult patients, ranging from psychotically immobilized individuals to those having adjustment problems stemming from a recent stressful life transition, such as retirement. While a number of other therapy modalities have been shown to be effective with older adults, the range of situations and individuals where variations of CBT have been used successfully is a very impressive feature of this treatment. A summary of the main studies looking at CBT for older adults is provided in Table 2.2. For a more comprehensive review see Laidlaw (2001) and Laidlaw (in press).

SUMMARY OF DATA FROM OUTCOME STUDIES AND META-ANALYSES

Evidence has accumulated to support the applicability of psychological treatments for late-life depression, but there is little evidence to specify whether any particular type of therapy is most effective for such patients. With reference to Table 2.2, it would appear that while significant differences may

UNIVERSITY OF WOLVERHAMPTON
Harrison Learning Centre

ITEMS ISSUED:

Title: Older people, nursing and mental health
ID: 7621879028
Due: 30/04/2018 23:59

Title: Evidence informed nursing with older
people
ID: 7624908436
Due: 30/04/2018 23:59

Title: Cognitive behaviour therapy with older
people
ID: 7624421884X
Due: 30/04/2018 23:59

Total items: 3
Total fines: £1.60
23/04/2018 14:16
Issued: 5
Overdue: 0

Thank you for using Self Service.
Please keep your receipt.

Overdue books are fined at 40p per day for
1 week loans, 10p per day for long loans.

not always be apparent between treatments there is good evidence that cognitive therapy is a very effective treatment for late-life depression.

MYTHS AND STEREOTYPES ABOUT AGEING AND PSYCHOTHERAPY

Professionals have traditionally been characterized as holding pessimistic views about the value and utility of psychotherapy with older people (Butler, Lewis & Sunderland, 1998), but recently a number of surveys have modified this opinion (Gatz & Pearson, 1988). The legacy of Freud's assertion that older people lack the mental plasticity to change or to benefit from psychotherapy (Lovestone, 1983) has deterred many potential therapists from working psychologically with depressed or anxious older adults (Woods, 1995). Although Knight (1996a,b) notes that while those who do not work with older people may argue that older patients are unlikely to benefit from psychotherapy, practitioners in the field are more optimistic and enthusiastic about the range of benefits older people can derive from this approach.

There are a number of reasons why older people have not always received psychological interventions for a range of emotional problems. In part, a lack of training of professionals and therapists in geriatrics and gerontology has contributed to the lack of psychological provision for older adults. Often it is assumed that depression is a natural consequence of the losses experienced by older people in terms of emotional attachments, physical independence and socio-economic hardships. The 'understandability phenomenon' (Blanchard, 1992) or the 'fallacy of good reasons' (Unutzer et al., 1999) is the notion that depression in older people is in some way to be expected and is a normal part of ageing. Assumptions such as these can influence the expectations of client, therapist and physician alike, resulting in a sense of hopelessness about treatment (Unutzer et al., 1999).

A number of myths can contribute to a sense that psychotherapy may be less effective with this section of the population. The final section of this chapter provides information to debunk these myths.

WORKING WITH OLDER PEOPLE: MYTHS AND PSYCHOTHERAPY

Myth 1: You Can't Teach an Old Dog New Tricks

The belief that it is too late for older people to change, or 'you can't teach an old dog new tricks', is potentially very corrosive to any progress that can be achieved within therapy. In many cases older people will not seek treatment at all, or if they do seek treatment they will often have much reduced expectations for change (i.e. 'you have to accept you're not getting any younger'). The idea that increasing age is synonymous with a deadening of learning is erroneous. The American Association for Retired Persons (AARP, 2000) commissioned a survey to examine life-long learning in adults aged 50 years and over. The majority of respondents (90 per cent) reported that they were interested in continuing learning. Of the people surveyed, it appears that older people want to learn for the simple joy of learning, to enhance their spiritual or personal growth, and to keep up with what is going on in the world. Thus, older people continue to learn and consider this to be important. Consider the fact that many respondents in the AARP survey replied online. The National Organization for Adult Learning in the UK has a section on their website specifically dedicated to what it calls 'inspiring learners'. The examples are certainly inspiring, such as the 94-year-old attending college for the first time in her life in order to learn how to use computers, or the lady who, at 73, fulfilled a long held ambition to learn ballet at a dance class! Powell (1998) highlights the example of the author, Betty Friedan, who set out on her first outward-bound experience at the age of 60 after a life spent as a confirmed city-dweller. The MacArthur Foundation study on successful ageing (Rowe & Kahn, 1998) states that weaker short-term memory in older people can be overcome by training to the extent that trained older people can perform at higher levels than younger people who have not received any memory training. As Rowe and Kahn (1998) state, while the stereotype is of older people unable or unwilling to cope with change, 'Research has demonstrated the remarkable and enduring capacity of the aged brain to make new connections, absorb new data, and thus acquire new skills'.

Myth 2: It Must be Terrible Getting Old

When your patient says 'I hate being old', or 'it's a terrible thing to grow old', this can often be taken as a statement of fact rather than an indication that they hold ageist beliefs and have set up an expectancy bias for themselves where they expect to be unhappy because of their age. This myth often means that when older people develop depression they accept this as a 'normal' part of ageing rather than a disruption of functioning. The result is that older people may be willing to put up with much less help and support, even accepting second-class citizen status for themselves. Older people are just as likely as younger people to hold biases about getting old, where 'old' is seen as incompetent or decrepit. In truth, getting old may require changes and may indeed at times be quite difficult, but apart from depressed older people I have yet to meet anybody who would rather be dead than old. To grow old is a privilege. With the global increase in longevity (see Chapter 1) it is becoming clear that constriction of handicap and disability to later and later stages of life is becoming the norm. In many ways we can be optimistic about what our young-old age holds for many of us (Baltes & Smith, 2002).

Myth 3: Older People Don't Want Psychotherapy

The NIH consensus statement (NIH, 1991) suggested that older adults would reject any help or treatment from mental health services. Rokke and Scogin (1995) assessed the attitudes of older and younger adults towards different types of treatment for depression. Interestingly older adults expressed more positive attitudes towards mental health services than younger people. Landreville and colleagues (2001) also investigated the acceptability of psychological and pharmacological treatments for depression to older people. Using a series of case vignettes, older people reported cognitive, cognitive-behavioural and antidepressant medications as all being acceptable treatments for late-life depression. Interestingly, the acceptability of treatment types varies according to the level of severity of depression symptoms; for more severe depression symptoms, older people rated cognitive therapy as more acceptable than antidepressant medication. Hence the myth that older people do not want psychotherapy and prefer to take medications instead appears to be just that—a myth.

Finally, if older people did not want psychotherapy there would be no clinical examples to publish in this book. It is probably a fair assertion to state that all people attend psychologists with a degree of reticence regardless of age. Often with older clients there is a pervasive notion that it is wrong to discuss problems outside the family unit and they can often feel considerable guilt at their perceived inability to deal with their difficulties themselves (Thompson, 1996; Yost et al., 1986). Therefore, more emphasis is placed upon socialization into therapy (Emery, 1981) right at the start of therapy and implicit or covert feelings regarding the notions of therapy are discussed. Zeiss and Steffen (1996a) emphasize the non-pathologizing stance of CBT and state that this makes this type of approach particularly helpful for use with older adults suspicious of being labelled as mentally ill. Often the therapist may need to set aside time within initial sessions to take an educational approach and explain what depression is and what impact it has upon the individual.

Myth 4: Older People Benefit More from Concrete Interventions in Therapy but not 'Abstract' Elements of Therapy such as Thought Monitoring

Following work with a group of depressed patients attending a day hospital, Church (1983) has suggested that dysfunctional thought records (DTR) are not relevant and are invalid for work with older adults. Church (1983) published one of the first papers focusing on process issues in cognitive therapy for late-life depression. The poor results that Church obtained with his sample has had far-reaching consequences as many clinicians have developed beliefs that older people are unable to deal with abstract aspects of therapy such as thought monitoring and challenging. In many respects, Church's paper unwittingly reinforces Freud's view that older people lack the mental plasticity to cope with psychotherapy. As with any individual of any age, in therapy the issue in the application and use of thought monitoring and challenging is *timing*. To use dysfunctional thought records without preparing the groundwork often results in failure of compliance with this task as homework. Often events from the weekly activity schedule (WAS)—a diary of a week in the life of the patient—in which pleasure ratings show a drop are good points at which to introduce the concept of thoughts impacting upon the individual producing negative mood changes (see Chapter 5).

Myth 5: To be Old is to be Sick or 'If I Had the Problems of Later Life, I'd be Depressed Too'

This myth is also known as the understandability phenomenon (Blanchard, 1992) or the fallacy of good reasons (Unutzer et al., 1999). Often an older client may have a number of physical conditions that can make depression or anxiety more challenging to treat. For example, when the patient has significant hearing or sight problems, this can often leave the therapist wondering whether their therapeutic skills are going to be at all useful. It is very easy to be drawn into feelings of hopelessness and therapeutic inadequacy when confronted by clients who appear to be unable to perform some activity of daily living that we may have taken for granted. In the example of patients whose vision is so poor as to require them to use prosthetic aids to allow independent functioning, this can be challenging to work with using a cognitive framework. The therapist might find themselves asking, 'How can I make therapy effective if we cannot use diaries to record behaviour or thoughts?' or 'How can I ensure that my patient can take part in behavioural experiments to test out possibly erroneous beliefs?'

It is sometimes easy to be drawn into accepting that increasing age is something to fear and dread, especially when 'objectively bad' conditions such as dementia, stroke and Parkinson's disease afflict your client. It is important to bear in mind that even where there are high rates of depression associated with certain medical conditions, the correspondence is not 1:1. Thus there is an important psychological component to how well an individual responds to the presence of physical illnesses. It is important to explore the meanings that the circumstances hold for the individual. Does the person have experience of illness in the family that is equated with disability and dependence? Often this age-cohort will have certain beliefs about illness that need to be addressed in therapy. Depression is not an automatic consequence to physical illness. Therapists are not immune to developing negative automatic thoughts themselves with regard to dealing with older people with multiple physical complaints. An important rule of thumb here is to ask oneself, 'Would this situation be acceptable or understandable in a younger cohort?' Often a therapist will state, 'My patient's problems are realistic, so thought monitoring and challenging is not helpful in these circumstances'. The net effect of these beliefs is that the patient's depression remains untreated. Sympathy, of course, can never be an adequate treatment for depression. This, however, is to forget that disability may have developed gradually so that the individual will most probably have had time to adjust and accommodate to it. To be explicit, depression is not a natural consequence of old age. Everyone who is depressed deserves treatment for this, however 'reasonable' the depression may seem in the circumstances.

Myth 6: Too Little Gain for Too Much Pain: Older People are at the End of their Lives, so the Ratio of Benefit to Cost is Very Low

Older people are often concerned that they are wasting the therapist's time as they may consider their problems to be primarily related to their age (e.g. 'I'm not depressed. It's just my age'). It is important that the therapist takes a validating position by not dismissing the patient's views or by simply providing reassurance. The therapist can ask patients what they consider would be a good way to make sure they made the most of their therapy sessions. From previous sections of this chapter, it should be apparent that therapists are not immune to developing unhelpful or interfering thoughts and beliefs that may influence *their* behaviour. It is important to examine our thoughts and our beliefs as these may have the effect of limiting what can be achieved both within sessions and over the course of treatment. In a very thought-provoking address at the World Congress on Cognitive Therapy in 1998, Christine Padesky suggested that the ultimate efficacy of cognitive therapy was enhanced or limited by the beliefs of the therapist practising cognitive therapy. It is arguable that skilled therapists who hold beliefs that cognitive interventions are potentially beneficial to the clients with whom they come into contact will be more inclined to adopt a 'try it and see' approach. This approach arguably enhances rather than limits therapy options that potentially have an impact on outcome.

SUMMARY

A lot of empirical evidence has been accumulated to suggest that older people can, and frequently do, benefit from psychotherapy for depression and anxiety. Since the time of Freud, psychotherapists have often viewed working with older adults as unattractive or as a waste of their efforts. Services have developed and been guided by the idea that emotional distress in later life is primarily a function of ageing, and myths and stereotypes have tended to interfere with therapists' abilities to work through issues and problems that arise in late-life depression. It is hoped that this chapter has helped therapists to apply CBT with older adults in the spirit of empiricism; unless you try you will never know what the outcome will be.

Chapter 3

COGNITIVE-BEHAVIOURAL MODEL FOR OLDER PEOPLE

INTRODUCTION

Conceptualizing treatment plans (formulation) for older people with depression can be challenging because of the presence of many complicating factors such as medical comorbidity, alterations in role status and the potential for stress in various intergenerational relationships. In working with older people, there may be important aspects of cohort beliefs and attitudes towards ageing that may influence behaviour. Making sense of all the data that may be available on the patient can be very daunting. Formulation allows the therapist and patient to focus on individual circumstances rather than getting stuck in a loss-deficit mode of thinking about the problems facing older people. For too long, this has been part of the 'practitioner heritage' when working with older adults (Knight, 1996b).

Understanding how people idiosyncratically respond to stressors is important for the successful outcome in any psychological treatment. While formulation is a skill valued by many clinicians, there is often a feeling that explicit written formulations may bias therapists from hearing information that runs contrary to the working formulation (Eells, 1997; Denman, 1995). However, formulations are hypotheses to be tested out for their clinical utility (Persons, 1993, 1991, 1989) and foster awareness of underlying issues that can

Cognitive Behaviour Therapy with Older People.
Ken Laidlaw, Larry W. Thompson, Leah Dick-Siskin & Dolores Gallagher-Thompson.
© 2003 John Wiley & Sons Ltd.

only enhance treatment outcome. This chapter presents a psychotherapy formulation model for use with older adults.

THE IMPORTANCE OF FORMULATION IN CBT WITH OLDER PEOPLE

Formulation is one of the key skills in cognitive therapy. If techniques such as Socratic questioning, graded task assignment, thought monitoring and challenging are the science of cognitive therapy, then formulation is the art. The importance of formulation in therapy is that it seeks to reconcile what is known about patients' beliefs and vulnerability factors with their thoughts, feelings and behavioural responses to current stressors (Persons, 1993, 1989). Formulation provides therapists with a tool to understand their patient quickly and efficiently. Persons (1991) also proposes that case formulation can improve treatment outcome: 'All else being equal, outcome ought to be better for a patient treated with an accurate formulation than a patient treated with an inaccurate formulation' (Persons, 1991, p. 103). Formulation also prevents 'therapeutic drift' in longer-term cases (Denman, 1995).

While formulation incorporates information that is congruent with what is known about an individual, formulation in therapy also seeks to reconcile and incorporate seemingly incompatible information within a reasonably broad and comprehensible understanding of an individual.

FORMULATION IS A THEORY

Eells (1997) provides a useful working definition of formulation and states 'A formulation is essentially a hypothesis about the causes, precipitants and maintaining influences of a person's psychological, interpersonal, and behavioural problems'. Essentially, formulation is a way to understand the idiosyncratic nature of the patient's difficulties (Warwick, 1995; Greenberger & Padesky, 1995a; Persons, 1989). A formulation is a theory that clinicians develop about their patients. If they are to be useful to clinicians, formulations should be descriptive and predictive and be able to identify potential pitfalls in therapy.

Formulations are beneficial to therapeutic outcome in the sense that they aid the important process of understanding between patient and therapist (Persons, 1993). Formulation serves an important function in terms of the therapeutic relationship or alliance enhancement. Therapeutic alliance is a term more commonly associated with psychodynamic orientations; however, it is gaining increasing acceptance as a 'pantheoretical construct' (Horvath & Luborksy, 1993). Barber et al. (2000) provide evidence that a good understanding between therapist and patient (alliance) significantly predicted positive changes in levels of depression.

Working from an explicit formulation, the therapist is able to make more accurate and earlier interpretations of a patient's actions and motives. The accuracy with which the therapist is able to make interpretations aids understanding and provides the patient with the feeling of being listened to and understood. This is a critical ingredient of a strong and productive therapeutic relationship. Rarely within therapy sessions is behaviour considered to be unimportant for understanding the patient's everyday style of relating outside of sessions. Jacobsen (1989) states that dysfunctional beliefs influencing a patient's everyday functioning are likely to determine specific behaviours of the patient in therapy. Safran and Segal (1996) likewise suggest that the patient's habitual style of relating to an other will result in interpersonal styles of relating and behaviours that are played out within therapy sessions.

ASSESSMENT FOR FORMULATION AND TREATMENT

Therapists can often be wary of asking too many historical questions for fear of getting lost in the mire of past issues. Alternatively, some therapists may consider that the only way the patient's current episode of depression can be understood is if the whole developmental history of the individual is explored. Formulation allows a middle way in which the individual's current episode is the main focus of treatment, but other more distal factors may permit a fuller understanding of the context to the development and maintenance of current difficulties.

It is good practice to attempt to formulate an understanding of a patient's difficulties as early as possible in therapy to avoid misunderstandings and to enhance the choice of treatment interventions. A collaborative approach to data collection can compensate for any inaccuracies in the early process of formulation. Table 3.1 illustrates the type of information that can be covered usefully when developing a formulation.

USING FORMULATION TO CONFRONT OBSTACLES TO PROGRESS

Formulation guides interventions and helps therapists to predict and avoid potential pitfalls (Persons & Tompkins, 1997; Persons, 1989). When a patient says 'It is terrible being old, I don't want to burden anyone with my troubles' there are two ways to deal with this. Without a formulation this can be dealt with as a negative thought and the approach seems evident: cognitive restructuring. With a cognitive formulation taking account of gerontology

Table 3.1 Information to collect when developing a cognitive case formulation

Type of information required	Content of information
Differential diagnosis	• What is the primary diagnosis? Is there evidence for the presence of other secondary axis I or axis II diagnoses?

Psychological assessment/problem list	• What is the reason you are seeing this patient? Description of problem(s) by patient
	• What other factors contribute to the current difficulties: cognitive, behavioural, physiological?
	    I. Core and conditional beliefs
	    II. Contingent reinforcement schedules
	    III. Excess disability in chronic medical conditions
	• Impact of problem; occupational, interpersonal, social?
	• What event(s) or stimuli account for the onset of your client's current difficulties. What are the triggers for this current episode? Have there been similar or previous episodes?
	• What are the client's vulnerabilities in terms of the current stressor(s) and in terms of previous episodes of depression and anxiety or previous response to stressors?

Background and context	• What developmental factors have contributed towards the existence of underlying beliefs, rules or standards currently contributing towards the client's difficulties? • How has the person coped with personally challenging situations in the past?
Cohort factors	• What generational beliefs may be important for understanding your client's response to their current difficulties? • Are there cognitive, social or physical limitations that may be important to take account of in the development of a treatment plan? • Are there any issues of loss, health, role/status, interpersonal functioning that need to be taken into account? • Are there any pertinent intergenerational role stressors?
Measurement	• What measures will contribute to an understanding of the patient's current difficulties and allow progress during therapy to be tracked? • Diaries, weekly activity schedule, mood monitoring form, thought diaries. Standardized measures (e.g. BDI, GDS, PSWI, BHS, etc.)
Sociocultural context	• What are the person's attitudes towards his or her own ageing? Is there evidence of the internalization of specific ethnically based or socioculturally grounded beliefs about growing old?
Therapeutic alliance	• What is the patient's style of relating? Is the patient open or somewhat defensive? Does the patient keep focused on one task or does he or she require prompts? Is the patient likeable?

Note: BDI = Beck Depression Inventory, GDS = Geriatric Depression Scale, PSWI = Penn State Worry Inventory, BHS = Beck Hopelessness Scale.

knowledge about older adults, the statement the patient has made needs to be addressed at an entirely different level and with entirely different behavioural and cognitive strategies. For example, does this statement reflect the interaction of core and conditional beliefs about themselves in terms of lovability (i.e. I am unlovable, and therefore if I am a burden to others they will reject me), or is this statement more representative of an expression of a widely held cohort belief (i.e. a belief held by a birth-year defined age group) that one should always stand on one's own feet. Alternatively, the statement may reflect an internalization of negative sociocultural beliefs about growing old where increasing age is seen as indicating a greater burden on others and society in general.

Obtaining a conceptualizing view of this statement requires clarifying questions to be asked. It would be useful to ask how long the patients have been concerned with being a burden to others. When they think of needing help, what sorts of thoughts and feelings are generated? Where does their notion of burden come from? Have they experience of caring for others and, importantly, what sorts of supports from peers and other family members do they seek out? In taking an explorative approach, it is necessary to assess for a wider understanding of statements rather than adopt an excessively technique-driven approach. In doing so important beliefs may begin to emerge that may help the therapist to obtain a more thorough understanding of the patient, thus potentially reducing the length of treatment while at the same time enhancing the outcome. The difference of approaches to this statement underlines the importance of formulation in cognitive therapy with older adults, and this important issue will be discussed in more detail later in this chapter.

HOW AND WHEN TO DISCUSS FORMULATIONS WITH THE PATIENT

Since cognitive therapy stresses a collaborative stance between patient and therapist, at some point the formulation must be shared with the patient, therefore the formulation ought to make sense to the patient (Warwick, 1995) and should address the primary concern of the patient that is related to the central irrational belief (Persons, 1989). A formulation can guide not only the types of interventions that a therapist considers important—given the idiosyncratic nature of a patient's difficulties—but can also serve to influence the timing of the introduction of interventions (Persons, 1993). It is important when sharing a formulation with a patient that the therapist is mindful to assess whether the patient has the requisite resources to challenge and deal successfully with the issue at hand.

Eells (1997) stresses that in deriving a clinical formulation a tension can often be engendered between immediacy and/or comprehensiveness. A balance needs to be struck by the therapist as to when he or she feels that enough information has been gathered from sessions to develop a written explicit formulation that will determine at least the early part of therapy. In a sense, a formulation will always be incomplete (Eells, 1997; Persons & Tompkins, 1997). It can be very tempting to wait for the 'final' piece of the puzzle to become clear before putting pen to paper, but often putting pen to paper invokes a process of thinking about a patient that may paradoxically provide a new perspective or the final piece of the puzzle. A related issue concerns when to feed back a formulation to a patient. The answer to this question is that one may feed back working formulations or parts of a working formulation as early as the beginning of the second or third session at least as a way of clarifying information or hypotheses.

There is no clinical algorithm that can prescribe the correct time to share a formulation. The time for this varies, owing to a number of factors such as the complexity of the patient's presentation, the therapist's confidence and experience in developing a formulation and whether the therapy will be enhanced by a sharing of ideas and hypotheses about the underlying nature of the patient's difficulties. *Therapists are probably ready to discuss a formulation when a single sentence defines the hypothesized nature of the patient's main difficulty.* It is very crucial that the therapist takes great care to ensure the patient's participation in the feedback of the formulation. Frequent use of summarizing statements that end in a question on the relevance of what has been fed back to the patient is recommended.

A useful tool for ensuring a collaborative participation between therapist and patient in producing a formulation is to use a whiteboard or a flipchart. The therapist may take the lead in putting some organizing titles (such as important early experiences) on the flipchart and ask the patient to fill in the blank spaces. To further ensure ownership of the formulation by the patient, incomplete aspects of the formulation can be agreed upon as homework for him or her to reflect upon. For example, it may be useful to ask patients to note the types of negative automatic thoughts they commonly notice and what sense they make of this repetition. Presenting a formulation using a single modality, i.e. a mini-lecture, provides information that quickly becomes overwhelming and off-putting. This is to be avoided by use of participation in multi-modal presentations within a session.

There is always a danger that a patient can be overwhelmed, or feel criticized, or devalued by a clinical formulation (Denman, 1995). To avoid this the therapist needs to constantly assess the patient's level of understanding of the relevance of this task. When working with older people, repetition of new information is usually a good idea (Thompson, 1996). The therapist must aim to provide information in easily digestible chunks before proceeding with further information. It goes almost without saying that technological jargon must be kept to a minimum while active participation in the process of understanding must be maximized. While discussing the formulation, it is important that any 'hot thoughts' about what patients think about their life being laid bare is identified and, if necessary, challenged. The judicious use of humour may help to defuse a potentially difficult session. When working with older adults formulation can take many forms and therapists have to use their own clinical judgement on the most appropriate time to feed back information and hypotheses. In many cases a formulation that takes into account the overt–covert distinction may be enough to attract the patient's attention. For cases where there are multiple problems, as is often the case when working with older adults, a formulation is especially useful as it prevents the therapist feeling overwhelmed.

A COGNITIVE MODEL FOR CBT WITH OLDER ADULTS

Working therapeutically with older people can be different from working with younger people in a number of important respects, such as the higher likelihood of physical conditions, changes in cognitive capacity, different cohort experiences and, in certain circumstances, getting the patient to re-initiate good practices rather than learn new practices (Thompson, 1996; Knight, 1996b). The fact that psychotherapists are much less comfortable dealing with physical problems and may be biased in terms of outcome when patients present with comorbid health problems (Haley, 1996; James & Haley, 1995) underlines the need to develop a model that will allow cognitive therapy practitioners to feel comfortable about using their techniques with older adults, whatever the circumstances.

The adaptations that may be required when working with older adults are more likely to be recognized when drawing up a formulation as this allows the therapist to conceptualize the main issues involved in each individual treatment package. The formulation that is suggested here aims to enhance the effectiveness of CBT when working with older adults. As such the CBT model, first described by Beck and colleagues (1979), is supplemented by information and understandings from gerontology. The information necessary to develop a formulation with older people is summarized in Table 3.2.

Cognitive Model

The Beck model for therapy (Clark et al., 1999; Beck et al., 1979) suggests that early experiences are important for the later development of beliefs and attitudes. Within the structure of Beck's cognitive model of psychopathology there are a number of levels of belief. At the primary level are the *core beliefs*, which are rigid and inflexible and usually begin with 'I am...People are...The world is...' An important secondary level is the *conditional beliefs*, so called because they often take the form of 'if...then' statements. This intermediary class of belief is often the rule by which a person operates in the world. Conditional beliefs represent the operation of core beliefs in action. For

Table 3.2 Clinical formulation with older adults

Elements in a formulation	Description of each element
Early experiences	Clinically relevant developmental events that the patient recognizes as important over the course of his or her lifespan. Experiences are linked to specific hypothesized core beliefs
Core beliefs	The therapist hypothesizes about the patient's most important personal beliefs, the world and/or the motivations of others
Conditional beliefs	The therapist hypothesizes how core beliefs are translated into action in the patient's everyday functioning. Most usually specified in the form of 'if…then' statements
Activating events/ precipitants	Therapist and patient work together to agree upon external events, situations or stressors that may have triggered current episode of depression and/or anxiety
Compensatory strategies	The therapist hypothesizes how the patient may have coped with certain maladaptive beliefs by converting them into functional behavioural strategies to gain positive contingent reinforcement from significant others
Negative automatic thoughts	The repetitive nature of negative thoughts reflects the operation of activated core beliefs during an episode of anxiety or depression
Cohort	The shared beliefs and experiences of age-specific generation. The importance of shared culture and developments in 'the time in which one lives' (Smyer & Qualls, 1999)
Role investment	The importance and function of roles carried on or lost by the patient as he or she ages
Health function	The physical health status of the patient is assessed in terms of independence and opportunities for autonomy
Sociocultural beliefs	The internalization or rejection of beliefs about ageing in the culture and society in which older people live
Intergenerational linkages	The stresses and supports of important close relationships across generations. Linkages that connect people with the society and culture in which they live

[handwritten margin note: Additional to main formulation]

instance, a person who has the core belief 'I am bad' may have the intermediary belief '*If* I let people get close to me *then* they will find out about me and reject me'. A further, intermediary, class is the compensatory beliefs (Beck, 1995): for instance, if a person states 'I am bad' the compensatory belief is 'I must protect myself from rejection'. The compensatory strategy may be to sabotage relationships with other people when they appear to be getting too close. When developing a formulation at this cognitive level, it is important that early experiences are linked to specific core beliefs that are in turn linked to specific conditional beliefs and then to compensatory strategies.

Another important concept in the cognitive model of psychopathology is the concept of negative automatic thoughts. Negative automatic thoughts reflect the existence of underlying dysfunctional schemas. Negative automatic thoughts can often be collected together to identify themes that are evident in an individual's belief system. The therapist uses this knowledge when formulating the patient's story in order to determine the cognitive-behavioural interventions that may be necessary.

The standard cognitive therapy formulation outlined above is supplemented with additional important information necessary when working with older adults, such as cohort beliefs, role investments, intergenerational linkages, sociocultural context and physical health. Each of these elements is considered in detail below.

Cohort

Knight (1999, 1996a) states that working with older adults means learning something of the folkways of people born many years before. For many older people there may be certain cohort beliefs that may interfere with psychotherapy outcomes such as 'It is wrong to discuss my personal business outside the family' or 'To seek help for problems is a sign of weakness of character'. Lebowitz and Niederehe (1992) state, 'The stigma of mental illness is especially strong in the current cohort of elderly people, who tend to associate mental disorder with personal failure, spiritual deficiency, or some other stereotypic view'.

Combining cohort beliefs about weakness and spiritual deficiency with core beliefs about failure requires the therapist who works with older adults to take the initiative in discussing the possibility of these beliefs interacting to prevent a patient gaining benefit from therapy. For instance, during the first two or three sessions, the therapist may find it helpful to explicitly ask the patient to state the sorts of ideas or beliefs that make it difficult to talk comfortably within sessions. Alternatively the therapist can take a psycho-educational approach and discuss the idea of cohort beliefs as a potential barrier to relating information of a sensitive nature. Unless the therapist takes the initiative during this early phase of therapy, the patient may be left feeling vulnerable and may be more likely to discontinue therapy prematurely.

Role investments

Role investment may also constitute an additional important variable to evaluate when working with older adults. Champion and Power (1995) state that vulnerability to depression is related to the extent to which an individual invests in certain highly valued roles and goals. Over-investment, that is, investment in certain roles and goals to the exclusion of all others, may constitute vulnerability for the development of depression. In their review, Champion and Power (1995) state that there may be a gender bias in the sorts of roles and goals in the investment. Women are more likely to invest in interpersonal relationships and men are more likely to invest in areas of achievement-orientation such as work. The relevance of this information when working with older adults is that with increasing age both men and women are at a higher risk of loss in these potentially important areas of investment and self-validation. Women are more likely to be widows and to live alone. Men may have lost over-valued roles after retirement. When working with older people it is useful to take a considered explorative approach to the sorts of roles and values that older people may have invested in over the years. Self-validation is an ongoing developmental task that does not halt when an individual becomes older.

Intergenerational linkages

Intergenerational relationships can often create tensions, especially when older generations do not always approve of, or understand, changes in family structures or marital relationships (Silverstein & Bengston, 2001; Bengston et al., 2000). Thompson (1996) notes that it is common for relationship strains between older adults and their adult children to precipitate a depressive episode. With the change in family and society demographics (increased longevity, smaller family sizes, increased rates of divorce and subsequent remarriage) grandparents and great-grandparents perform an important role in our societies and provide strong intergenerational linkages across families (Bengston, 2001; Bengston & Boss, 2000). The result of demographic changes in society has meant that older people often spend more time with younger generations than ever before and have more diverse roles (Parrott, Mills & Bengston, 2000).

Older generations tend to value continuity and transmission of values whereas younger generations value autonomy and independence. In addition, successive generations often achieve higher occupational standings and this again creates a gap in understanding between generations (Silverstein & Bengston, 2001; Bengston et al., 2000). When working with older people, therapists may find themselves discussing their patients' relationships with their adult children without a full understanding of the sorts of idiographic and structural tensions that can exist across generations. To ignore these tensions as just evidence of the 'generation gap' is to miss out on important stressors in the lives of older adults. Hence, in this formulation model, this element is explicitly identified.

Sociocultural Context

The variable of interest in this context is primarily the person's own attitude towards ageing. Often patients will explicitly state that growing old is a terrible experience. Expressions such as these can appear to be realistic appraisals of a difficult time of life but in fact are very corrosive statements that conceal the internalization of sociocultural negative stereotypes about growing old. Older people themselves can develop a form of the 'under-standability phenomenon' where they assume that if they are unhappy or depressed, then this is a normal part of ageing. Unfortunately beliefs such as these often prevent individuals from seeking treatment or, at the very least, from making the most of treatment when it is offered. The therapist needs to explore the patient's sociocultural context at the start of therapy. Formulations of beliefs about ageing are very important if therapy is to proceed in a timely and efficacious fashion. The sociocultural context also takes into account the values of the therapist. One must work to develop a realistic understanding of ways of treating older people.

Physical Health

Increasing age brings with it an increased likelihood of developing chronic medical conditions. There are some conditions that are mainly diseases of old age, such as dementia, stroke, myocardial infarction and other cardiac diseases. However, it does not follow that all older people have a chronic medical condition that has a limiting functional effect. In any formulation with older adults, it is important to enquire about the presence and impact of medical conditions. Medical conditions such as epilepsy often carried a social stigma among previous generations, and in these instances an individual may hold important beliefs about the presence of certain medical conditions. It is not uncommon for older people to hide illnesses through embarrassment caused by long-held misconceptions.

APPLICATION OF THE MODEL IN PRACTICE

The elements of a clinical formulation are laid in a schematic (see Figure 3.1) using the following case example as a guide.

Mrs K is a 73-year-old retired healthcare worker. She became depressed shortly after an incident when she was working for a charity. She became convinced that she had given the wrong information to someone who had asked her advice and immediately decided to retire before she made some serious errors (some evidence of an internal negative stereotype of ageing). As she cut back on activities she became more depressed and tended to isolate herself from her friends. She started to become depressed about her depression (Teasdale, 1985), seeing herself as weak and a failure. She would often compare herself unfavourably with her deceased mother whom she often stated had experienced 'real hardships' in her life and had never become depressed. She also strongly believed that people should never 'burden'

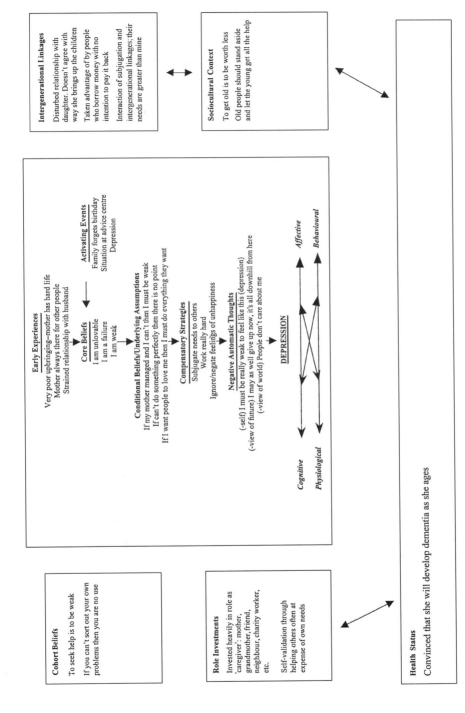

Cohort Beliefs

To seek help is to be weak

If you can't sort out your own problems then you are no use

Intergenerational Linkages

Disturbed relationship with daughter. Doesn't agree with way she brings up the children

Taken advantage of by people who borrow money with no intention to pay it back

Interaction of subjugation and intergenerational linkages; their needs are greater than mine

Sociocultural Context

To get old is to be worth less

Old people should stand aside and let the young get all the help

Early Experiences

Very poor upbringing–mother has hard life
Mother always there for other people
Strained relationship with husband

Activating Events

Family forgets birthday
Situation at advice centre
Depression

Core Beliefs

I am unlovable
I am a failure
I am weak

Conditional Beliefs/Underlying Assumptions

If my mother managed and I can't then I must be weak
If can't do something perfectly then there is no point
If I want people to love me then I must do everything they want

Compensatory Strategies

Subjugate needs to others
Work really hard
Ignore/negate feelings of unhappiness

Negative Automatic Thoughts

(-self) I must be really weak to feel like this (depression)
(-view of future) I may as well give up now, it's all downhill from here
(-view of world) People don't care about me

DEPRESSION

Affective

Behavioural

Cognitive

Physiological

Role Investments

Invested heavily in role as 'caregiver': mother, grandmother, friend, neighbour, charity worker, etc.

Self-validation through helping others often at expense of own needs

Health Status

Convinced that she will develop dementia as she ages

Figure 3.1 Cognitive formulation using cognitive model for CBT with older people

anyone else with their problems. In a sense, she identified with a cohort belief that to be depressed is evidence of a weakness of character, and that people ought to stand on their own two feet. Mrs K also had a disturbed relationship (negative intergenerational linkages) with her family and would often overcompensate for any difficulties in their relationships by entirely subjugating her needs to them. She appeared to endorse the view that her needs were secondary to those of other people. This was evidenced by the fact that she would often 'lend' money to her great-niece, despite the fact that the money was never returned. Mrs K would state 'her needs are greater than mine'.

The cognitive formulation seen in Figure 3.1 was derived and discussed with Mrs K. It takes into account *precipitating factors, predisposing factors* and *maintaining factors*. The formulation also takes account of age-related factors and cohort beliefs. The formulation is descriptive of the nature of her current difficulties and also predictive in the sense that from the hypothesized conditional beliefs one might predict that she will characterize her difficulties as weakness and might therefore be more likely to see these as unchangeable. Mrs K might also present other challenges to the therapist, as she appears to hold the view that getting old is synonymous with developing dementia. From a previous interaction with Mrs K it became clear that she would over-react whenever she made any mistakes (note the extreme reaction in her charity work) and often assumed that she was starting to develop a dementia. It is not unusual for people with direct dementia caregiving experiences to develop fears about dementia and to become concerned over what they perceive as their poor memory performance (Barker et al., 1994).

Core beliefs are described that highlight the global, stable and internal nature of her attributions (see Rehm, 1977). Mrs K has always set high expectations for herself and her expectations regarding the extent of change and the pace of change in therapy need to be explored. She is also very compliant and in therapy the therapist might predict that she will find it difficult at first to take a full part in therapy, as she may go along with what the therapist suggests in terms topics in sessions. Challenging interpersonal core beliefs (Safran & Segal, 1990) is discussed in more detail in Chapter 7. Over-compliance by Mrs K requires the therapist to work hard to ensure Mrs K's active participation in therapy and in ensuring that her needs (apart from the need to please) are being met in therapy. In the early stage of therapy the therapist may make this one of the goals for treatment.

Also of note in this formulation is the delineation of compensatory strategies that Mrs K uses to cope with dysfunctional attitudes and core beliefs. Behavioural experiments can be developed to challenge the utility of Mrs K's compensatory strategies. The compensatory strategies ought to be considered as more malleable than core beliefs, but less malleable than negative automatic thoughts, and consideration needs to be given to the correct time to challenge these coping strategies.

The therapist can use all the insights from this formulation when planning interventions and can decide to apply some simple behavioural experiments initially to increase Mrs K's confidence in her abilities. The subjugation of her needs reflects an important core belief that she developed from her understandings of her mother. In addition, she faces stresses in intergenerational relationships that reinforce her belief that in order to gain the approval of others she needs to do whatever they wish. In a discussion of this formulation, Mrs K found it interesting to draw parallels between herself and her idealization of her mother. She could see that this was unhelpful to her when she was dealing with depression as she was labelling herself as weak and inadequate—a view not shared by her closest friends.

CONCLUSIONS AND SUMMARY

Formulations are a relative newcomer in terms of cognitive therapy. Formulations that take account of the challenges facing older adults hold the promise of providing an improved treatment outcome. Formulations also provide therapists with a chance to avoid feeling overwhelmed by the wealth of clinical data they may be dealing with when working with older adults. However, formulations are beneficial to therapeutic outcome in the sense that they aid the important process of understanding between patient and therapist. Given that older adults may at times feel devalued and unwanted by the value placed upon youth in our societies, this experience can be a very powerful agent for change. The new cognitive model developed here will be discussed in detail and applied throughout the rest of this book.

Section Two

COGNITIVE THERAPY FOR LATE-LIFE DEPRESSION

Chapter 4

CBT FOR LATE-LIFE DEPRESSIVE DISORDERS

INTRODUCTION

Depression during later life is often referred to as the 'common cold' of geriatric mental health. Faced with the many losses and hardships that one may encounter during the later years, periods of being downhearted, sad or blue may be expected with greater frequency and regularity. Whether or not these episodes meet criteria for a diagnosis of depressive illness is an issue currently under continued exploration. There are controversies as to whether the criteria for a diagnosis of a mood disorder ought to be different for the elderly, whether the measuring devices currently in use are appropriate, or whether additional categories of depressive disorders should be included in the classification systems. These debates are fuelled by observations that the expression of depression may indeed be different in the elderly, with those characteristics reflecting depletion being emphasized more than those reflecting intense changes in affect (see Powers et al., 2002, for a review). In the absence of firm guidelines specific to the diagnosis of depressive disorders in this age group, the presence of depressive symptoms alone unfortunately may be frequently overlooked when considering the advisability of a treatment programme for older persons. The need for attention to this issue becomes more apparent in the light of current epidemiological research.

Cognitive Behaviour Therapy with Older People.
Ken Laidlaw, Larry W. Thompson, Leah Dick-Siskin & Dolores Gallagher-Thompson.
© 2003 John Wiley & Sons Ltd.

SIGNS AND SYMPTOMS OF DEPRESSION IN THE ELDERLY

When one thinks about symptoms of depression, the first one that invariably comes to mind is 'being sad, downhearted and blue'. However, depressed older adults do not always present with sadness as the predominant feature (Lebowitz et al., 1997). Sadness may even be denied altogether, or only added reluctantly after substantive questioning as the belief systems of some older cohorts may constrain many from acknowledging that a particular pattern of complaints was anything more than just the typical aches and pains of 'normal ageing'.

Symptoms associated with depression are often grouped conveniently into four general categories: emotional, cognitive, physical and volitional (Blazer, 2002). When assessing depression in older people, it is important to look for other features, such as irritability or anger, somatic complaints with no apparent medical basis, memory complaints with no other indications of cognitive difficulties, expressions of hopelessness and complaints of being unable to do things, diminished interest or pleasure in usual activities, increased worries, pronounced slowing when engaging in activities or general lack of personal health care (Gallo & Rabins, 1999). Also, restrictions in social and vocational roles normally associated with ageing may influence how both the patient and clinician evaluate the presence of impaired functioning in different roles.

Observable indicators of depression can occasionally be difficult to evaluate with older people. For example, when considering appearance, a stooped posture may be the result of a medical condition; unkempt appearance may reflect a response to a less demanding schedule; and bowel problems may occur because of improper diet and water intake. All of these 'symptoms' may or may not be due to depression. Similarly, confusion may reflect possible nervous system (CNS) changes rather than changes in affect level. Signs of psychomotor retardation, such as slowed speech and movements, shuffling gait and constrained movements, may be due to pain or possible dysfunction in the extrapyramidal motor system that may or may not be accompanied by changes in affect. Signs of psychomotor agitation, such as picking and pacing, can also be a result of CNS changes. In working with older people care must be taken to rule out other possible causes of these signs before attributing them solely to depression.

The clinician should not overlook the possible implications of depression, especially as symptom clusters frequently do not appear in number or duration to meet criteria for a diagnosis of major depressive disorder as currently specified in the DSM or the ICD classification systems. Blazer (2002) emphasizes that this 'subsyndromal' condition in the older adult warrants serious consideration from health and mental health professionals when developing treatment programmes. For example, Gallo et al. (1997) found that older adults who reported feeling hopeless or worthless had thoughts of death or suicide, and only two other depressive symptoms were at increased risk for disability, distress and death even in the absence of dysphoria or anhedonia.

In the DSM classification system (APA, 2000) depressive disorder categories are discounted if they are clearly due to a general medical condition. Furthermore, they must also be of sufficient magnitude to 'cause clinically significant distress or impairment in social, occupational, or other important areas of functioning' (DSM-IV-TR, p. 356). Herein lies a difficulty in formulating a diagnosis for an older person, which may contribute in part to the negative relationship between age and prevalence of depressive disorders in adult community samples. Many of these symptoms do occur in the elderly as a result of other problems, and may often be discounted for this reason, when in fact their presence may be aggravated or amplified by a mood disturbance, thus when working with older adults therapists must exercise good clinical judgement when arriving at a diagnostic decision. More comprehensive discussions of this issue can be found elsewhere (see Blazer, 2002; Thompson et al., 2002).

ASSESSMENT OF DEPRESSION IN THE OLDER ADULT

Detailed discussions concerning the problems and issues involved in assessment can be found elsewhere (Blazer, 2002; Karel et al., 2002; Powers et al., 2002; Pachana, Gallagher-Thompson & Thompson, 1994). An excellent compilation of screening instruments for special populations, many of which address depressive symptoms among other behavioural problems, are included in a special issue of the *Psychopharmacology Bulletin* (Raskin & Niederehe, 1988).

Screening instruments are useful in detecting the possible presence of depressive symptoms, and completion of one of these by the patient can sometimes indicate to the health professionals that more in-depth assessments might reveal the presence of significant depressive symptoms. Several that have been used with older populations include the Geriatric Depression Scale (Yesavage et al., 1983), the Center for Epidemiological Studies—Depression (CES-D; Radloff, 1977), and the Beck Depression Inventory (Beck, Steer & Brown, 1996). In addition, the Cornell Scale for Depression in Dementia (Alexopoulos et al., 1988) is particularly useful when screening for depression in patients who are experiencing serious cognitive impairment. More recently, the CES-D-Revised has been developed to correspond with DSM-IV criteria for depression (Eaton, Smith & Muntaner, 1999; cited in Gallo & Rabins, 1999). This instrument shows promise for use as a screening instrument with older populations.

If a mood disorder is suspected, then a more detailed evaluation is in order. The process should involve a review of current medical problems and treatments, living conditions and other available resources including social and instrumental support systems, a general mental status examination, brief screening of cognitive capabilities followed by more comprehensive cognitive assessment if indicated, and a careful assessment for current and past mood disorders. It is, however, beyond the scope of this book to discuss this process in detail, and useful discussions concerning the interview assessment process can be found elsewhere (Blazer, 2002; Karel et al., 2002).

COGNITIVE BEHAVIOUR THERAPY OF LATE-LIFE DEPRESSION

The question is often raised as to whether CBT must be modified to be effective with older adults (see Chapters 2 and 3, and Laidlaw (2001) for a fuller discussion of this issue). While wholesale adaptations are considered unnecessary, there are some procedural modifications that can make the model more effective. Table 4.1 provides a summary of some of the procedural modifications that may be necessary when applying CBT with older adults. For a review of the important issues when working with frail older adults, see Grant and Casey (1995).

PHASES OF TREATMENT IN CBT FOR LATE-LIFE DEPRESSION

CBT is conceptualized as having three distinct phases: early, middle and late. The time allocated for each phase depends in part on the condition of the patient and/or general resource availability. Many older adults require about 16 to 20 sessions to obtain remission of depressive symptoms. Some may require less, or perhaps the institutional policy calls for termination when notable improvement in symptoms (rather than full remission) has occurred. In that case, fewer sessions will be available. Regardless of the number of sessions, certain process and content goals need to be met so that progress can be made.

Early Phase: First Three Sessions (Approximately)

First and foremost, it is necessary to adequately socialize the patient into therapy. Older patients are often not familiar with psychotherapy and how it works, and may experience anxiety in anticipation of what will transpire. Thus, socialization is very important to the establishment of a working therapeutic alliance. It involves the following five components:

1. Eliciting expectations about treatment. These may be based on experiences years ago with outmoded forms of treatment, and/or not reflect current

Table 4.1 Procedural modifications to CBT for older people

Age-related issue	Modification to strategy
Memory problems	Present new information slowly in different ways and use frequent repetitions to enhance encoding and free recall
	Use concrete mnemonic devices, such as caricature drawings or other specific visual and auditory aids. Remember the maxim: Say it, show it, do it
	Provide patients with folders or notebooks for storing home practice and in-session materials. Encourage review and rehearsal as homework. Use a flipchart frequently to illustrate points
	Tape sessions and encourage patients to review these. Encourage patients to take the tapes home for further study
Multi-morbidity	Involve the interdisciplinary team. For example, if physical symptoms are aggravated due to a medication issue, direct communication with a geriatrician may quickly provide the requisite information to correct the problem. Or if the patient experiences problems due to inadequate resources, communication with a social worker on the team may be sufficient to initiate an appropriate intervention to rectify the problem
	Always consider whether excess disability is a factor in the patient's presentation
Internalized ageism	Dispel some of the myths of ageing for the patient by introducing knowledge from more recent research. Books like *Successful Aging* (Rowe & Kahn, 1998) and documents such as *Active Ageing* (WHO, 2002), *Ageing: Exploding the Myths* (WHO, 1999) can be immensely helpful to depressed elderly clients in developing more positive expectations and reducing hopelessness
Story-telling	Older adults often have a strong inclination to provide extensive details about important life events. This characteristic tends to be particularly prominent when they are conveying information in a situation where they expect another person to provide some form of assistance
	Provide frequent summaries of information presented by the patient and ask for feedback to clarify any difficult points. Set up ground rules that give the therapist 'permission' to interrupt and redirect the focus of discussion

    thinking about the active involvement of both therapist and patient in the treatment process.

2. Explaining the collaborative nature of CBT. The therapist is not the 'expert' but rather an experienced guide who will provide opportunities for learning and for new ways of thinking to occur.
3. Clarifying that CBT therapy is time limited (not open-ended). It helps to actually write out projected dates for the full course of treatment in order to

emphasize the need for every session to 'count' towards the treatment goals.

4. Highlighting the 'here and now' focus of CBT. This is not a form of therapy that focuses on one's past; rather it is problem focused and solution oriented.
5. Establishing goals so that there is a 'road map' to follow in the weeks ahead.

A second key aim of these first few sessions is to learn about the patient and his or her life history in order to begin to develop a trusting working relationship that is built upon mutual respect. At this point, patients typically ask the therapist personal questions (age, marital status, number of children, where you grew up or went to school, etc.). Contrary to what most of us may have learned it is very important to respond honestly to these enquiries in a warm and supportive way (neither revealing too much about one's personal life nor stonewalling the patient). Being evasive at this point stimulates fear and distrust. The third critical ingredient involves explaining the CBT model and how therapy will proceed. Using diagrams (such as the model presented in Chapter 3) is helpful to illustrate how thoughts, feelings, and behaviours interact to maintain depression. It is recommended that therapists encourage questions so that the model becomes clear to the patient, along with providing a rationale for homework that emphasizes its importance.

Next, when eliciting the patient's chief complaints it is usually practical to limit the complaints to two or three. Make sure that goals are formulated so that they can be achieved (e.g. learning ways to challenge negative thoughts that affect my relationship with my spouse is more concrete than 'getting along better with my husband') and is therefore a more achievable goal.

Finally, it is important to address practical issues that may make therapy difficult such as lack of reliable transportation and/or significant responsibilities to provide care to a loved one with major physical or cognitive impairments. The patient will appreciate your concern and your assistance in problem solving whatever barriers may be present.

Middle Phase: Sessions 4–16 (Using a 20-Session Model)

Once these tasks have been accomplished, part of the homework for the therapist is to prepare a case formulation (or working model of how depression is being maintained in this particular individual's life) to guide selection of intervention strategies. It is here that one or more specific cognitive and/or behavioural skills are taught to the patient, with the aim of practising them (both within and outside of sessions) until they are learned sufficiently well so that the patient can work through and resolve one or more of the initial target complaints. In our treatment manuals, we refer to this as the 'skills not pills' phase. We also talk about having an array of 'tools' in one's 'toolbox', including thinking skills, feeling skills and doing skills (see Appendix 2 for a list of appropriate resources). These techniques are described in more detail in Chapter 6.

It is also important to keep track of the time-limited nature of treatment during this phase. Since many depressed older adults are lonely (often living alone and with a small social network) the therapist may take on the role of being the patient's confidante. This can be challenging, since the primary focus is not on the relationship per se, but on using the relationship to encourage development of new skills to better challenge negative thinking and to enable the patient to become involved in more adaptive behaviours. During this time it is tempting for the therapist to 'just sit back and listen' to the stories told by the elder, rather than focusing in on the business at hand. However, the needs of patients can be better served once the therapist selects the skills to commence with. Typically, for those with moderate to severe depression, starting out with behavioural skills (such as increasing the frequency of engagement in everyday pleasant events) will be more successful than beginning with dysfunctional thought records. However, the reverse seems to hold for those with milder levels of depression at the outset: they often benefit quickly from modifying negative thoughts and developing more adaptive ones in their place.

During Phase II, various recording forms are introduced (see Chapters 5 and 6) and patients are taught how to use them as part of their commitment to homework and self-improvement. Other key issues during this phase (besides skill development) include: reinforcing the importance of doing regular homework or home practice; dealing with the difficult patient (otherwise known as 'resistance'); and recognizing when and how to recommend cognitive processes such as acceptance or forgiveness rather than focusing on changing negative thoughts.

Homework issues arise when there is poor planning, lack of time, competing outside responsibilities (as is the case with family members who are providing ongoing care to disabled elderly relative) or low motivation to change. The patient may feel that it is not worth while spending time doing things outside the sessions because nothing will really improve the situation. Other issues (and suggestions for dealing with them) are included in Chapter 13.

Dealing with resistance is a major issue, as it is in most other psychotherapy modalities. It usually occurs when individuals are extremely sceptical about therapy outcome, either because they think the therapy is ineffective for the kind of problems they are experiencing or they believe that they are burdened with an intractable situation. A frequent situation that fosters resistance occurs when a patient is referred with multiple somatic problems with no apparent medical basis. Often the patient is convinced that his problem is organic and has nothing to do with psychology. Attempts to develop counter-positions are usually futile, but encouraging the patient to engage in techniques, such as distraction or relaxation that may reduce his pain or concern, is a useful starting point. It is critical that reference points for evaluating change in the somatic condition be developed so that the patient can determine the effectiveness of the techniques. Once the patient sees the value of a particular technique he may be more inclined to consider alternative views of his current predicament.

Fortunately, the collaborative problem-solving approach for addressing therapy goals can minimize some of the stumbling blocks. Gently challenging the patient to assume a scientific attitude and collect more data to support or refute his position can help to diminish resistive behaviours. For example, a 75-year-old musician had developed a pervasive sense of worthlessness following his retirement five years prior to therapy, which left him seriously depressed and unable to care for himself. His family insisted that he seek help, and he came grudgingly, knowing that nothing could help him. Any and all attempts to examine his irrational negative cognitions had no impact on his attitudes towards himself or his low level of behavioural functioning. The therapist enquired whether there was any person or any type of feedback that would require him to reconsider his belief about himself. After some mild 'wrangling' with the therapist, the patient reluctantly volunteered that if two particular individuals were to evaluate him positively, he would have to reconsider his position. After gentle challenges from the therapist, he agreed to ask them for feedback. Before doing so the therapist and he developed the questions to be asked and the criteria for evaluating their responses objectively. The information he received was so overwhelmingly positive that no attempts to discount it on his part were successful, and he was forced by his own reasoning to consider alternative ways of evaluating his worth. Subsequent to this point he became cooperative in completing home practice and considering rational reconstructions for his negative dysfunctional thoughts. Within two months from this pivotal exercise, his depressive symptoms had decreased, and he was considering the possibility of doing volunteer concerts.

It is not uncommon for the therapist to become exasperated with many older individuals who have seemingly antiquated and inflexible belief systems. In moments of hidden frustration the therapist is not immune from sudden bouts of age stereotyping, and should be prepared to examine how such 'counter-transference' might aggravate or precipitate resistance in the patient. Remember that it is important to recognize any tendency to stereotype the patient and try to avoid it. When things are not going smoothly in therapy sessions it is important that therapists remain open-minded and optimistic and deal with their own dysfunctional cognitions when therapy appears not to be progressing. Therapists can remind themselves to maintain a problem-solving attitude. What's good for the goose is good for the gander. Thus all cognitive-behavioural therapists recognize the importance of maintaining a high tolerance for frustration.

Therapists can use changes in personal feelings towards the patient as an opportunity to refocus on what the patient may be doing to create this and what this reveals about the patient's way of interacting with others. The therapist may wish to reflect on how the presenting problems described are influenced by the patient's style of interacting with others. This may provide useful data for challenges to the patient. The use of acceptance and/or forgiveness as therapeutic strategies are often important for older adults. Invariably their lives are filled with numerous current negative events that simply cannot be changed (e.g. having to move out of the family home because they need to be in an assisted living environment, or facing the deaths of numerous friends (and possibly other family members) as the years advance). Acceptance and forgiveness are often involved when patients are struggling with the meaning of past negative events to which they may have done their best to adapt, but which still haunt them and cast a negative influence in the present. An example should illustrate this point.

Mabel, aged 70, has for years been estranged from her older brother who lives in a distant city and has recently been diagnosed with terminal cancer. Part of Mabel's depression is due to the fact that she has a conflict between wanting to reconcile with her brother before his death, while at the same time 'feeling justified' in maintaining her long history of anger and resentment. It turns out that the reasons for this estrangement were very legitimate: the brother, a bachelor at the time, had molested Mabel's young daughter over a period of about 6 months while acting as her babysitter. For most of her adult life, Mabel was unable to forgive either herself (for not recognizing what was going on and intervening sooner) or her brother, whom she bitterly resented for the trauma he had caused. The daughter, now in her forties and married with a family of her own, similarly vacillated between negative emotions towards her uncle, and also, at times, a sense of wanting to forgive him and allow the family to reconcile and to heal. The daughter (more than Mabel) recognized that her uncle was genuinely remorseful for what had happened. He had no history of such behaviour before or since the episodes in question, which appeared to be due to his inability to cope with losing his job and becoming alcoholic for several years. In fact, he had done many things to show his repentance (e.g. went into therapy to deal with his behaviour and to learn more appropriate ways to relate to women and girls; sought pastoral counselling and forgiveness from his church). He accepted this total rejection from his sister and her family as a form of punishment (in those days, relatives were typically not prosecuted for such behaviour), but over the years, had made many attempts to reconcile with Mabel that she had rebuffed. Later in life he married and lived a model life in another city. In CBT Mabel learned to assess whether or not it was important to stay angry—even though she clearly was justified in adopting that stance many years ago. She was asked to examine whether she could see value in accepting the past as it was (not sugar-coating it, but acknowledging that people close to us can make terrible mistakes sometimes) and finally coming to terms with it. She was also asked to consider forgiving her brother: not condoning his behaviour but putting it in context, appreciating what he had suffered and how he had learned from his mistakes. Finally, Mabel's daughter encouraged her mother to do these things for the sake of the family as a whole, as she believed that this would be beneficial to all concerned. This is in fact what happened, and it did turn out well for Mabel, although it was very difficult to do.

This is but one example; many similar experiences have occurred in our clinic, suggesting that this 'theme' may be more prominent with older adults who have, after all, a lifetime of situations to accept and many, many relationships and experiences to come to terms with. Had we gone the traditional CBT route of challenging her thoughts without focusing on the additional step of encouraging her to both accept the past and actively forgive her brother, we believe we would not have had the same kind of therapeutic success that was achieved with Mabel.

Late Phase: Sessions 17–20

In the final stage of therapy, there are two main goals to accomplish: (1) preparation for, and completion of, treatment termination; and (2) planning for relapse prevention. At this point the chief complaints will have been satisfactorily resolved (or at least significant improvement has been noted) so that termination can proceed. If the patient has become worse rather than better, or if new crises have developed, additional sessions of CBT may be needed or a referral may be required for other kinds of mental health services. However, for the most part, depressed outpatients will have learned an array of skills to help them to cope with affective distress, and will be ready to terminate at this point.

Skill is required to terminate sessions effectively with older adults. This is true for several reasons: (1) the likely importance of the therapeutic relationship in their lives which they do not necessarily want to have come to an end; (2) the difficulty they are likely to have in finding another person with whom to share personal thoughts and feelings; and (3) fear of future episodes of affective distress that will make them dysfunctional again and in need of additional mental health care.

We have the following recommendations for handling termination:

1. Space the final four sessions apart by, say, two or four weeks each, rather than continuing to meet weekly until the last session. This will encourage the patient to make more independent use of the cognitive and behavioural skills they have learned, with less reliance on direction from the therapist. It will also reveal the kinds of difficulties they are likely to have when therapy is officially over. These challenges and struggles can be brought into the final sessions and worked on.

2. Consider offering several 'booster sessions' over the next year or so, at periodic intervals, so that the patient can have scheduled appointments to look forward to should the need arise. They can always be cancelled if things are going well. This is very reassuring to patients who do not need to have an emergency in order to resume therapy. It also offers opportunities for reinforcement of skills.

3. Allow time to discuss relationship issues in the final sessions, and even if the patient seems reluctant to do so, place this item on the agenda for those final sessions. At this point in therapy the therapist can share something of what he or she has learned from working with this patient. It is gratifying to older people to know that they have something to offer to highly trained professionals who themselves are 'not too old to learn'.

Skill is also needed to prepare adequately for relapse, which is common among those with affective disorders, and to help the patient think in terms of 'relapse prevention'. There are several components in this work. Firstly, patients are asked to record (in whatever way they can, and often with the therapist's assistance) the main skills they learned in treatment. They also are asked to think about which ones they are likely to use again on their own. Typically patients name two or three that they prefer to use. Secondly, patients are then asked to think about and actually anticipate future situations that are likely to cause them to become highly depressed or anxious again. These are also recorded. Finally, a 'Survival Guide' is created jointly by the therapist and the patient as part of homework in the final phase of therapy. Key skills are recorded in a special notebook (or in some other relatively permanent place) and they are then lined to the anticipated troublesome situations. For example, if the patient fears that she will become depressed again as her health continues to deteriorate, she is asked to think about what she could do at that time to forestall a full-blown depression. In this case, the patient might record in the notebook: 'I will do a thought record so that I can if I'm thinking in all or none terms again. I will also examine the evidence and try to figure out what I still can do, rather than focus only on what I cannot do. In that way I won't always think the worst.'

This is a clear example of how the strategies she plans to use 'fit' the anticipated situation and are likely to be helpful to her in coping with it with less (or no) depression. Another patient, who may have used more of the behavioural techniques successfully, might complete her Survival Guide in this way: 'When I go to visit my granddaughter this year in New York, I am going to try not to become depressed like I usually do. I get upset over her lifestyle: she has a fine education but seems to be wasting her life, living with an artist and doing odd jobs around the city. This time, I will focus on having an enjoyable visit with her, and not on what she is doing that I disapprove of. After all, I do love my granddaughter and I do not want to spoil these infrequent visits with critical comments.' For this particular client, this was a very helpful strategy that she actually employed.

Finally, the door can be left open, if possible, for patients to recontact the therapist personally if they do significantly worsen in the future, so that they could hopefully return to treatment with few hurdles to cross. Knowing that they can contact the therapist, even if they never do, is very comforting to most older adults as they end therapy.

SUMMARY

From the foregoing, it is clear that when applying CBT for late-life depression there are a number of age-specific issues that need to be taken into account, not least of which is the issue of diagnosis of depression. Depression in older people is often under-recognized and under-treated because of the difficulties in making this diagnosis. CBT works best when clear goals are set, and arriving at a diagnosis is an important step along the way to deriving appropriate treatment interventions. As older people can be aged anywhere between 60 and 100 years plus, this group can be very homogeneous and it is very likely that you will meet people who do not require any modifications to CBT in order to benefit from this treatment. It is equally likely that modifications will be required, and these have been spelled out in this chapter. As CBT is not open ended, there are important differences in the phases of this treatment and all lead to the eventual outcome of discharge.

Chapter 5

BEHAVIOURAL TECHNIQUES

INTRODUCTION

In this chapter, the focus is on behavioural techniques within cognitive behaviour therapy. Often it is behavioural experiments that let patients see that change is possible and produce the necessary shifts in patients' conceptual thinking to allow further change to take place for progress in therapy to occur. It is important to remember that behavioural techniques are not just useful at the beginning of therapy but at all stages. For example, in dealing with core beliefs and dysfunctional schemata, well-chosen individualized behavioural experiments are a very important tool for challenging longstanding beliefs. In cognitive therapy words are not enough, the emphasis must be placed on action during all the phases of therapy. Cognitive therapists are defined by their active collaborative approach to therapy and much of the activation takes place via behavioural interventions. In that sense the B in CBT is well placed; right in the centre, in the thick of things. Befitting a chapter focusing on behavioural techniques within therapy, the emphasis is very much on the practical aspects of applying these techniques in action.

THE BEHAVIOURAL MODEL OF DEPRESSION

Lewinsohn and colleagues (Lewinsohn & Gotlib, 1995; Lewinsohn et al., 1986; Lewinsohn et al., 1985; Lewinsohn & Hoberman, 1982; Lewinsohn, Sullivan &

Cognitive Behaviour Therapy with Older People.
Ken Laidlaw, Larry W. Thompson, Leah Dick-Siskin & Dolores Gallagher-Thompson.
© 2003 John Wiley & Sons Ltd.

Grosscup, 1980) developed the most systematically well-elaborated behavioural theory of depression. The Lewinsohn model (Lewinsohn & Gotlib, 1995; Lewinsohn et al., 1985, 1986) stresses the functional relationship between depression and everyday life events and suggests that events that disrupt functioning, particularly if the disruptions result in an increase of negative events or a reduction in positive events, is likely to increase vulnerability to the development of depression (Zeiss et al., 1996; Lewinsohn et al., 1985).

The behavioural model for depression takes account of the fact that a substantial portion of the most salient positive reinforcers in any person's world are interpersonal in nature, and this is equally true if not more so for older people (see Chapter 3). Depression is more likely to occur following the disruption of valued roles and goals in a person's life. More specifically, a low rate of response-contingent positive reinforcement in major areas of life or in valued activities and goals and/or a high rate of aversive experiences lead to dysphoria and a reduction in behaviour which results in depression (Lewinsohn & Gotlib, 1995).

Lewinsohn's theory suggests that as people become depressed they reduce their participation in activities and hobbies, cutting themselves off from things that provide a sense of enjoyment and meaning in life. As a person's mood level drops further, a vicious cycle develops (i.e. lower mood, increased apathy and reduced motivation, further isolation and reduction in pleasurable activities). In addition, at first, carers, relatives, friends, etc., are quite concerned and give the person a lot of attention (negative reinforcement). The depressed person then becomes increasingly aversive to be with and tends to become more isolated (Lewinsohn, Sullivan & Grosscup, 1980). This tends to lower mood even further, which in turn continues to reduce activity level, and so on until a vicious circle develops that leads to a prolonged mood disturbance and the development of numerous other symptoms of depression.

Empirical research evidence suggests that interventions based on the behavioural model are efficacious for the treatment of depression in adult and in older-adult populations (Rokke, Tomhave & Jocic, 2000; Teri et al., 1997; Gallagher, Hanley-Peterson & Thompson, 1990; Thompson, Gallagher & Breckenridge, 1987; Teri & Lewinsohn, 1986; Gallagher & Thompson, 1983; for reviews see also Karel & Hinrichsen, 2000; Gatz et al., 1998; Scogin & McElreath, 1994; Gotlib & Hammen, 1992) and much research has focused on the efficacy of the coping with depression course that has been developed to implement and evaluate the effectiveness of this intervention (Antonucci, 1998).

THE IMPORTANCE OF INCREASING ACTIVITY LEVELS WITH OLDER PEOPLE

Specific behaviour interventions in CBT place emphasis on increasing a person's level of engagement in pleasurable events. The strategy is to help the person to plan to do something enjoyable at least once a day. Just putting in a few extra pleasant events in a person's week can make a big difference to the quality of the person's mood and life.

Older people generally tend to live quite sedentary lives following retirement (Gauthier & Smeeding, 2000), thus depressed older people are likely to report very low levels of social engagement and activity and are at risk of becoming extremely socially isolated, especially if they live alone. Identifying potentially pleasant events (PEs) means finding activities that people like to do, then encouraging them to do those things to make them feel better. Pleasant events don't need to be big events like going on holiday or decorating a house. In fact many people have small pleasant events that they take for granted, like reading the newspaper or having a leisurely lunch. Working in the garden, talking on the telephone to friends or family or washing the car can be a pleasant event for people. *Anything that a person likes to do is a pleasant event*.

A further benefit from the use of activity scheduling with older adults can be obtained from behavioural experiments that challenge 'ageist' beliefs. An important age-specific belief that may be considered at the level of cohort or generational beliefs is that 'you cannot teach an old dog new tricks'. By referring to Chapter 2, a fuller discussion of this issue is outlined. However, when older people engage in behavioural experiments that are set up as 'no lose' experiments (see below), it is impossible not to learn something important about their behaviour. Thus an important outcome of engaging in behavioural experiments with older people in therapy is that this important myth about ageing is challenged and deconstructed.

IDENTIFYING CONNECTIONS BETWEEN MOOD AND ACTIVITY LEVELS

An important benefit of having patients monitor and assess their current levels of activity (using a weekly activity schedule; see Figure 5.1) is to make the connection between mood and activity levels. The technique of activity monitoring is a very useful early homework exercise. The rationale of this task can be made very simply and clearly to the patient. It is useful for the therapist to get a 'feel' or a sense of how much the person is doing during the day and during the week. By asking a patient to complete a weekly activity schedule (WAS), the therapist gathers this information in a very natural way and thus avoids wasting valuable session time by reducing the number of questions about a person's general activity level. The patient can usually see the rationale of finding out how much a person is doing when he or she is depressed or anxious. For the therapist, the use of the WAS as a homework task also provides a lot of useful information about how patients cope with completing a simple homework task. The WAS also serves to orient patients

	Mon .../.../...	Tues .../.../...	Wed .../.../...	Thurs .../.../...	Fri .../.../...	Sat .../.../...	Sun .../.../...
7.00 – 8.00							
8.00 – 9.00							
9.00 – 10.00							
10.00 – 11.00							
11.00 – 12.00							
12.00 – 1 p.m.							
1 p.m. – 2 p.m.							
2 p.m. – 3 p.m.							
3 p.m. – 4 p.m.							
4 p.m. – 5 p.m.							
5 p.m. – 6 p.m.							
6 p.m. – 7 p.m.							
7 p.m. – 8 p.m.							
8 p.m. onwards							

Figure 5.1 Weekly Activity Schedule

into an important part of cognitive therapy: completion of homework. To create an activity level baseline the patient needs to complete a WAS to provide a baseline assessment. Figure 5.1 gives an example of a WAS.

The WAS provides a measure of the patient's activity level and it can also be used in later sessions to record mastery and pleasure ratings for activity. By adding mastery and pleasure ratings it is possible to derive mood fluctuations during a person's recording period. In terms of recording in the WAS, *Mastery* is a sense of achievement gained from doing something. *Pleasure* is an indication of enjoyment gained from doing something. It is important that the therapist reviews a completed WAS at the start of the therapy session. It can be helpful and illuminative if the therapist asks the patient questions about the typicality of the recording of the week's activity. The therapist will also want to know the high point and the low point of the recorded week.

USING ACTIVITY SCHEDULING TO IDENTIFY THOUGHTS AND FEELINGS

Recording activity or inactivity on the WAS can also be used as a convenient way to introduce the concept of thought monitoring. The WAS can help a patient to make the thought–feelings–behaviour connection more easily. For example, Mrs S, a 69-year-old woman suffering from a severe level of depression, was asked to record her activity levels using WAS forms. Mrs S recorded her levels of enjoyment and sense of achievement (mastery and pleasure ratings). The therapist and Mrs S noted that an activity that used to provide a sense of both pleasure and achievement—knitting—was no longer providing any of this as Mrs S recorded this giving a maximum 2 out of a possible 10 on a scale of not at all enjoyable (0) to very enjoyable (10). When the therapist investigated this further he noted that whenever Mrs S made a mistake she developed the negative automatic thought, 'that's it, I've got a dementia, I can't even do simple things now'. Consequently Mrs S had stopped knitting as the experience of making mistakes at what she considered to be a simple task was proving too depressing and anxiety provoking. When the therapist asked how she would have thought about this before she became depressed, Mrs S brightened immediately and said, 'I wouldn't have given it a thought, I used to make mistakes all the time, all knitters do'. From this episode Mrs S developed an awareness of the connection between behaviours and mood and how her thoughts can have an influence on subsequent behaviour. Her mistakes in knitting made her feel anxious and low, and as her thoughts maintained the low mood she avoided knitting again for fear of feeling bad; hence she cut back unnecessarily on an activity which, approached in the correct way, could act as a source of pleasure. Importantly, Mrs S also learned from this episode that thoughts do not always fit the facts.

This exchange with Mrs S helped her to refrain from jumping to the conclusion that whenever she made a mistake it meant that she had started to develop dementia. From this incident, it became clear that psycho-education was required about dementia.

THE MOOD-MONITORING FORM

While the WAS has its uses within CBT it also has its limitations. Often there is very little space for an adequate description of events that may have affected an individual's mood over the course of a day. The Mood-Monitoring Form serves as a useful way of helping older people to get used to the idea of recording their thoughts and helps to bridge the conceptual gap between recording behaviours and recording thoughts (see Figure 5.2). The Mood-Monitoring Form can also be useful in helping patients to observe that as they take part in doing more pleasant activities, this has a positive effect on their mood. An example of a completed Mood-Monitoring Form is shown in Figure 5.2.

INCREASING ACTIVITY LEVELS

In CBT, increasing pleasant events (PEs) serves a number of important therapeutic functions for working with older people with depression. Increasing PEs shows a person that activity (behaviour) and mood are linked and that by changing behaviour, the mood levels can be influenced. With this approach, people learn an important lesson in how to control and limit negative mood cycles in depression. As an enabling technique, activity scheduling or increasing PEs is one of the most important tools to combat the effects of depression.

Guidelines to Identifying Potentially Pleasant Events

1. The PE must be Realistic

The person may enjoy travel and holidays but realistically people cannot do this every day. In this case it might be more realistic to help the person to plan short bus trips into town by the scenic route if possible.

2. Choose a PE that can be Increased

If you choose an event that already occurs on many days, it may prove quite difficult to increase the number of times this event occurs. It is much better to

1. Please rate your mood for each day, i.e. how good or bad you felt, using the 9-point scale shown below. If you felt good, put a higher number on the chart below. If you felt 'so-so', mark a 5. And if you felt low or depressed, mark a lower number

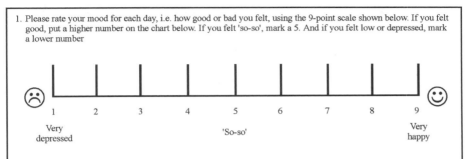

Very
depressed

'So-so'

Very
happy

2. On the two lines next to your mood rating for each day, please briefly give two major reasons that might have had an influence on your feelings. Try to be as specific as possible.

Time of day	Mood score	Reasons why I felt this way
11 a.m.	3	It rained all day today and I never got a chance to meet my friends for lunch
3 p.m.	7	I phoned my friend today and she could see me today and we had a great chat. It was nice to get out of the house
4 p.m.	8	Went to a new exhibition on the life of Winston Churchill at the public art gallery. I really enjoyed it. Being here took my mind off my own problems
8 p.m.	3	Got home and haven't spoken to a soul. I've just waited for the phone to ring
Average for the day	5	An up and down sort of day. I see that if I go out and do something rather than wait for something to happen (like the phone to ring) I generally feel better

Figure 5.2 Daily Mood-Monitoring Form

help the person to focus on building up hobbies or behaviours that may have decreased recently.

3. Choose only the TOP TEN Events for your List of Pleasant Events

Help the person to identify ten pleasant events to put on a personal list. Ask the person to put the events in order with the most enjoyable event at the top. Remember that the event at the top of the list may not be the most ideal event but the most pleasant event that the person can do on a regular basis. *Allow the person to change the list if more events are discovered as the person goes along.*

CREATING A LIST OF PLEASANT EVENTS

Ask your patient to list the things that are most enjoyable to do. This is most productively done collaboratively during the session. However, it can also be set as a homework task. Get the person to list things that would be enjoyable even if he or she is not currently engaging in them. If a person cannot identify TEN items, get him or her to list as many as possible. Listen for any new ideas that can be added.

The therapist may find it useful to use the completed WAS to identify things that give the person some enjoyment. A good tip is to ask the patient to complete a WAS with ratings of activities for mastery and pleasure (M & P) on a 7-point scale—with 0 representing no pleasure and 7 representing maximum enjoyment. Once the patient is able to complete a WAS, ratings for M & P can be added after a few weeks.

Tracking the List of Pleasant Events

Once the patient can identify his or her TOP TEN list of pleasant events, the next step is to record the occurrence of these events. The patient should complete the WAS as before, but this time note the occurrence of events from the list of pleasant events. It may sometimes be helpful to use the WAS to schedule in times when the patient might be encouraged to do something from the 'top ten' as a specific homework task.

IDENTIFYING OBSTACLES TO ENGAGING IN PLEASANT EVENTS

It is not uncommon, particularly for depressed people, to say they cannot do something. It is too difficult or they do not see what good it will do. It is useful to have a discussion to identify how such people think they might benefit from doing these activities. The therapist can assist patients to construct a 'pros and cons' form to help them to identify what they will gain from the activity. This can be set up as a 'no-lose experiment'. If the patients do it, they will then see whether or not it is of benefit. If they don't do it, information will still have been gained as the therapist and patients can collaboratively work out what the difficulties were. By getting the patients' agreement to try, this can be viewed as, at least, a step forward. As this is a no-lose situation, it should be emphasized as such to the patients.

It might be useful to identify obstacles in advance. This gives the patients and the therapist a chance to trouble-shoot. The therapist ought to check the patients' understanding of what is required of them. At this stage the therapist needs to ask the patients a series of questions, such as: What personal obstacles could keep me from increasing my pleasant events? Are these obstacles unhelpful thoughts, feelings or maybe even a physical barrier? Finally, the therapist needs to ascertain how relevant the planned homework task is to the patients' current problems.

PROBLEM-SOLVING TECHNIQUES

When patients are feeling overwhelmed by their difficulties, it is often hard for them to see potential solutions that will help to make the situation more positive or hopeful. This section presents a five-step technique that will facilitate the development of more alternatives and options for managing a situation or solving a problem (McKay, Davis & Fanning, 1997). You might teach your patients this well-known acronym in order to help them to remember the steps in problem solving:

State the problem (in specific terms)
Outline goals and aims (How does the patient want the problem to change?)
List the alternatives (What are the possible strategies?)
View the possible consequences (the pros and cons)
Evaluate the outcome (Has it worked?)

Step 1: State or Define the Problem

The first task is to state or define the problem *as clearly and as specifically as possible*. This step can often be the most challenging, as sometimes several different problems can be embedded into one. Patients can be helped to sort out each problem and pick the one that appears to carry the greatest distress. *The therapist can help by asking the patient to try to state the problem in a single sentence.*

Step 2: Outline the Goals

Next, the therapist works with the patient to set goals for change, i.e. how would the patient like the problem to change.

Step 3: List Possible Solutions

This step allows possible solutions to be evaluated based on any criteria the patient chooses. Brainstorming is the key strategy used here where potential solutions to a problem are proposed. *The key to brainstorming is NOT to evaluate each potential solution, but just allow suggestions to be presented.* In brainstorming there are a number of rules that can be outlined to the patient beforehand:

(1) don't evaluate any possible solution, the aim is to
(2) come up with any solution, the more creative the better, and
(3) quantity is required in brainstorming, so that
(4) ideas can be combined and improved upon.

The patient may evaluate whether he or she has time to devote to one solution or another, or may evaluate each solution based on money, energy, or the amount of help that would be needed from other people, etc. As each item is examined, some of the alternatives proposed may seem unrealistic, and therefore will get a lower rating than others. In rating the options, the patient should assign ranks to them, or may simply choose plusses or minuses to represent the evaluation.

Step 4: Select one Alternative and View the Possible Consequences

In this step, patients should select the first alternative solution and see what develops. At any time patients can choose to return to their list of options and select another possible solution and work it through. The idea here is to select the most promising option(s) and work out what is required in order for the patients to put these solutions into action. It is important to identify pitfalls and obstacles beforehand and it is sometimes helpful to role-play by applying the new strategy. A problem-solving worksheet is contained in Appendix 1. It is important to ask the patients if they are satisfied that the strategy they have decided upon has been beneficial. This departure from the old way of doing things can often present patients with new and unanticipated difficulties. By discussing each strategy in terms of short- and long-term pros and cons, problems may be avoided. In many cases information is not fully available until the patients actually try to implement their new strategies.

PROGRESSIVE MUSCLE RELAXATION: STAGES AND APPLICATION

Relaxation as a therapeutic procedure was first developed by Jacobsen in 1929. However, despite consistently demonstrating the utility of this method, Jacobsen's work made little impact in psychotherapy. It was not until Wolpe (1958) incorporated a modified version into systematic desensitization that relaxation received widespread recognition. Progressive Muscle Relaxation (PMR) involves patients becoming aware of the contrast between tension and relaxation of muscles. In addition, when patients are told to 'relax', the therapist often modifies his or her voice accordingly by speaking in a softer tone, thereby introducing a degree of 'suggestion' into the technique. The aim is to take the patient gradually through a series of exercises designed to enable him or her to actively reduce any anxiety by relaxing. The first stage helps the patient to relax using PMR. The patient is seated in a comfortable armchair and the therapist models how the different muscles groups should be tightened and then relaxed. The patient does the tension and release exercises with the therapist and afterwards any questions the patient may have are answered about the technique. Emphasis is on dealing with problem areas. The patient is then given a tape of the therapist's voice and instructed to practise twice a day. It is recommended that the tape given to the patient should be the therapist's own voice doing PMR. Since the patients are learning a new skill, it is recommended that they practise relaxation when they are not feeling too anxious. Relaxation practice can form the homework exercises at the end of therapy sessions. In order for PMR to be effective, the patients must be taught how to recognize the early signs of anxiety and apply the relaxation procedures to cope with the anxiety instead of letting it overwhelm them. Interested readers are referred to Andrews et al. (1994) for an excellent overview and explanation of the application of relaxation procedures.

Identifying Tension

It is often very helpful to understand the sources of anxiety and types of danger signals experienced using a Tension Diary. The Tension Diary allows patients to record their most stressful times, their least stressful times and their physical symptoms of tension (see Appendix 1).

Caution using Progressive Muscle Relaxation Exercise

There are many effective methods of relaxation, but the therapist should be somewhat cautious in selecting an exercise for older adults. For older adults with joint or muscular difficulties it can be quite difficult to engage in exercises requiring the physical tensing and releasing found in progressive muscle relaxation. In these instances it is recommended that exercises focusing on visual imagery or concentrating on cue-controlled breathing can be used. In order for patients to gauge whether relaxation is helpful, it is suggested that patients are encouraged to develop a habit of doing a pre- and post-tension rating using the scale below. A Relaxation Practice Log develops this scale further (see Appendix 1). Remind patients that the more relaxation is practised, the more relaxed they will feel immediately following the exercise. Also, with increased practice, there will be a decrease in the time it takes to reach a relaxed state. Encourage the use of the Relaxation Practice Log to gauge progress.

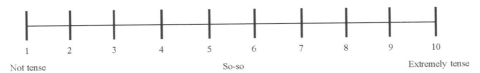

| 1 | 2 | 3 | 4 | 5 | 6 | 7 | 8 | 9 | 10 |

Not tense   So-so   Extremely tense

Relaxing using Diaphragmatic (Cue-Controlled) Breathing

This is a fairly simple technique to teach patients to use. It can be used either as an alternative or an adjunct to PMR. A typical introduction to breathing techniques is to help the patients to become aware of the changes to their breathing if they become aroused and start to hyperventilate. When people typically become anxious their breathing often becomes more rapid and shallow. During an anxiety attack a person's abdominal muscles tighten and constrict, thus interfering with the natural action of the diaphragm. The person's chest often becomes tight and contributes to the fear that he or she is about to suffer a heart attack, and unless this cycle is interrupted it can lead to hyperventilation and, ultimately, a panic attack. The procedure for learning diaphragmatic breathing is as follows:

1. Get the patients to practise slowing their breathing rate by taking moderate breaths in and out. (Breathe in through the nose and out through the mouth.) It is helpful if the patients initially lie on the floor or some other reasonably supportive surface and practise their breathing initially by placing a small book on their stomach and concentrating on noticing their stomach rising as they breathe in and falling as they breathe out. It is generally helpful if the therapist models this technique in the session.
2. Therapists may wish to draw an outline of the way the diaphragm muscle stretches and flattens to allow the lungs to expand (during the in breath) and becomes curved to push the air out of the lungs (during the out breath).
3. Encourage patients to gently breathe in and out at a moderate pace. Encourage them to find their own slow but steady pace. The patients can count their in and out breaths. Try to get the patients to breathe in for three seconds and out for three seconds, and remind patients to say 'Relax' as they breathe out.

SUMMARY

This chapter has reviewed three main behavioural intervention strategies, increasing activity level and increasing pleasant events, problem solving and using applied progressive muscle relaxation. The chapter has focused on the usefulness of these techniques within cognitive therapy. As techniques they can be used as stand-alone therapeutic interventions; however, they are much more effective if incorporated into a well-elaborated treatment plan. The following chapter looks at thought monitoring.

Chapter 6

DEALING WITH NEGATIVE THOUGHTS

INTRODUCTION

This chapter provides specific information about eliciting and modifying negative thinking that often accompanies (and reinforces) depression in older adults. Although it is often thought that older patients do not benefit as much from the 'cognitive' work of CBT (Koder, Brodaty & Anstey, 1996; Church, 1983) due to supposed age-associated cognitive impairment, such as rigidity of thinking, this notion is challenged in this chapter with the inclusion of a variety of suggestions to make cognitive work both comfortable and effective with older adults. That is not to say that it may not be difficult at times and tax the creativity of the therapist; however, by maintaining flexibility and a positive attitude, changes in negative thinking patterns in older people can indeed be accomplished. Case examples are included throughout the chapter to support this view.

CHARACTERISTICS OF NEGATIVE AUTOMATIC THOUGHTS

People of any age who are prone to depression are more likely to interpret their life experiences in an unduly negative manner. However, this can be a

Cognitive Behaviour Therapy with Older People.
Ken Laidlaw, Larry W. Thompson, Leah Dick-Siskin & Dolores Gallagher-Thompson.
© 2003 John Wiley & Sons Ltd.

particular problem for older adults, whose thought patterns may have existed, relatively unchallenged, for many years. The negative cognitive triad (Beck, 1987, 1983; Kovacs & Beck, 1978)—which includes the patients' thoughts about themselves, their experiences, and the future—tends to be pessimistic to an extent beyond what most people would regard as appropriate for the particular situation. For example, many older persons with depression view normal changes associated with ageing (e.g. diminution of hearing and visual acuities and/or some decline in everyday memory skill) as catastrophic, resulting in a distorted self-concept. They report regarding themselves as very undesirable because of these changes, and are not able to integrate their self-concepts in an adaptive manner, as non-depressed counterparts are able to do. Since thoughts about oneself, one's experiences, and the future tend to be interrelated, distortions or unrealistically negative perceptions and beliefs in one area influence beliefs in another, reducing enjoyment of life generally. Individuals may contend that 'old age is a depressing time of life' or say 'it is terrible getting old', and present these beliefs as facts rather than as age-related negative automatic thoughts. Negative thoughts like these can be very difficult for therapists to dispute unless they possess specific knowledge about normal ageing (see Chapters 1 and 2). It is important early in therapy to note any occurrences of age-related negative thoughts and challenge them using standard cognitive restructuring questions such as:

- What is the evidence for and against this thought?
- What is the effect of holding this belief?
- How does it help individuals to think in this way?
- What would their advice be when their children look forward to their own later years?

Finally, the therapist can point out that beliefs such as 'it is terrible getting old' reflect general habitual ways of thinking (errors of processing such as black and white thinking, overgeneralizing, etc.).

Older depressed persons make the same sorts of information-processing errors (see Table 6.1) that were identified by Beck in his cognitive model for depression in general adult populations (Beck, 1987, 1983; Beck et al., 1979). For example, John, a 72-year-old male patient diagnosed with major depression, indicated that his depression began when he *passed* his driving test to renew his licence. He had made four errors out of a maximum of six errors that are 'allowed' for an individual to pass. John 'selectively abstracted' the interpretation that this was evidence of his declining mental abilities, leading to his belief that he probably had dementia, which led to him become depressed. In talking about this in therapy, John indicated that this was the 'beginning of the end'—and from that point on he believed that his so-called diminished cognitive capacity was going to lead to diminished functional capacity, and eventual nursing home placement (overgeneralization and catastrophizing). Negative automatic thoughts tend to be relatively automatic

Table 6.1 Information-processing errors common in depression

Cognitive distortion	Description of distortion	Example of distortion
Arbitrary inference	Drawing a specific conclusion in the absence of evidence	Friends walking across the street fail to say hello. Patient thinks, 'They purposely avoided me'
Selective abstraction	Focusing on a detail out of its context while ignoring more salient information	Patient is given an appraisal at work that is extremely positive and yet ignores the praise and focuses instead on criticism
Dichotomous reasoning (black and white thinking)	Propensity to categorize all experiences in one of two categories	Patient thinks unless my appraisal at work is totally positive then I am a failure at my job
Overgeneralization	Drawing a conclusion in the absence of substantiating evidence	Friends walking across the street fail to say hello. Patient thinks, 'That's it, none of my friends want anything to do with me now'
Personalization	Propensity to relate external events to oneself	Patient finds out that his adult son is seeking a divorce and thinks, 'I let my son down, I'm a failure, I didn't do my job as a parent properly'
Magnification and minimization	Either exaggerating or down-playing the personal significance of an event for the patient	Minimization: Patient conquers a phobia and states, 'It's no big deal, most people aren't afraid of heights' Magnification: Patient forgets a relative's birthday and says 'I am a terrible, selfish person'
Catastrophizing	A propensity to think of the worst possible outcomes for situations	Patient has chest pains and thinks, 'I am having a heart attack, I'm going to die unless I get help'
Negative imperatives	A precise and fixed idea of how things ought to be in the world (should and must statements)	Patient slightly damages his car when parking and says to himself 'I should never do this. I must never make any mistakes here'

in depressed persons: that is, the individual does not consciously say to himself or herself that 'I am going to selectively abstract now' or 'I am seeing only part of the total situation'; the thoughts occur without the patient's awareness, until they are brought to the person's attention through thought monitoring and challenging. John was not aware that his supposed failure on the test was in fact the underlying situation giving rise to his increasingly negative views of himself. However, his wife began to notice that he was less enthusiastic about going out with friends (since they lived in California, driving was often involved) and that he lost interest in mental activities he used to enjoy, such as doing crossword puzzles. He became increasingly withdrawn and fearful about meeting his everyday responsibilities (gardening, paying bills, etc.), saying to his wife that he was no longer doing them 'right'.

It is important to use 'common sense' language to describe negative thinking patterns. For example, patients who frequently see things in 'all or none' terms (extremes of black and white) are committing the error that we call 'this-or-that/no in-between'. Those who label themselves negatively are 'name-calling' and those who think in terms of what they 'should-a'/'would-a'/'could-a' done are experiencing the 'tyranny of the shoulds'. Other common errors include: generalizing (drawing conclusions from few facts), emotional reasoning ('I feel this, so it must be true') and the 'fortune-telling' error: just as things turned out in the past, that is how they are going to turn out in the future (also sometimes referred to as 'mind reading'—meaning I know what you are thinking about me or my performance or about what will happen next without even asking or letting the situation unfold).

IDENTIFYING NEGATIVE AUTOMATIC THOUGHTS

Since older adults may be so accustomed to thinking in certain ways, they may feel particularly unconfident in their ability to 'change' their way of thinking (age-related negative thought—you can't teach an old dog new tricks). The three-column Dysfunctional Thought Record (DTR) is a very helpful tool for this purpose as it is less intimidating to patients than a five-column DTR, especially in the early stages of therapy. Column headings are modified as follows to make it easier for older adults to complete the record:

A: Situation	B: Beliefs	C: Emotions
A brief description of the stressful event	Thoughts associated with the stressful event	Emotions/feelings associated with the stressful event

Older adults can generally describe A and C readily, but not B, so it is helpful to start with A and C and work backwards to get at B. For example, Joan is a 67-year-old widow with a degree in social work who was experiencing a dysthymic disorder. She came in for treatment after being repeatedly turned down for employment following her husband's death two years previously. Initially she could describe the pain and depression, the sense of loss she felt because she could not return to her prior job (which she had left five years previously in order to be a full-time caregiver for her husband) and her bitter disappointment that she could no longer find work in her profession. However, what that meant to her, and how she now thought and felt about herself and her future, proved more elusive to specify explicitly (column B). She was encouraged to imagine the event happening right now, in session, as a way to capture the relevant thoughts. At first this was too painful and she was unable to do it. However, after three sessions she was able to identify some of her repetitive thoughts (which now were so strong that they prevented her from continuing to seek employment or even a volunteer position). Joan found that she was labelling herself as 'a loser' as well as 'a failure' because she had not found a position. She was also overgeneralizing: 'I will never find work, look how long it's been.' There was a degree of hopelessness evident in Joan's thinking patterns as she would comment 'What's the use? My efforts have failed so far so why continue even trying?' Once Joan became aware of these thoughts, she was able to learn to challenge the veracity of her thoughts. An important point to recognize in this case is that Joan's negative automatic thoughts were not age-related but specific to her difficulties in finding an appropriate position. Thus, when working with older people, therapists would do well to remember that older adults are a very heterogeneous population and in some cases CBT requires minor modifications.

Older adults have a tendency to confuse thoughts and feelings: often when first learning to do a DTR, they put 'thoughts' in the 'feeling' column and vice versa. They may not be used to thinking about how their mood changes as a function of everyday events, so it can be helpful initially to have them begin by doing a Mood-Monitoring Form (see Chapter 5 and Appendix 1) where each day they rate their mood and indicate why they think they felt that way. This simpler approach often lays an excellent foundation for the later use of DTRs. Therapists need to educate older people about the distinction between thoughts and feelings, and use gently probing questions to elicit them, while providing feedback. For example, the therapist may say: 'In reviewing your thought record I can see that some of your thoughts are in the third column, such as "I feel like a failure"—that is really an evaluative judgement about yourself and not a feeling. Some feelings that may be associated with that thought would be: disappointment or resentment ("I've tried my best and look where it got me" could be an additional thought here as well) or guilt ("I don't work hard enough so no wonder I'm a failure" might be a related thought).' This distinction needs to be understood before proceeding.

Many older adults are sensitive about writing things down, either due to embarrassment that they will misspell words or not write clearly, or because of physical or perceptual problems impairing their ability to write as easily. The patients ought to be reassured by the therapist that they are not 'grading' their work for spelling or punctuation. There are alternatives to writing down ABC's, such as: talking the material into a tape recorder and bringing the tape, cued up to a relevant example, to the next session. They can be asked to phone in every day at a certain time and complete an ABC (three-column thought diary) over the telephone—even into an answering machine if the therapist does not have time to talk with them personally.

In some instances, patients may be forgetful when keeping a thought diary. They can be helped to remember to do the assignment by using 'post-it' note reminders in their bedroom, on the refrigerator door, or in the bathroom. Others seem very disorganized and may benefit from a notebook where all such DTRs can be recorded, and/or a set of file folders which they are asked to bring to each session so that materials can be better organized. These same techniques are very helpful as the patient progresses in therapy from using the three-column DTR to the five- and six-column versions used later in treatment.

DEALING WITH AGE-RELATED NEGATIVE AUTOMATIC THOUGHTS

Some older adults (and their therapists) believe that depression is a normal part of ageing. Therapists may hold age-related negative automatic thoughts, such as 'if I had all of his problems I'd be depressed too', that can interfere with the outcome of therapy. Likewise, older adults may see their age as reason in itself for the development of depression and may state 'It's just my age' when first asked what they think may have caused them to feel depressed. In these circumstances depression seems to be a reasonable response to some unfortunate situations. However, this is a *trap* that therapists and patients can easily fall into: as at any other age, it is *not* the situation itself that is causing depression (or stress or anxiety) but, rather, it is how the person *interprets* and *responds* to the situation that makes all the difference. At this point, therapists may ask: 'But what about the facts of this person's situation? He or she has significant health problems, is less able to get around and do things that were once enjoyed, and has a spouse with dementia. How can things be improved? Is helping the patient with his or her depression a realistic treatment goal?' To these questions we respond by saying: 'CBT can improve the patient's quality of life because if we can significantly reduce the symptoms of depression, he or she will function more optimally and be able to see things and do things in ways not clouded by depressogenic thinking, which makes functioning that much more difficult.' Thus, therapists are recommended to take a proactive, hope-engendering stance with patients in objectively difficult situations: only if the therapist can honestly convey the belief that things can change through CBT will it be successful.

The case history of Robert G will illustrate how this process can work. He was wheelchair bound as the result of a severe stroke at age 65, and was extremely depressed regarding his supposed 'failure as a man' since he could no longer work, was unable to have normal intimate relations with his wife, and had a lot of difficulty communicating—though, given enough time, he was able to express his thoughts quite well verbally. At first the therapist was as hopeless about the future as Robert was, which, of course, was not beneficial to either. In this instance, because he could not write or use a tape recorder very well but could dial the phone and speak into it, that was the method used for the DTR. Robert had to be convinced that CBT had something to offer, which was accomplished by helping him understand that certain limitations were very 'real' and due to the stroke itself, whereas others were 'excess disabilities' brought about by his depression. Thus, if the depression could be reduced, some of his functional abilities could and would improve (for example, finding meaningful roles in the world and in his family; finding other ways to be intimate with his wife, etc.). Getting Robert to complete DTRs on a regular basis was a major accomplishment that took about four weeks of encouragement and problem solving to attain.

The following is a sample of Robert's DTR:

A: Situation	B: Beliefs	C: Emotions
Can't drive myself places or work any more; I'm dependent on my wife	I'm a failure as a man; I should just be put into a nursing home so my family doesn't have such care burdens	Depressed 80%; hopeless 80%

Robert's wife was also involved in his treatment: she was depressed as well about his status and, although well-meaning, could not seem to help him much. Robert had been a very independent, successful businessman who was used to 'being in charge' and was not pleased at all with his major dependency needs. Mrs G was used to being on her own a great deal and was finding that she had to reconnect with her husband now and work to re-establish a loving relationship. Thus, the stroke took its toll on each of them individually and on their relationship generally. Mr and Mrs G were seen individually, as well as being seen together, and DTRs were kept singly and eventually conjointly (those having to do with relationship issues). Mr G was asked to rate the strength of his negative emotions, and when recording the content of his thoughts he was also asked to rate a degree of belief in his thoughts. Later in treatment (see below) when thoughts are challenged and modified by the patient, it is important to see if the subjective ratings of strength of emotions and degree of belief in veracity of thoughts also change. With patients who are timid about numbers or who do not seem comfortable with the 0–100 scale, this can be simplified by rating intensity from 0 to 10.

DETECTING PATTERNS AND THEMES IN NEGATIVE THOUGHTS

Negative automatic thoughts (NATs) that are recurrent are most in need of challenging and modification, as they are often linked into a more general theme, revolving around low self-esteem or pessimism about the future. That is why patients are asked to complete at least one thought record each day which the therapist reviews at the start of the next session so that commonalities across days of the week, or when describing interactions with particular persons or situations, can be identified. For example, Mary, age 76, was a caregiver for her husband with dementia for about five years when she was referred for Adjustment Disorder with Depressed Mood due to stress associated with caregiving. After about three weeks of keeping thought diaries it was clear that two major themes characterized her records: (1) whatever she did for her husband was not enough, and (2) she was unable to give herself permission to do any regular pleasant activities (e.g. keeping a regular bridge date with her women's club). Her major negative feeling was guilt regarding both of these.

TYPICAL THINKING ERRORS IN DEPRESSION

Once themes are identified, the next step is generally to review them carefully to determine which thinking errors or unhelpful thought patterns they typify. This can be explained to patients in terms of 'dirty tricks' that they play on themselves without really being aware of it. A particularly common thinking pattern in depressed older adults is the frequent use of the 'if only' approach— 'if only I had done more like I should have, or done a specific thing that I could have done, the situation would be different'. Family caregivers express this often: if only they had provided better care for their loved ones, they would not have died as soon as they did, or they would have suffered less. Other older adults with regrets about the past frequently torture themselves with this way of thinking: 'If only I had married someone else I would not be alone now' or 'If only I had taken that other career path, I would be better off financially now.' Another common pattern involves relationships with adult children: 'If only I had brought them up differently they would not be in trouble now.' These kinds of thoughts are particularly difficult to challenge since they often hold a modicum of truth. This type of thinking reflects a type of hindsight bias in which the individual berates himself for making 'wrong' decisions with the benefit of information that he has now but was not available when he had to make his decision. However, since no one could have predicted the future on the basis of what was happening at the time, the patient needs to learn to accept what was done (or not done).

CHALLENGING UNHELPFUL AND UNREALISTIC THOUGHTS

In order to challenge unhelpful thoughts and develop more adaptive and functional patterns of thinking, the therapist must teach the older adults specific skills that can be used for this purpose (see also Coon et al., 1999; Thompson, 1996).

Examine the Evidence

The therapist asks the patients, literally, what information or data is there to support the negative belief. The patient is also asked what data he or she can develop or think of that does not confirm the truth of the NAT? This straightforward technique is popular with older patients since it is a relatively easy discussion to engage in which allows them to draw their own conclusions after completing the process.

Examine the Consequences of Maintaining X Belief

The therapist points out to the patient: even if X is true, what is to be gained (what is the benefit) from maintaining this thought? For example, if the person believes that 'old age is a depressing time of life' then he or she is not likely to be motivated to engage in a treatment programme targeting depression until this thought is modified. Thus, a self-fulfilling prophecy is in effect. But if the patient can conclude that this thought is not entirely true in all circumstances, then he or she may be willing to 'give therapy a try' (e.g. 'If I start with something small, that I can really do, like get involved again with my grandchildren's lives, maybe the future won't continue to look so bleak').

'Put Someone Else in my Shoes'

The therapist encourages the patient to imagine how another person would look at the same situation (cognitive distancing) and how that person might respond to it. What perspective might that person take on the beliefs in question? For example, what would the patient say to a close friend if she chastises herself for not being a good enough carer if the friend were in similar circumstances to those that the patient finds herself in right now? Would the patient say to her friend, 'You're just not good enough?' If not, the therapist can explore with the patient the reason that she would not chastise her friend in the way she has chastised herself. The therapist can use the analogy of a good boss and a bad boss. A bad boss picks up on an employee's failures and makes the employee's life difficult; a bad boss also never seems to be around when things are going well and so praise is never received. A good boss, on the other hand, recognizes when mistakes are being made and tries to learn lessons from what has gone wrong. A good boss is also ready with praise and encouragement and nurtures change. The therapist can point out to patients that the way they treat themselves is like a bad boss, but the way they treat others is like a good boss and they ought to be a good boss to themselves too. This can lead to a homework assignment: namely, discussing the thoughts in question with a neighbour, a close friend, or in a support group, where other perspectives on the same issues can indeed be found. Another helpful adaptation here is to ask patients to think of a famous person in history who may have suffered the way they are suffering. Depending on their interests, they may already be familiar with artists, composers, actors and actresses, or political figures who did in fact face similar situations but who triumphed over them, or at least learned things about themselves in the process of experiencing them. Many older adults are interested in history and are very much aware (when they are asked to think about it) of how these famous people handled things.

Consider Alternatives

With this technique a patient is helped to generate as many alternative thoughts as possible. Whether or not the patient actually believes them is left to a later stage (this is a form of brainstorming). When several thoughts have been elicited and written on the board or in the patient's notebook, he or she is then asked to consider each one in turn: how likely is this one to be true, or at least more appropriate for the situation? Suppose the patient is convinced that he is a failure deep down inside because he is no longer engaged in paid employment—he is 'only' doing volunteer work since his retirement. Other alternative views could be: (A) I am healthy enough to do volunteer work, what am I complaining about? (B) I am appreciated more at the volunteer centre than I ever was at work! (C) I really don't want to go back to full-time work; it was a grind and I was happy to finally retire. Maybe I need to explore part-time or consulting work. After all, employers won't come to me; I need to reach out to them. Any of these alternatives is more adaptive than the belief that he is a failure. Often just by going through this exercise, new paths are opened up for exploration.

Review Past Successful Coping Methods

This is a particularly useful technique for older people in objectively difficult situations, such as those in very poor health or with very severe depression. People often gain encouragement and hope by taking time to reflect on how they handled past adversities: usually other major stressors occurred earlier in life and somehow they were faced and lived through, and the person functioned again. This technique is invaluable with older patients, who have gone through many difficult situations in the past. Quite likely, what worked to reduce their distress and enabled them to think more adaptively in the past will almost certainly work again in the present.

Positive Affirmations

This is a very helpful method to instruct patients when they are in situations that, in fact, are not going to change (or are only going to get worse). For example, those with degenerative diseases may be helped more by learning a calm acceptance of their situation, plus how to use encouraging self-statements to continue to be as active as possible, than by trying somehow to convince themselves that things are not 'all that bad'. Similarly, those who may have lost a loved one unexpectedly in an accident or some other form of untimely death may benefit from this approach, as well as those whose lives are filled with multiple stressors. In those instances, the therapist can work on changing the negative thought patterns and encouraging substitution of positive affirmations. Many times patients can generate their own substitutions, based on religious faith or philosophical convictions.

Summary

Traditionally, these techniques are generated in session, so that the patient can use them between sessions as they continue to record negative thoughts on their DTRs. At this point, the number of columns on the DTR is expanded to five. Besides the ABC's described earlier, there is a column 4 which is labelled 'D: Adaptive Thoughts' and a column 5 which is labelled 'E: Outcomes' (meaning, how did the strength of both the negative beliefs and feelings *change* as a result of going through this exercise?). A completed thought record is shown in Table 6.2, in the case example of Alice.

ALICE

In this case example, Alice, a 70-year-old recently widowed woman, learned to challenge her negative thoughts effectively. When discussing this completed diary with her therapist, Alice noted that her 'dirty tricks' included: mind-reading (he does not really love me); overgeneralizing (am I really being ignored?); the 'if-only's' (if only my husband were still here...) and 'name calling', calling herself a basket case.

However, some older adults want to take things further and want to discuss the 'bottom line'—'how is this CBT going to impact on my life and my ability to function?' For these individuals there is a six-column version of the DTR: in addition to the five columns described in Table 6.2, there is an additional column, labelled F (see Appendix 1), which stands for Functioning: Does changing my thoughts really make a difference in my daily life? This is called the 'Why Bother?' question.

In the case of June, her F column read this way: Changing my thoughts will change my behaviour in two ways: (1) I am going to plan for some evening

Table 6.2 Dysfunctional Thought Record: 5 columns

A: Situation (Where were you, what were you doing, who else was there?)	B: Beliefs (As your mood changed what thought was in your mind?)	C: Emotions (Emotional consequences of beliefs)	D: Adaptive thoughts (What can you say that will be more helpful?)	E: Outcomes (Re-rate the strength of the negative beliefs and feelings now)
Home alone waiting to receive usual 'Sunday night phone call' from her adult son, Albert, who is a 50-year-old married man with three teenagers, and a businessman who travels frequently. It is 10 p.m. and he has not called.	He does not really care about me, after all I did for him throughout his life!	Frustration: 80%	Albert could be on the road and not thinking about the time difference; maybe he will still call, or maybe he is in flight somewhere, or maybe he is exhausted and already asleep	Frustration: 40%
	How can he ignore his mother this way? Doesn't he realize I have feelings too?	Dejected and depressed: 80%		Dejected and depressed: 25%
	I miss my husband and when I talk with Albert I am reminded of him. If only John were still here! I don't know what to do; I'm a basket case right now!	Lonely: 75%	Just because he misses an occasional Sunday night call does not mean I am being ignored. He generally calls because he *does* know how important it is to me. I need to 'give him a break' as my grand-kids say	Lonely: 50%
			I am not a basket case. I need to remember that I have coped reasonably well so far with John's death. I can hold him in my heart and encourage myself to begin to develop my friendships	I am encouraged that I am starting to think more about the future and getting more active. Maybe next week will be better!

activities with my friends and (2) I am *not* going to be angry with Albert when we finally do talk on the phone. Instead, I will listen to his explanation and be appreciative that he calls as regularly as he does. I will try to be supportive of him too—his life is not easy.

In sum, the use of the six-column technique has proved very effective with older adult patients. They see the 'chain of events' from A to F and can see the sequential effect that each component has on the others. Learning both this method and the various techniques for generating adaptive alternative thoughts form the backbone of CBT with depressed older adults.

USING BEHAVIOURAL EXPERIMENTS IN COGNITIVE RESTRUCTURING

Skilfully planned and carefully executed behavioural experiments are also needed to help patients to gather actual data that will enable them to modify their thoughts more rapidly and also (as a secondary benefit) become more active in their daily lives. The therapist enrols the patients in 'becoming scientists' by putting their perceptual biases 'on hold' while they collect information on the validity of their negative thoughts. A patient who is very lonely, for example, and refuses to attend social gatherings because he believes that he will be ignored and end up feeling even more depressed, may be given the assignment of attending an upcoming social event that he normally would not attend. When there, the patient is then asked to strike up a five-minute or shorter conversation with at least two people whom he does not know while at the same time impartially observing what happens. He is then asked to write it down as soon as possible thereafter, and discuss it with the therapist at the next meeting. In most cases, the data gathered disconfirm the belief. The anticipated rejections tend not to occur. This is strong evidence that the patient's thinking was awry, which is very encouraging when it comes to challenging other NATs.

Other kinds of behavioural assignments that can be used involve discussions with estranged family members, or actually seeking paid or volunteer work. In these instances, since the responses of the other people involved are not under the therapist's control, it is necessary to prepare patients for a range of possible outcomes, including some that may be disconcerting, such as not getting the job, or being rebuffed by one's adult daughter (at least initially). In preparing patients for such behavioural experiments as homework tasks, extensive use of in-session role-playing and modelling are crucial so that they not only learn to overcome their cognitive barriers, but also learn the necessary behavioural skills to ensure a useful learning experience, such as active listening, in the case of the strained family relationship, or appropriate assertiveness, in the case of the job interview. The patients can be reassuringly told that these behavioural assignments are not completely under their control in terms of their outcome, and therefore if they go wrong the patients are not totally at fault. While it is scary to not be in total control, they should ease up on the pressure on themselves as they are really on a fact-finding mission. Whatever happens, it is an opportunity for learning, and for more corrective feedback that will be useful in future situations.

Other uses of behavioural assignments have been presented in Chapter 5, including pleasant activity scheduling, and more details on how to change core beliefs and basic negative schemas are included in Chapter 7.

SUMMARY

In this chapter the basic techniques of cognitive therapy, thought monitoring and challenging are reviewed. The chapter provides clear guidance on applying cognitive therapy with older people. The evidence provided here via the use of a number of well-chosen case examples refutes the notion that older people are too concrete in their ways of thinking to benefit from the use of cognitive restructuring techniques. The case examples highlight the fact that older people make the same sorts of thinking errors in depression as younger people. The techniques are the same and are equally effective. The following chapter on core beliefs provides a complementary view of therapy work with older people.

Chapter 7

CHANGING CORE BELIEFS AND ASSUMPTIONS

INTRODUCTION

A Chinese proverb says *'those who remember the past are masters of the future'*, and this proverb provides the rationale for uncovering and working with contextual factors in cognitive therapy with older people. In cognitive therapy, while the focus is generally on 'the here and now' element of the patient's difficulties, it is recognized that there is often a pre-existing vulnerability or a developmental context to current psychological problems. In working with older people, therapists may be at a loss as to whether they ought to work on modifying dysfunctional beliefs in their patients that may have formed a lifetime ago and may in certain circumstances have served a certain purpose for the individual. However, just because dysfunctional beliefs (and core beliefs, or self-schemas) may be almost as 'long in the tooth' as the individual endorsing them, this does not mean that people cannot benefit from fine-tuning of beliefs and attitudes that may make them vulnerable to mood disorders. This chapter focuses on strategies for identifying and modifying dysfunctional attitudes (conditional or intermediate beliefs which consist of rules and attitudes) and core beliefs/self-schemas (absolutist, rigid and inflexible beliefs mainly focusing on beliefs about the self). This chapter is one of the very few in the literature on CBT for older people that explicitly deals with dysfunctional

Cognitive Behaviour Therapy with Older People.
Ken Laidlaw, Larry W. Thompson, Leah Dick-Siskin & Dolores Gallagher-Thompson.
© 2003 John Wiley & Sons Ltd.

attitudes and core belief in late-life depression (see also Dick & Gallagher-Thompson, 1995; Dick, Gallagher-Thompson & Thompson, 1996).

COGNITIVE THEORY AND CORE BELIEFS

Self-schemas or core beliefs are formed early on in one's developmental history and continue to form and develop throughout childhood and early adulthood experiences (Beck, 1987). They are organized mental models (in terms of thoughts and images) or representations of an individual's prior experiences (Segal & Ingram, 1994). This results in the development of self-schemas which, in turn, influence information processing so that the way people make sense of the world, and other people's actions, is schema driven (Clark et al., 1999; Segal & Ingram, 1994; Safran & Segal, 1990; Beck, 1987; Kovacs & Beck, 1978). When unhelpful or unnecessarily rigid or inflexible beliefs develop (termed dysfunctional attitudes) this leaves people vulnerable to developing depression and anxiety and, if left unmodified, individuals are at increased risk of relapse and recurrence of psychological problems (Clark et al., 1999; Padesky, 1994; Persons, 1989; Kovacs & Beck, 1978). In depression, schema content is predominantly related to themes of loss or guilt. In anxiety, schema content is predominantly related to threat or anticipated danger (Clark et al., 1999; Kovacs & Beck, 1978).

The cognitive therapy model is a stress-diathesis one and, as such, core beliefs (or self-schemas) are considered to act as pre-existing vulnerabilities that may be latent, or dormant, until activated by a life event or stressor in the patient's recent experience (Beck et al., 1979; Kovacs & Beck, 1978).

> For vulnerable people, these life events precipitate a pattern of negative, biased, self-referent information processing that initiates the first cycle in the downward spin of depression. Nonvulnerable individuals react with an appropriate level of distress to the event, but do not spiral into depression.
>
> (Segal & Ingram, 1994, p.665)

Core beliefs or self-schemas can be used to explain why individuals respond markedly differently to apparently similar stressors (Beck, 1987; Kovacs & Beck, 1978). Thus the idiosyncratic development of the meaning of situations and stressors is very important in understanding patients' reaction to events in their daily lives. For example, if a person has a personal schema relating to weakness (e.g. I am weak) and a dysfunctional assumption related to the core belief (schema) that is 'If I do not have someone to depend upon then I will not be able to cope' one would expect that bereavement will be very difficult for this individual to cope with, *regardless of the age of that individual*. Therapists need to watch for their own age-related assumptions interfering with the process of therapy with older people. Thus when working with older people who are depressed following a bereavement, one ought not to assume that this is a 'normal' response to loss in older people but rather one that reflects a much earlier and emotionally 'primitive' pre-existing vulnerability to loss. As ever in cognitive therapy, a functional analysis of responses to situations that result in the generation of high levels of negative affect is recommended (see Chapter 6 of this volume).

IDENTIFYING DYSFUNCTIONAL ASSUMPTIONS AND CORE BELIEFS

Persons and Miranda (1991) recommend that therapists gather as much information about dysfunctional beliefs as early as possible in treatment because of the mood–state hypothesis (Miranda & Persons, 1988). The mood–state hypothesis suggests that as a patient's mood begins to lift he will have more difficulty accessing and reporting core beliefs unless a negative mood–state is being experienced (Miranda, Persons & Nix Byers, 1990) or activated (Persons & Miranda, 1992). The mood–state hypothesis carries implications for the treatment of depression and provides the rationale for the therapist to work at eliciting hot thoughts during moments of strong emotion during sessions. Persons and Miranda (1991) outline four main strategies for identifying and understanding dysfunctional beliefs: (i) direct questioning (confrontation; recalling; evoking negative state); (ii) gaining information from the nature of interaction within the therapeutic relationship (see also Safran & Segal, 1990; Muran et al., 2001); (iii) use of homework exercises; and (iv) using the cognitive formulation to infer connections between the patient's overt problems and hypothesized covert beliefs (see also Persons, 1989). Sentence completion methods can be a very valuable, efficient and direct way to identify dysfunctional beliefs. As homework, it might be productive in early sessions to ask the patient to complete statements such as I am..., People are..., The world is....

An interesting way to gain insight into the underlying beliefs patients hold about themselves is to borrow a technique from Kelly's personal construct approach and ask patients to complete a 'script' as a homework task. In this task, the therapist takes care to supply the following instructions to patients to enable them to provide a characterization of themselves. If you use this technique with your patients be sure to encourage them to write in the third person. This can be useful if the patients find it embarrassing or difficult to talk about certain perceived aspects of themselves, or their perceived character defects. The exact instructions given to patients are:

> *Write a character sketch of (Patient's name) just as if you were the main character in a play. Write it as it might be written by a friend who knows you very intimately and very sympathetically, perhaps better than anyone ever really could know you. Start by writing, (Name of Patient) is:*

Core themes can also be inferred from the repetition contained within negative automatic thoughts or from recurring difficulties within and across sessions. For example, Mrs T is a 69-year-old retired and widowed civil servant, who was referred because of chronic low mood over the last two years. She has a history of non-response to antidepressant medication and she described her main problems as poor motivation, anhedonia, poor energy and impaired sleep. Mrs T often states that she did not see things ever likely to improve for her. She has been avoiding social contact, and currently prior to taking part in any activity she considers the pros and cons of social participation before eventually opting to do nothing. As a result, Mrs T is becoming more withdrawn and isolated.

Over the course of treatment the therapist identified and raised the issue of Mrs T apparently not following through on things. The common theme appeared to be 'Why bother, it's never going to work out for me anyway'. Mrs T was quickly able to identify several instances in which she managed to get so far with tasks only to turn her attentions elsewhere, such as: taking medication for a short period and then stopping (it didn't have an immediate effect); replacing curtain poles in her house (identifying a new type of pole, buying poles and then stopping halfway through the 'job'); and leaving the garden in a half-finished state. The therapist also brought up the issue of Mrs T's pattern of cancelling appointments at short notice. Mrs T agreed that she had not been attending psychology appointments when she knew she needed to with the result that she was getting so far, feeling the benefit of individual sessions and then not following through. When her mood was lowest she didn't attend for appointments as she felt that she wouldn't manage if she became upset in the sessions.

The underlying theme was discussed and explored further using a technique known as the Downward Arrow Technique (DAT: Burns, 1980). The reasons for the patient's failure to carry through with tasks was explored as shown in Figure 7.1.

From the interaction presented in the figure, the therapist has drawn out a *recurrent theme* from the patient's actions and together they have identified an automatic thought. The recurrent theme is detected by the use of a repetitive series of questions about the person's idiosyncratic meaning that is derived from situations or events or thoughts. The therapist has engaged the patient in a *Socratic dialogue*, in which the patient becomes more aware of implicit messages she is giving herself. Idiosyncratic implicit messages reflect covert or underlying dysfunctional beliefs about oneself. A conditional belief could be stated as 'If I cannot manage to do things by myself, then I am weak'. The core belief that has been uncovered is, 'I am weak/failure'.

The next step is to help the patient to challenge the utility of these beliefs and assumptions. How helpful is this belief to her? What are the consequences of holding this belief (particularly in difficult circumstances). It may be useful to distinguish between current circumstances now and times in the past when these beliefs (however maladaptive now) may have served some function. In

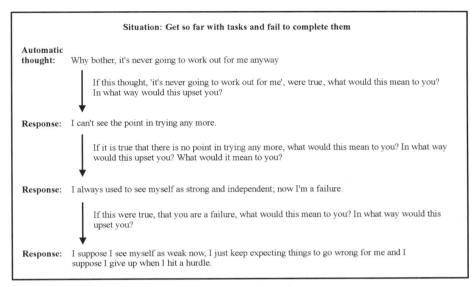

Situation: Get so far with tasks and fail to complete them

Automatic thought: Why bother, it's never going to work out for me anyway

If this thought, 'it's never going to work out for me', were true, what would this mean to you? In what way would this upset you?

Response: I can't see the point in trying any more.

If it is true that there is no point in trying any more, what would this mean to you? In what way would this upset you? What would it mean to you?

Response: I always used to see myself as strong and independent; now I'm a failure.

If this were true, that you are a failure, what would this mean to you? In what way would this upset you?

Response: I suppose I see myself as weak now, I just keep expecting things to go wrong for me and I suppose I give up when I hit a hurdle.

Figure 7.1 The Downward Arrow Technique (DAT)

working this way with older adults, the notion of growing wiser not just growing older gives a kinder context to discussing changes in core strategies. Thus recognizing that certain beliefs are no longer useful and need to be modified is an example of growing wiser. It is beneficial if the patients think of their years lived as a large 'dataset' of examples of ways of dealing with difficulties over a lifetime of change and development, rather than as evidence that they are too long in the tooth to change now.

Understanding the context is very important in that it can also guide the therapist in ensuring compliance and completion of homework tasks. For example, at a very basic level, if patients are hypothesized to have a core fear of failure, then this understanding can be used when identifying potential pitfalls they may experience in either completing or reporting on the homework. As a homework step Mrs T worked with the therapist to identify a task that she would complete by the next session. The homework task set was a small piece of decorating in her home. At the next session, Mrs T reported that she had been able to manage this task satisfactorily but that she was aware that she had felt at certain points an urge to leave the task when she got anxious that she was doing a poor job. She noticed that, as she carried on, her anxiety subsided and she finished the task with a sense of achievement. By working at a deeper level than negative thoughts (the cognitive products of schemas: Beck, 1987) the therapist and patient were able to identify a threat to a successful outcome in this case and were able to put in place a behavioural experiment that counteracted the belief that she was unable to improve things by herself and for herself.

DIFFERENTIATING OVERT AND COVERT PROBLEMS WITH OLDER PEOPLE

Within cognitive therapy, problems and difficulties can exist at two levels, overt and covert (Persons, 1989). This distinction is a very simple yet powerful technique to challenge habitual ways of thinking, feeling or behaving. It is also a useful distinction to employ when a negative automatic thought seems to recur across a number of problem situations. Overt difficulties, such as symptoms of depression, anxiety and phobias, are often the main reason a person seeks treatment. Overt difficulties can be organized within a cognitive framework that incorporates cognition, mood and behaviour. Each component of the overt level is reciprocally linked (see Persons, 1989). Thus a change in one component, such as mood, results in a change in cognition and behaviour that in turn results in a consequential change in mood. The interaction of these elements provides the therapeutic rationale for cognitive and behavioural strategies. However, to incorporate longer lasting change in symptoms and conditions, the therapist has to take account of underlying mechanisms that may be influencing overt problems.

Covert difficulties, such as the patient's core beliefs, conditional beliefs and compensatory strategies, are the underlying psychological mechanisms that essentially maintain a person's difficulties. Covert difficulties are manifested in specific cognitive, affective or behavioural ways. For example, during treatment sessions with Mrs T, the therapist notices that she appears to be experiencing difficulty discussing any topics in depth. She appears to 'flit' between one topic and another within the therapy sessions and the therapist is naturally concerned that the patient is not allowing herself enough time to fully discuss problems to any degree of resolution. When the therapist discusses his concerns with the patient some underlying themes are quickly uncovered. The patient states that she is concerned with what the therapist thinks of her. There are a number of ways to deal with this. The therapist could reassure the patient about his respect for her, but this does not address the important underlying issues. When discussing the issues within the session, the therapist draws out the overt–covert model and detects a dysfunctional belief manifesting itself in certain behavioural strategies and coping styles. The interaction between covert beliefs and current overt difficulties is illustrated in Figure 7.2.

As can be seen from this figure the use of this model highlights important issues to be addressed in therapy and the model serves as a good introduction to the importance and relevance of the concept of underlying difficulties for understanding the nature of a patient's difficulties. The therapist can usefully explore the connection between overt difficulties and underlying beliefs over a number of sessions, and it is important that the patient is able to work with the therapist collaboratively in developing further links between overt (or presenting problems) and apparent underlying (covert) difficulties. The use

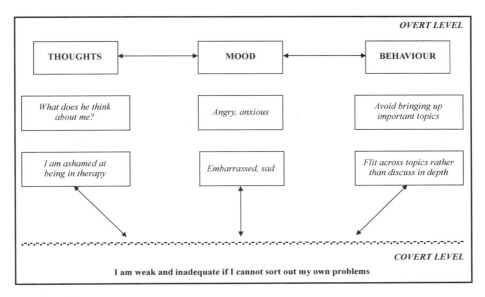

Figure 7.2 Understanding how covert beliefs and overt difficulties interact

of the 'overt–covert' model can allow the patient access to a fuller under-standing of her difficulties.

CORE BELIEFS AND ISSUES IN THE THERAPEUTIC RELATIONSHIP

Consistent with behavioural models of depression (Lewinsohn & Gotlib, 1995; Lewinsohn et al., 1986), important and salient positive reinforcers in a person's world are considered to be our interpersonal relationships with others. Important types of schema found in depression are the 'interpersonal schemas' (Safran & Segal, 1990; Safran et al., 1990). The interpersonal schemas are considered to constitute representations of self–other interactions (Safran et al., 1990) that can result in maladaptive and repetitive difficulties in relationships with others. Dysfunctional interpersonal attitudes or negative interpersonal self-schema can be changed by using the therapeutic relation-ship as a test-bed in which to understand interpersonal patterns of behaviour and test out changes to habitual patterns of relating to others (Muran et al., 2001; Safran & Muran, 1996; Safran & Segal, 1990). If a patient is considered to have core beliefs relating to badness or weakness she may be afraid to open up to a therapist for fear of being rejected or thought of as inadequate. For example, Mrs K (see Figure 3.1) had an interpersonal schema, 'If I want people to love me, then I must do everything they ask'. In therapy, a historical test of her schema—a list of critical life events that may have influenced the development of her belief (Dick et al., 1995; Padesky, 1994; Young, 1990)—was drawn up between the therapist and Mrs K and the impact this belief had upon Mrs K's interactions with others, including with her therapist, was assessed. Mrs K could see that there was a potential problem in holding this belief and gaining what she needed out of the therapy sessions. As a result, Mrs K was encouraged to take a much greater part in determining the agenda for each subsequent session and was encouraged to find ways to tell the therapist if she disagreed with him. Mrs K was encouraged to identify signs that her interpersonal schema was being activated and to act against this. She was also supported in asking some of her closest friends to ensure that she did not always comply passively with the group.

MODIFYING DYSFUNCTIONAL ASSUMPTIONS AND BELIEFS

The process of identification of assumptions and beliefs leads directly into modification. There are a number of techniques for achieving this. Importantly, if the patient decides to focus on core belief work it is important to specify, in advance, goals and aims to be considered. For instance, the person who holds the belief 'I am bad' may aim for a change in that belief to 'I am always good'. However, this may be an unrealistic aim, and a more realistic and comfortable new belief may be 'I am OK, just like most people'. Likewise, when working with assumptions, the therapist needs to help the patient to specify the realistic change with which she would be comfortable. For instance, if a patient holds the belief, 'If I don't do what others want then I am selfish', she would probably be uncomfortable with putting herself first, always. Therefore a more acceptable assumption might be 'If sometimes I can't do things for others it doesn't mean I am a bad person'.

There are a number of cognitive restructuring strategies for dealing with beliefs and assumptions that the patient will be familiar with by this stage of treatment. A very useful cognitive restructuring technique is to ask *'What's the evidence supporting your beliefs?'* and *'What's the evidence against this belief?'* You can also ask your patient to think about the effect of holding this belief. Standard cognitive restructuring techniques are covered in Chapter 6 of this volume and these work well in dealing with self-schemas.

Once the therapist and patient have clearly specified the main core beliefs it can be helpful to set up experiments to evaluate their validity. For example, asking the patient to confront their beliefs by acting in opposite ways can often be stated in a less threatening way by asking the patient to act *As if...* In setting up behavioural experiments, the therapist is asking the patient to confront long-held beliefs and assumptions that are often difficult to change. Thus it can be very productive and very reassuring to *role-play* scenarios (with the therapist adopting the role of the patient) prior to asking the patient to try out new strategies in real life.

Padesky (1994) provides a very clear and explicit description of the continuum method of schema change in cognitive therapy. This is a relatively new technique for modifying dysfunctional assumptions. The first step in this method is to identify clearly the core belief that is troubling the patient and the therapist ascertains the degree of conviction in the core belief. Thus the patient is asked to give a self rating on a continuum that reflects opposite extremes of the core belief. In the case of someone holding a core belief of badness, the two poles are good and bad. Padesky (1994) directly works with the adaptive pole of the continuum of the negative core belief. 'Thus, rather than using a continuum which ranges from 100% unloveable to 100% loveable, it is often more productive to use a continuum which ranges from 0 to 100% loveable' (Padesky, 1994, p. 270). Thus, it is better for a patient to believe that she is 10 per cent lovable than 90 per cent unlovable. In using this technique the therapist aims to get the patient to evaluate the validity of her belief and to introduce a degree of flexibility that was previously absent. Continuum work can be developed over the course of a number of sessions and may be mixed with other methods such as behavioural experiments and cognitive restructuring. For a more thorough discussion of this method, the interested reader is recommended to consult Padesky (1994). Without doubt the continuum method holds a lot of promise in modifying long-held beliefs, and there are no apparent contra-indications in the use of this method with older adults.

In therapy much emphasis is made on identifying negative core beliefs and maladaptive behaviour, especially as this is often the perceptual viewpoint of the patient. In dealing with beliefs and assumptions it is very important to alert the patient to the presence of evidence inconsistent with her beliefs. This technique of monitoring and recording instances of behaviours and events that are inconsistent with negative core schemas is termed *positive logging* (Greenberger & Padesky, 1995).

Finally, when working with older adults in modifying core beliefs an interesting and helpful intervention is to introduce the idea of schemas as self-prejudice (Greenberger & Padesky, 1995; Fennell, 1995; Padesky, 1993b). In essence the idea is that by holding certain maladaptive assumptions or core beliefs, patients are prejudiced against themselves. In working with older adults the notion of older people being prejudiced may be close to their hearts and provides a good solid base for discussing how difficult it can be to change people's attitudes to older people even when there is good contradictory evidence. Often older people are strongly against any form of prejudice and a useful and provocative discussion is encouraged. The therapist then may state: *'You know, sometimes I think you are prejudiced; against yourself. Let me tell you what I mean . . .'*

It might be helpful to talk about a particular type of prejudice and the consequences of this. For example, if someone believes 'all old people are a burden on society', they tend to look for evidence that supports this view (such as, older people have more hospital consultations than anyone else, or that pensions are a drain on a country's wealth). In discussing this example, the therapist might wish to draw the patient's attention to the idea that evidence to the contrary of a prejudice is often either discounted or distorted so that the prejudice is maintained even in the face of contradictory evidence. For example, the fact that, in countries ravaged by HIV, older people are now the main carers for the ophans (WHO, 2002; HelpAge International, 2002), prejudiced people may well respond by saying, that's just in Africa. Of course evidence is accumulating for the importance of older people to wealth in society (see Chapter 2 in this volume).

The therapist directs the patient's attention back to her own particular core belief, and asks her to think of ways in which she might have discounted evidence contradictory to her negative self-belief. Has she modified or distorted evidence so that she continues to see herself as bad? To make this technique more effective, Socratic questioning (Padesky, 1993a) is used to help the patient to think more constructively, for example: 'What do you think, prejudice has to do with your difficulties?'; 'What do you think is the reason I am raising this issue with you?' At this point the therapist can work with the patient to help her make the connection between her beliefs and prejudice as above. Once the connection is made, the schema change methods identified above are used. With older adults this technique is very relevant and carries high face validity.

SUMMARY

Change in interpersonal core beliefs results in an elaboration of the view of self, with a move away from a rigid and constricted view of self, to a view of self that is more flexible, multifaceted and differentiated (Muran et al., 2001). A number of techniques have been described that aim to provide elaboration and modification of rigid inflexible beliefs. In working with older people there is a very limited amount of published work that comments on the modification of core beliefs. Most of the methods described in this chapter are standard schema change methods in CBT. The usefulness of this chapter is to be found in the fact that all the examples describe the development of these techniques with older people. It is this feature that makes this chapter unique.

Section Three

COGNITIVE THERAPY
WITH SPECIAL ISSUES

Chapter 8

ANXIETY, WORRY, PANIC DISORDER AND OLDER PEOPLE

INTRODUCTION

This chapter focuses on the identification and treatment of anxiety disorders, particularly generalized anxiety and agoraphobia, in older adults. Treatment consideration is given to working with older adults who present with significant physical conditions in addition to anxiety symptoms. Anxiety is relatively common in later life (Lau, Edelstein & Larkin, 2001; de Beurs et al., 2000; Blazer, 1997, 1994), and some authors suggest that generalized anxiety presents more commonly than depression (Blazer, 1997). Anxiety is also commonly found to be comorbid with depressive disorders (Schaub & Linden, 2000; Pearson, 1998; Blazer, 1997; Lindesay, 1991). Although depression and dementia in later life are conditions that can cause a patient and his or her family great distress, the presence of anxiety and worry also causes significant distress to the individual (de Beurs et al., 2000, 1999; Beck & Stanley, 1997). As with depression in later life, anxiety in later life is under-detected and under-treated (Small, 1997) and research into the psychological and pharmacological treatment of anxiety in later life is sparse (Dada, Sethi & Grossberg, 2001; Stanley & Beck, 2000; King & Barrowclough, 1988).

Cognitive Behaviour Therapy with Older People.
Ken Laidlaw, Larry W. Thompson, Leah Dick-Siskin & Dolores Gallagher-Thompson.
© 2003 John Wiley & Sons Ltd.

PREVALENCE OF PANIC, ANXIETY AND WORRY IN OLDER PEOPLE

While it would appear that anxiety conditions such as panic disorder and obsessive-compulsive disorder are relatively uncommon in the youngest-old (65–74) and even less so in the oldest-old, generalized anxiety disorder (GAD) and specific phobias (particularly agoraphobia) are relatively common (Stanley & Beck, 2000; Blazer, 1997; Lindesay, 1991; Lindesay, Brigs & Murphy, 1989). The Epidemiological Catchment Area (ECA) study (Regier et al., 1988) reported on the prevalence of three types of anxiety disorders (specific phobias, OCD, panic disorder) in community dwelling individuals aged 18 years plus, including many participants aged 65 years and older. While the one-month prevalence rates of anxiety disorders were lowest in the older adults age group in comparison to all other age groups, there was an overall prevalence rate of 5.5 per cent for anxiety disorders. In the ECA study, phobic disorders were the most common anxiety disorders among older adults and women were more likely than men to develop anxiety disorders by a ratio of 2 : 1 (Flint, 1994). The ECA study did not measure the prevalence of GAD. Hopko et al. (2000) state that GAD is the most common of the late-life anxiety disorders and Blazer (1997) states that when all people over the age of 65 years are considered, then GAD is more common than major depression. Lindesay, Brigs and Murphy (1989) found the highest rates of GAD were found in adults aged 75 years plus. As a counterpoint to these findings, Wisocki (1988) measured worry in an outpatient sample of older adults and found them to have relatively few anxieties or worries. Wisocki (1998) states that the relative absence of worrying in her sample may reflect the fact that older adults have over the years developed effective coping strategies to deal with worry and are much more able to accommodate to changes in their environment.

Schaub and Linden (2000), reporting data from the Berlin Longitudinal Ageing Study (BASE), compared younger-old people (70–84 years) with oldest-old people (85–103 years) and found that the prevalence of anxiety disorders reduced with age. Of this sample, anxiety was characterized by phobic and worry symptoms. In common with other published studies, rates of panic disorder were relatively low (Blazer, 1994; Lindesay, 1991; Regier et al., 1988). The fact that rates of panic disorder are relatively low does not mean that this condition is unimportant or rare in later life. Panic attacks may be present in agoraphobia and in other anxiety conditions such as GAD and constitute an additional emotional burden for the sufferers. In addition, anxiety in later life exhibits considerable comorbidity with depression and Flint (1999) has suggested that late-life GAD is usually associated with depression. In contrast to other age groups, however, there are lower rates of panic disorder comorbid with depression in later life (de Beurs et al., 1999; Pearson, 1998; Beck & Stanley, 1997; Blazer, 1997; Flint, 1994; Lindesay, Brigs & Murphy, 1989).

ASSESSMENT AND MEASUREMENT OF ANXIETY IN OLDER PEOPLE

The therapist working with patients with anxiety in later life may wish to measure symptom change following the use of psychological interventions. For a more in-depth review of this important topic the interested reader is referred to Kogan, Edelstein and McKee (2000) and Stanley and Beck (2000). Recently, attention has focused on the need for adequate assessment of anxiety in later life (Stanley & Beck, 2000; Shapiro, Roberts & Beck, 1999; Flint, 1994). There is a specific paucity of information about the specific assessment of the needs of older adults as many of the main anxiety scales have been adopted from the general adult literature (Stanley & Beck, 2000; Fuentes & Cox, 2000; Beck & Stanley, 1997; Hersen, van Hesselt & Goreczny, 1993). The thoughtful clinician may well be concerned that the presence of comorbid physical conditions may result in artificially elevated scores on measures of anxiety designed originally for a population largely free of chronic medical conditions (Stanley & Averill, 1999). It is also possible that older adults have distinct cognitive and affective profiles that may make the use of certain scales problematic (Shapiro, Roberts & Beck, 1999). There are only two measures of anxiety that have been specifically designed for use with an older adult population. Wisocki (1986, 1988) developed the worry scale (WS) and Sinoff et al. (1999) have developed the Short Anxiety Screening Test (SAST).

The worry scale (Wisocki, 1988) assesses worry across three broad domains: financial, health and social worries. Stanley, Beck and Glassco (1996) demonstrated the ability of this measure to differentiate older adults with GAD from those without. Beck and Stanley (1997) report that this scale holds promise as an assessment of worry in older adults. Stanley et al. (2001) demonstrate that for older adults diagnosed with GAD, the worry scale demonstrates good reliability over time and has strong internal consistency.

The SAST was developed as a brief means of identifying older adults with anxiety problems, especially in the presence of depressive symptoms. The instrument takes 10–15 minutes to administer and has been developed by using selected commonly recurring questions from a range of anxiety measures. Sinoff et al. (1999) claim that the SAST shows good sensitivity (i.e. the ability of a measure to correctly identify those individuals suffering from a certain condition) and good specificity (i.e. the ability of a measure to correctly identify those individuals not suffering from a certain condition). As yet the SAST has not been widely applied or evaluated but shows some promise in terms of its clinical utility.

There are a number of other measures that can be useful with older adults such as the Beck Anxiety Inventory (BAI: Beck et al., 1988). This has been shown to demonstrate acceptable sensitivity and specificity for detection of anxiety in a range of settings (Stanley & Beck, 2000). Wetherell & Arean (1997) provide evidence that the BAI demonstrated sensitivity for the detection of anxiety in medically ill patients. Steer et al. (1994) also showed that the BAI differentiated medically and psychiatrically ill older adults. The Penn State Worry Inventory (PSWI) developed by Borkovec and colleagues (Meyer et al., 1990) while predominantly a measure of worry rather than anxiety per se has demonstrated good utility of use with older adults (Stanley, Beck & Glassco, 1996; Stanley et al., 1997, 2001). While Stanley et al. (2001) suggest that the PSWI has good internal consistency, there are questions regarding its test–retest reliability. The PSWI alone provides a means of assessing worry as a construct distinct from that of depression. The Hamilton Rating Scale for Anxiety (HRSA: Hamilton, 1959) has been criticized as a measure of anxiety in late life as there is a high reliance on somatic components of anxiety (Kogan, Edelstein & McKee, 2000; Stanley & Beck, 2000), nonetheless Beck, Stanley and Zebb (1999) provide evidence that the HRSA is able to differentiate older adults with GAD from those without. Unfortunately the HRSA would appear to have high levels of overlap with the Hamilton rating scale for depression (Hamilton, 1961) calling into question the ability of these measures to discriminate anxiety and depression among older adults (Stanley & Beck, 2000). The Hospital Anxiety and Depression Scale (HADS: Zigmond & Snaith, 1983) was originally developed for use with medically ill populations and as the HAD items were originally designed to minimize the influence of concomitant medical illness, this instrument is a potentially very useful measure of anxiety when working with physically compromised older adults. Studies evaluating the use of the HAD with older adults have tended to focus on the depression subscale to the relative exclusion of the anxiety subscale of the HAD (Kenn et al., 1987; Flint & Rifat, 1996). Davies and colleagues (1993) did evaluate the anxiety subscale of the HAD, but found that the HAD-A subscale showed poor specificity for anxiety as it identified depression more often than anxiety. Disappointingly the HAD scale may actually be a rather unsuitable screening measure for anxiety in later life. The Spielberger State-Trait Anxiety Inventory (STAI: Spielberger, 1983) has also been rather extensively evaluated for use with older adults (Stanley et al., 2001; Fuentes & Cox, 2000; Shapiro, Roberts & Beck, 1999; Beck & Stanley, 1997; Hersen, van Hesselt & Goreczny, 1993) and would appear to be quite useful.

TREATMENT FOR ANXIETY DISORDERS IN LATER LIFE

Older people receive and consume anti-anxiety medications, particularly benzodiazepines, at far higher rates than any other section of the population (Kirby et al., 1999). As Hersen, van Hesselt and Goreczny (1993) comment, this fact by itself indicates that anxiety disorders are a major problem in later life. Taylor et al. (1998) reported that benzodiazepine use increases with age and that more women than men are prescribed this substance; in their sample, many people were using this medication long term and, among new users, continued use was very high. While benzodiazepines are the most frequently prescribed medication for anxiety in later life (Dada, Sethi & Grossberg, 2001; Flint, 1994) there are a number of concerns over their use with older adults. Adverse side-effects of benzodiazepines prescribed for older adults include increased levels of confusion, risks of falls, respiratory problems, agitation, physical dependence and abuse, and in some cases hallucinations (Dada, Sethi & Grossberg, 2001; Sheikh & Cassidy, 2000; Schwab et al., 2000; Pearson, 1998; Flint, 1994). Blazer (1997) recommends prescribing benzodiazepines for short periods of time because of the risks of dependency and because their efficacy is reduced by habituation and tolerance over time.

Another class of drug that has been used to treat GAD is buspirone (Brawman-Mintzer, 2001; Blazer, 1997). The major contra-indications to the use of this agent are that it is rarely effective to switch someone from benzodiazepines to buspirone. This medication is poorly tolerated by older adults as many patients first experience nausea with its use, long before any therapeutic benefit is achieved, and it can take up to four to six weeks for a therapeutic effect to become evident (Blazer, 1997; Small, 1997).

COGNITIVE THERAPY FOR ANXIETY IN LATER LIFE

One of the first studies to evaluate the effectiveness of individualized cognitive therapy for late-life anxiety disorders was presented by King and Barrow-clough (1991), showing that 7 out of 10 patients benefited from the use of psychological methods of treatment. Standard procedures for treating panic disorder as outlined by Clark (1986, 1989), such as cognitive restructuring for dealing with catastrophic misinterpretation and safety behaviours, were applied effectively with this patient group. Results suggested by this pilot study show that anxiety in older adults can be effectively dealt with by non-pharmacological means, even where anxiety and depression coexist. As the authors point out, seven of those patients who improved after receiving cognitive therapy had previously had no benefit from pharmacotherapy. Thus, as a treatment alternative to standard pharmacotherapy, CBT compares very favourably.

Stanley, Beck and Glassco (1996) compared cognitive therapy with non-directive supportive therapy for the treatment of generalized anxiety disorder in later life. They utilized group treatment approaches in which treatment was provided over 14 sessions with each session lasting 90 minutes. Both groups reported benefit from the psychosocial interventions, and there were no significant differences between the groups on standardized measures of anxiety and worry.

Recently Gorenstein, Papp and Kleber (1999) reported upon a 13-session cognitive behavioural treatment package for anxiety in later life. The components of this treatment approach are very similar to that for the treatment of anxiety in the general adult population. While Gorenstein and his colleagues do not report results for their treatment package as yet, of interest to the clinician is the emphasis on the managing excessive worry and dealing with rational and 'realistic' fears associated with normal ageing. These authors are currently collecting data to evaluate the effectiveness of their treatment package. In their patient sample, they state that worries are centred around common themes evident in those who work with older adults such as anxiety about health, family (intergenerational disturbances) and financial worries.

Available data on the effectiveness of cognitive therapy for late-life anxiety disorders is currently limited, meaning that firm conclusions cannot be drawn at this stage (Stanley & Averill, 1999). Research on cognitive therapy for late-life anxiety disorders is surprisingly impoverished given that cognitive therapy appears to be such an effective treatment for the general adult population (Borkovec & Ruscio, 2001; DeRubeis & Crits-Christoph, 1998; Clark & Ehlers, 1993). There are many more papers published that comment on issues of treatment rather than evaluating efficacy or effectiveness (Stanley & Novy, 2000; Sheikh & Cassidy, 2000; Stanley & Beck, 2000; Stanley & Averill, 1999; Gorenstein, Papp & Kleber, 1999).

USING COGNITIVE THERAPY TO TREAT ANXIETY IN OLDER PEOPLE

Lindesay (1991) found that the most common trigger for the development of agoraphobia in older adults was a previous acute episode of physical illness such as a bone fracture or a myocardial infarction. Traumatic episodes such as personal attacks and falls in the home were much less common causes of agoraphobic symptoms.

When working with older adults with problems such as a phobia, it is always useful to enquire about antecedents in the form of traumatic events. For example, Mrs D is a 70-year-old retired beautician. She had developed a fear of leaving her home on her own for any prolonged period of time. Her main difficulty appears to be using public transport on her own. Mrs D admitted that she could travel by car if her husband was present and she felt confident enough to take a long train journey but she would find it impossible to make even a short bus journey by herself.

Prior to seeking professional help, Mrs D had tried to 'force' herself to go on a bus journey but had 'panicked' and got off the bus at the very next stop. She estimated she was on the bus for less than five minutes. In discussing this problem with Mrs D it became clear that she had developed her fears of using public transport after an incident that had taken place at her local shops about one year previously.

While at the local shops Mrs D was gripped by acute stomach pains and felt an immediate and uncontrollable urge to defecate. Unfortunately, Mrs D did not manage to find a public toilet in time. Eventually she was able to clean herself as best she could and walked home. She did not think of this incident too much until she was at her local shops again one week later. She became aware of anxiogenic thoughts such as 'What if I had been on a bus at the time?' and 'What if I had been in a shop queue?' Note that these anxiogenic thoughts are preceded by a 'what if' type statement and while they focus what could have happened, the implications for the future uncontrolled possibility of this incident happening again are implicit in these thoughts. In the cognitive model of anxiety as proposed by Beck, Emery and Greenberg (1995) anxiety thoughts reflect themes of danger. Mrs D also reported experiencing vivid dreams of not being able to get to a toilet when out at the shops. Following the occurrence of these thoughts, Mrs D decided to leave the shopping area and walk home, 'just in case'. In later sessions, the statement 'just in case' became a prominent signal that Mrs D was engaging in 'safety behaviours' such as making sure that she visited the bathroom immediately prior to going out. If for any reason there was a slight delay in her going out, she visited the bathroom again, *just in case*.

When Mrs D went out to social clubs she would only be able to stay if she managed to secure a seat near the bathrooms. Mrs D avoided places like the cinema and the theatre as she was afraid that she would be unable to vacate her seat promptly enough if she needed to visit the bathroom, and only visited localities where she had a mental map of all the local public toilets. Paradoxically, engaging in safety behaviours left Mrs D feeling much more out of control of her body and, consequently, much more anxious.

The treatment plan consisted of development of a graded hierarchy of feared situations and the adoption of a series of homework tasks that allowed Mrs D to confront her fears in a controlled and manageable way. As a first step in treatment, it was necessary to provide Mrs D with some education about anxiety. The early sessions were taken up with understanding the role and impact of anxiety in her difficulty. Following explorative questioning Mrs D revealed that she visited the bathroom frequently, 'just in case' the urge to go to the bathroom came upon her. Of course by engaging in this behaviour Mrs D cut herself off from disconfirming evidence of her fear that she was unable to exert any control over her bowels or her bladder. This paradox was explained to Mrs D and naturally led into the development of a data-gathering exercise as homework. As a first homework session, Mrs D was encouraged to practise holding off from visiting the bathroom for as long as possible. Mrs D successfully managed to hold off for 30 minutes in the first instance and this provided the 'evidence' that it was possible to take a bus trip alone into the town. By the end of Session 3, the homework task was to attend the bathroom only once before going out and to make a short trip to the town. By Session 4, Mrs D stated 'I'm really quite thrilled by my progress' and realized that she could quite comfortably hold off visiting the bathroom for 90 minutes. By Session 5, Mrs D stated that she was able to visit shops that were much further away and now she had very little fear of bus trips. She had managed to become aware of the role that the thought 'just in case' had in making her feel much more out of control of her difficulty. By Session 6, the final session, Mrs D stated that she was now able to visit places even when she did not know where the toilets were. She stated 'I am doing things now without a thought that a few months ago were beyond me.'

COGNITIVE MODELS FOR ANXIETY

The cognitive theory of panic, as developed by Clark (1986), states 'Individuals who experience panic attacks do so because they have a relatively enduring tendency to interpret certain bodily sensations in a catastrophic fashion' (Clark, 1993). In addition to the importance of catastrophic misinterpretation of bodily symptoms, there are other key features of the cognitive model, such as the concepts of hypervigilance and over-monitoring of bodily functioning, safety seeking behaviours and avoidance. Often in working with someone who has developed panic disorder, it is important to *differentiate the first panic attack from subsequent panic attacks*. The initial panic attacks may explain why the fears developed in the first place, but the subsequent panic attacks explain how the problem is maintained.

Clark's (1986, 1993) model makes three predictions:

1. Panic patients will be more likely to interpret bodily sensations in a catastrophic fashion than individuals who do not experience panic attacks.
2. Conditions that activate catastrophic misinterpretations of bodily sensations will lead to an increase in anxiety and panic in panic disorder patients.
3. Panic attacks can be prevented by reducing patients' tendencies to interpret bodily sensations in a catastrophic fashion.

The three predictions outlined by Clark (1986) are very important in the treatment of panic disorder. Thus prediction (1) indicates that the clinician ought to take a full initial assessment of the patient's report of the body sensations that are experienced during a panic attack. It is also evident from predictions (2) and (3) that in order to help patients to deal with panic attacks the exact nature of the anxiety that is generated during a panic attack needs to be identified explicitly and the catastrophic interpretations modified to become more realistic and appropriate. Important information to be gathered here is whether the patient engages in any safety behaviours during a panic attack and the extent of hypervigilance of bodily symptoms during any activity. Safety behaviours are active avoidance strategies performed during an anxiety episode that an individual believes he needs to do in order to offset a catastrophic occurrence. For example, Mr S was a keen ballroom dancer who had been diagnosed with panic disorder, and became anxious whenever he felt his heart racing during dancing. Upon noticing this change in his heart rate, Mr S slowed his dancing down as the thought occurred to him 'Unless my heart slows down I am going to have a heart attack'.

COGNITIVE MODELS FOR GAD/WORRY

The most notable feature of GAD is the pervasive nature of worry (Andrews et al., 1994). The 'inner life' of GAD patients is consumed by the need to avoid impending catastrophe or danger (Borkovec & Newman, 1999). The problems people experience with GAD is best summarized by the words of one patient who stated, 'I am no longer able to make a decision; when I do, I immediately wish that I had done the other thing...I have no peace.'

A central role for cognitive therapy in the treatment of GAD is dealing with worry. Worry precludes emotional processing and interrupts problem solving. Borkovec, Ray and Stober (1998) have identified some information-processing characteristics of chronic worriers that interfere with learning and hence maintain anxious arousal, these are:

- a pre-attentive bias to threat cues, sometimes outside of immediate conscious awareness;
- rapid cognitive avoidance of detected threats;
- negative interpretations of and predictions from ambiguous and even neutral information;
- worrying increases cognitive rigidity and hence interferes with processing of alternative information;
- superstitious thinking about worrying.

There is no general cognitive model for GAD apart from that proposed by Wells (1997) who distinguishes Type 1 worries from Type 2 worries. Type 1 worries concern the welfare of partners or other family members or health, or financial type worries. Type 2 worries concern the nature of worry itself. The patient becomes concerned that worry is likely to result in his becoming mentally ill, or he will worry himself sick. Wells (1997) states that a Type 2 worry is 'worry about worry'. The therapist may find it useful to discuss this idea with the patient and identify which type of worry he finds most distressing. Wells (1997) also notes that many individuals consider worry to perform a useful function of preparedness despite the evidence from research suggesting that chronic worry is rarely if ever helpful or useful (Borkovec & Newman, 1999).

MANAGING WORRY IN LATER LIFE

Basevitz and colleagues (2000) investigated worry among 95 community-dwelling older adults. Intolerance of uncertainty and beliefs regarding the merit of worry were strongly associated with trait worry. These authors note that regrets and negative life experiences among older adults were weaker predictors of pathological worry.

When anxiety, worry and insomnia accompany depression, many people report negative thoughts, significant physical tension and intensified feelings of guilt and self-reproach. People often describe themselves as feeling 'overwhelmed' by worry and unable to find a way to reduce its impact on their daily functioning. It is also common for these feelings to be so intense that people find it hard to imagine a time when they were absent. It is important to engage the patient in a discussion of how they would know when they are anxious or angry. Do the same types of situations bring on these intense feelings? Many people report patterns of emotional reactions to specific situations. Becoming aware of when these are experienced will help the patient to take control of them. Cognitive behaviour therapy clearly emphasizes attending to how patients are thinking, but excessive thinking about feared events or imagined impending catastrophes can lead to another problem: *worry*.

WORRYING AND 'WHAT IF...' TYPE THOUGHTS

One sign of over-thinking or 'worrying' occurs when a thought or a set of thoughts stay around without any clear solution. The therapist can educate the patient to look out for 'worry-thoughts' such as 'What if...' type questions. Worrying involves 'stuck' thoughts that increase anxiety or sadness. Worry leads to rumination and while a solution sometimes arises, this is exceedingly rare. The patients often tell themselves that they should stop worrying, but this is a hard thing to do unless they use certain strategies. An important first strategy is to teach the patient relaxation.

Using Relaxation to Treat Anxiety in Depression

Relaxation can be an effective tool to break the vicious cycle of worrying and help the patient to feel more in control of their emotions. In cognitive therapy, relaxation is an important resource and can be viewed as an adjunct procedure—a means to an end. When introducing the concept of relaxation the therapist ought to take a few moments to discuss any fears or misconceptions the patient may have about relaxation. Emphasize to the patient that relaxation is more than just 'unwinding' to music or taking her mind off things for a while. The therapist will be teaching the patient specific skills she may wish to use to help her to ease anxiety and stress.

Recognizing the Physical Sensations Associated with Anxiety

We know when we are tense or angry because of our physical symptoms. Is there tension in our body? Does our head ache? Is our breathing too quick? These physical symptoms are typical signs of anxiety or anger. These physical symptoms are called 'stress signals'. Spend a few moments talking with the patient about her stress signals of anxiety and frustration. The therapist can also make use of a metaphor here.

> In homes nowadays, many people have fire alarms and these are sensitive to smoke, but smoke does not always mean fire and sometimes, for example, when we burn toast, the alarm goes off. This can be annoying but we can judge when we ought to react to these alarms. Obviously, it's good to have a smoke alarm even if it occasionally sounds when there is no danger. Likewise our bodies have an alarm built in: stress and anxiety. In some people it goes off when there is no real danger. The trick is to judge when to react and when not to. By learning relaxation we can tune our alarms to become less sensitive to false alarms.
>
> (After Butler & Hope, 1997)

Therapists can explain to patients that alarm signals are the body's way of announcing that the people affected must stop what they are doing, calm down and refocus their thoughts. When an alarm signal arises, it is time to introduce a 'stop sign', either a behaviour or a thought that will put the breaks on the negative feelings. Some examples of 'stop signs' are taking a deep breath, leaving the room, turning the lights off for a moment, or even a combination of all of these things.

In addition to relaxation there are important cognitive techniques that help the patient to keep his or her thoughts in perspective. Mainly these techniques use education, verbal reattribution and behavioural experiments. Worry is a mental activity, so it can be useful for therapists to help their patients to distinguish between the content and process of worry. The content of worrying thoughts may be amenable to testing in a similar fashion to identifying and modifying negative automatic thoughts in depression, but focusing on content alone is often unsatisfactory. In the process of worrying, one thought tends to lead to another. For the therapist dealing solely with the content of worries, it can feel like trying to pluck a fish out of a stream by hand; the therapist almost catches it and it appears to slip out of his or her grasp at the last minute. After many attempts at fishing this way, and many near misses, the therapist can end up feeling defeated and dejected. In dealing with worry, time needs to be spent in the therapy session discussing the whole sequence of worrying and how this process can quickly escalate out of all proportion. It is useful for therapists to help their patients to make links between not just the content of worrying thoughts but the escalation of distress.

KEEPING WORRIES IN PERSPECTIVE

Fears about *Not* Worrying

The therapist might want to explore patients' fears about worrying, particularly they may have superstitious fears that if they don't worry about something this will leave them vulnerable and unprepared. A useful technique here is to ask patients to think back to the past: Have they been in this or a similar situation before? How did that turn out? The therapist might find it useful to discuss some research that was carried out by Borkovec and Newman (1999). The researchers asked participants to monitor daily worry predictions to see how often their worst fears were realized. In *84 per cent of the time*, outcomes were very much better than predictions. In *78 per cent of the remaining situations*, participants still found that they coped better than they had predicted or expected. You might wish to pause to discuss this with your clients before letting them know about the rest of the research findings. In the *3 per cent* of cases where people's worst fears came *close to being* realized, in no instance did worrying about the event help them to deal with the situation more effectively. The therapist may find it profitable to spend some time discussing what sense the patients make of this research. Can they relate to it, are there any similarities to their own experiences? It can also be helpful to discuss with the patients that worry is paradoxical in that it feels as if it helps to generate solutions, but in actuality anxiety generated by worry prevents people from thinking realistically and adaptively about situations.

Thought Stopping

This technique involves actively halting 'the worries' and moving to thoughts about other things. One strategy is to teach patients that once they recognize that they are worrying, they should try to say 'Stop!' out loud. This may feel very unusual at first but it can be very effective. The therapist can suggest that patients practise saying (to themselves or out loud) 'I am thinking about (the worry) right now, instead I want to think about (new thought)'. This new thought should be repeated several times or written down on a cue card. Eventually the patients can think 'Stop!' to themselves.

Importance

Another useful exercise is to ask patients to work out how important are the things they are worrying about. The therapist might ask them: Will you still be worrying about these in 10 years time? Will you even remember them then? How many things in your life have you worried about that lasted 5–10 years or more? Will you be still worrying or bothering about this fear in a year from now? What about in a month's time?

Estimating Probability

A patient may be overestimating the likelihood of his fears being realized. For example, David was a 67-year-old retired sports-coach with a persistent fear that an ex-athlete he had fallen out with held a strong grudge against him. David felt certain that this person was sure to act on his grudge against him by getting his body-building son to 'visit' him. David held this fear of attack for a few years. This provided the opportunity in therapy to work out the probability of David's fears being realized. It was possible to work out how many days David had held this fear (and hence the number of opportunities for attacks). There are different ways to calculate the opportunities for danger. David could calculate the number of opportunities for the colleague's son to attack him on a *daily basis* over the last two years. Hence, 365 days in a year $\times 2 = 730$, or David could work this out on an *hourly basis*. If David works an 8-hour day, then this figure is *5840* opportunities over the past two years in which he could have been attacked at work. If one were to assume (as David has) that an attack could come at any time of the day or night, then there have been 730×24 ($17\,520$) opportunities for attack over the last two years.

Following this discussion, David was able to work out for himself that his fears were exaggerated. As fear and anxiety are always future directed, it is important to get the patient to make predictions about upcoming events and compare the patient's predictions with actuality. The therapist asks his or her patients about any things they are worrying about over the coming week. If there is an identifiable fear, get the patients to verbalize this specifically. Ask them to state their fears/worries explicitly in a single sentence. This is their prediction. Get them to rate their beliefs in the likelihood of its occurrence. Make it a condition of the homework that the patients will record exactly how their feared situations turned out.

The Worry Half-Hour

Sometimes people feel better after they have worried about things a little. 'Worry time' is a scheduled time during the day to focus worrying. Instruct patients to make a 'worry list' and avoid thinking about them for the moment. Then, they could schedule some time every day to look at the list and really think about the worries on the list. It is important that patients *limit the time* to a specific amount, stick to this time limit, and plan something to do at the end of the worry time. We suggest that patients set a kitchen timer whose sound will mark the end of 'worry time', and remind them to shift their attention. For example, as a homework task, a therapist could ask the patient to plan 30 minutes in the evening to worry right before a favourite television show. The patient is instructed to look at worry items on his or her list and think about each one, but he or she should stop as soon as the TV programme starts. Many people find this technique helpful, although it may feel a little strange at first.

Using Imagery

The therapist can help the patients to conjure up images that allow them to let their worries go. This is a very simple procedure but some people are better able to use it than others. The therapist can suggest to the patients that they imagine all their worries as leaves on a tree in Autumn and to imagine the leaves (worries) blowing away one by one in the wind far off into the distance. Another image is for the patients to imagine they have written all their worries on a sheet of paper and placed them in a time capsule to bury in the middle of a field. In other exercises the patients imagine that they have written all their worries on a sheet of paper and cast it, and all their worries, into the sea from a rowing boat, or put the paper into a fire and watched it blacken and crumble and fly up the chimney. The therapist can encourage the patients to suggest their own images that they can play around with and alter as they wish. The therapist may find that these exercises work better when applied with some relaxation exercises. In addition to using imagery, the therapist can raise the utility of worry with the patients: What is the benefit of spending hours a day worrying about some future event? A useful way to help the patients to gain control of their worries is to ask them: 'Is there anything you can do about your situations right now?' If the answer is 'no', the therapist can remind the patients that they will gain nothing but distress by continuing to worry. If the answer is 'yes', they can do something right now, then delaying action or procrastinating is only likely to result in distress and a loss of a sense of control. In this case, the therapist works with the patients to determine steps they can take to tackle the problems they are worrying about. If the patients are not able to take action immediately, the therapist can specify a plan of action and help them to use other worry control techniques in the meantime.

SUMMARY

This chapter has identified the nature and extent of anxiety disorders in later life. It is evident that late-life anxiety is under-detected and rather more inadequately psychologically and pharmacologically managed even than late-life depression. It would appear that the main treatment offered to older adults suffering from anxiety is benzodiazepine medication despite widespread fears and concerns about the applicability and adequacy of this treatment approach with older people. For many therapists working with older people, anxiety is a common condition, but until relatively recently very little has been written in the clinical literature about the psychological treatment of anxiety in later life. Recently mainstream cognitive therapy techniques have been applied with very promising results for the treatment of anxiety in older adults. While the limited numbers of studies that have evaluated psychotherapy for this disorder provide us with only tentative conclusions about the worth of therapy, cognitive therapy is already providing good results in terms of outcome. One can be optimistic that CT is an effective treatment for older adults with anxiety. The ease with which standard CBT techniques for anxiety and worry are applied with older people is a testament to the flexibility and utility of these techniques.

Chapter 9

INSOMNIA AND SLEEP DISORDERS

INTRODUCTION

This chapter addresses the issue of sleep problems in later life. In working
with older people in psychotherapy settings it is surprising how commonly
patients complain of sleep difficulties. It is also surprising how many older
adults use pharmacological means of assisting sleep. Use of medication to aid
sleep directly contradicts the empirical evidence for effective treatment of
sleep difficulties in older people, and yet older people are commonly
prescribed medication for insomnia. This chapter sets out specific information
on the use of CBT techniques for effective sleep management. A case example
outlines how sleep problems may manifest themselves when working with
older people.

SLEEP PROBLEMS IN OLDER PEOPLE

Older adults commonly report inadequate sleep. Approximately 12–25 per
cent of healthy older adults report chronic insomnia and higher rates are likely
to be found for older people with concurrent medical or psychiatric conditions
(Mellinger, Balter & Uhlenhuth, 1985). Factors affecting an older person's sleep
include normal age-related changes in the biology of sleep, medical
conditions, multiple medication use, psychiatric conditions, as well as changes

Cognitive Behaviour Therapy with Older People.
Ken Laidlaw, Larry W. Thompson, Leah Dick-Siskin & Dolores Gallagher-Thompson.
© 2003 John Wiley & Sons Ltd.

in lifestyle such as retirement or widowhood (Blazer, 2002; Morin et al., 1999; Bootzin et al., 1996; Miles & Dement, 1980). Although it is commonly known that sleep disruptions can aggravate or even precipitate severe mood fluctuations, these are often overlooked in the treatment regimen for late-life depression, perhaps because they occur so frequently in this population. Effective techniques are available to assist patients in sleep regulation, and an aggressive focus on sleep problems can be remarkably helpful in the treatment process. Clinicians should be alert to any complaints of a sleep problem in the older patient, and address this with appropriate diagnostic and treatment strategies. We will provide a brief discussion of the usual age-related changes in sleep, along with the characteristics of late-life insomnia and current treatments available. A detailed review of insomnia or other sleep disorders is beyond the scope of this chapter, but the interested reader may wish to refer to Lichstein and Morin (2000).

In DSM-IV (APA, 2000) insomnia is defined as a complaint of insufficient, non-restorative sleep for at least one month that is disruptive to occupational or social functioning. In order to be diagnosed with insomnia, other sleep disorders (e.g. sleep apnoea) or muscular disorders (e.g. restless leg syndrome or periodic limb movement disorder) are ruled out. Insomnia can present in three ways: (1) *sleep onset insomnia* is defined as difficulty falling asleep; (2) *sleep maintenance insomnia* is defined as frequent awakenings during the night or waking too early (than desired) in the morning and returning to sleep is problematic; and (3) *mixed type insomnia* is defined when both sleep onset or maintenance is disturbed. In addition, primary insomnia is differentiated from secondary insomnia. *Primary insomnia* occurs when sleep loss is not concurrent with another medical condition, psychiatric condition or substance use. *Secondary insomnia* occurs when sleep disturbance is associated with other conditions mentioned above (Reidel & Lichstein, 2000).

THE BIOLOGY OF SLEEP AND CHANGES IN SLEEP WITH AGE

Sleep is characterized by stages of light sleep and deep sleep that repeat throughout the night. As one progresses from light sleep (stages 1 and 2) to deeper sleep (stages 3 and 4), background brain activity, as measured by an electroencephalogram (EEG), transforms to slower, high-amplitude waves. As deeper sleep is attained, there is some oscillation between deeper and lighter sleep stages. After about 90 minutes of sleep, rapid eye movement (REM) sleep begins to occur, which is characterized by dreaming, increased heart rate and blood pressure, and rapid breathing.

Undisturbed sleep is the key process that governs overall functioning. The human body is sustained by night-time sleep and daytime wake cycles called circadian rhythms. Non-REM sleep enhances the immune system, and REM sleep is noted for regulating day-to-day mood functioning (Bootzin et al., 1996). While sleep loss over a one- or two-night period is not worrisome, consequences of continued sleep loss includes daytime fatigue, impaired functioning, and an increased tendency for mood fluctuations.

Sleep in later life is quite sensitive to chronic physical problems (Miles & Dement, 1980). Older persons experience greater frequency and duration of night-time awakenings, and age-related reductions in REM sleep and dreaming increase an older person's vulnerability to the development of mood disorders (Reidel & Lichstein, 2000; Bootzin et al., 1996). Older adults are commonly labelled as inefficient sleepers, as they are likely to maintain a 'regular bedtime' regardless of fatigue, thus extending their time in bed without sleep. Secondary insomnia is of great concern in later life, not only due to impaired sleep from physical discomfort, but also when mobility problems increase time in bed throughout the day. Likewise, as mobility and activity decline, increased daytime napping can affect a regulated sleep schedule, which in turn increases the development of psychiatric symptoms.

MEASURING SLEEP

The sleep diary is a cost-effective, self-report measure designed to assess an individual's sleep–wake schedule (Figure 9.1). It also captures information regarding daily caffeine intake as well as the use of sleep aids prior to sleep or during the night to manage awakenings (Rogers, Caruso & Aldrich, 1993; Haythornthwaite, Hegel & Kerns, 1991; Spielman & Glovinsky, 1991). Sleep diaries can be extremely helpful in determining the importance of sleep disturbance in individuals suffering from a mood disorder. Sleep diaries are widely used in research and treatment settings, and correlate well with observed sleep from polysomnography (Rogers, Caruso & Aldrich, 1993; Haythornthwaite, Hegel & Kerns, 1991). As polysomnography is a costly procedure involving the measurement of physiological processes throughout the night—such as brain activity, eye movements, blood pressure, respiration, and periodic leg movements—this procedure is recommended only if sleep apnoea is suspected (Blazer, 1998; Bootzin et al., 1996).

TREATMENTS FOR INSOMNIA

Previously considered a first-line intervention for insomnia, medication is no longer recommended as the sole treatment for late-life insomnia (Bootzin et al., 1996). The long-term use of hypnotics results in increased tolerance and habituation requiring incremental increases of medication in order to produce the desired effect on sleep disruption.

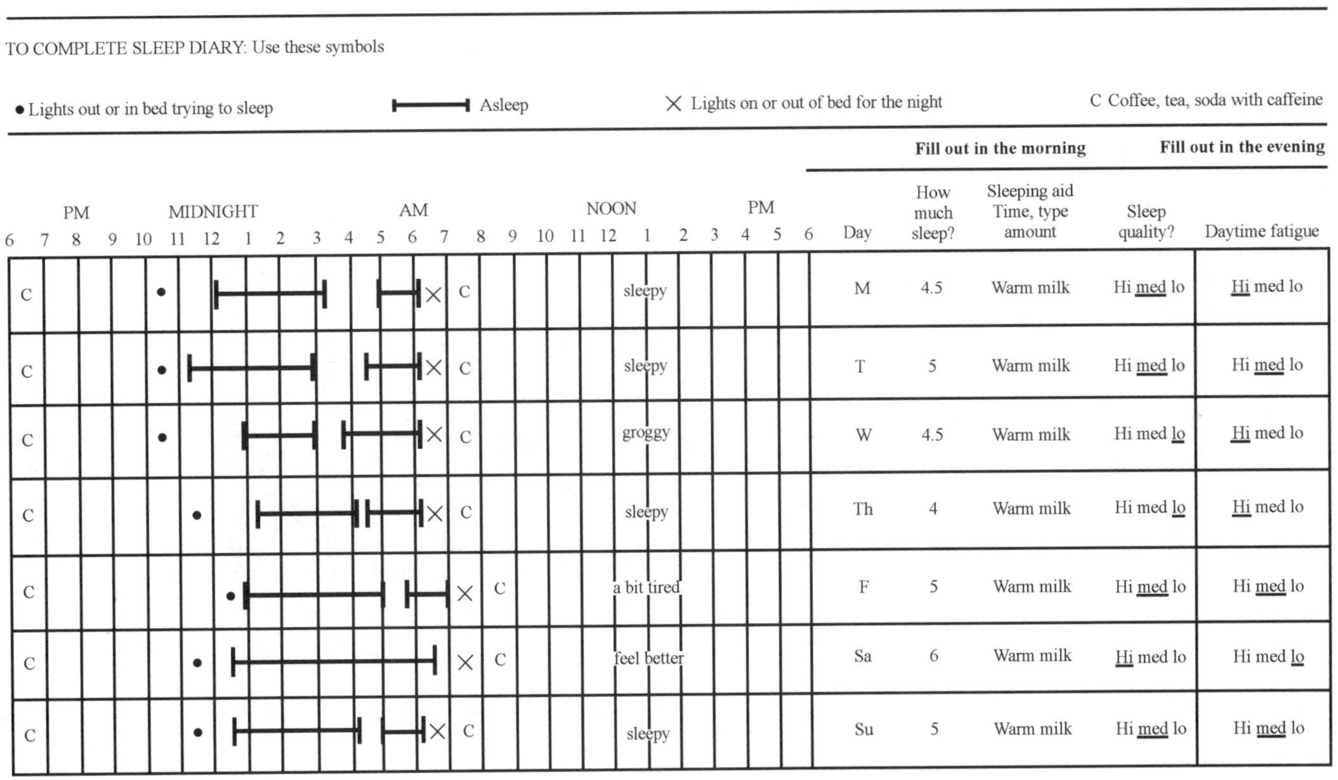

TO COMPLETE SLEEP DIARY: Use these symbols

• Lights out or in bed trying to sleep

| Asleep

X Lights on or out of bed for the night

C Coffee, tea, soda with caffeine

Figure 9.1 Mrs J's Sleep Diary (adapted from Spielman and Glovinsky (1991))

Worryingly, hypnotics alter the 'architecture' of sleep, reducing both the stages of slower wave (deeper) sleep and REM sleep. As these effects mimic changes in sleep that naturally occur with age, prescribing hypnotics for late-life insomnia becomes exponentially problematic. Side-effects of hypnotics include an increase in confusion or unsteadiness as well as an increase in susceptibility for psychological dependence. While newer hypnotics have fewer 'morning-after' side-effects, empirical evidence strongly points to the use of behavioural and cognitive interventions rather than medication alone (Blazer, 1998; Nicholson, 1994).

Behavioural interventions such as sleep hygiene, stimulus control, sleep restriction, relaxation and cognitive restructuring can be extremely effective with older adults who complain of difficulty in sleeping. In particular, behavioural interventions can be useful with patients where medication usage may be problematic.

Sleep hygiene refers to 'good sleep behaviours'. Older adults are taught (1) the normal and pathological aspects of sleep, (2) the effects of caffeine and fluid intake close to sleep, (3) the potentially harmful effects of long-term medication use, (4) the detrimental effects of napping and (5) the importance of keeping a consistent sleep–wake schedule that includes setting an alarm for the same time seven days a week (Blazer, 1998; Bootzin et al., 1996). A discussion of the older person's personal preferences regarding his or her sleep environment is discussed, such as comfortable sleeping temperatures, noise level, lighting, mattress firmness, etc. The realistic effects of impaired sleep are also taught to help older adults to distinguish between normal, occasional sleep loss and true insomnia.

Stimulus control is an intervention designed to strengthen the association between the bed and the bedroom as a cue for sleep. Additionally, it is designed to help the person to rely on the physical cues of fatigue and sleepiness rather than on a standard bedtime to promote sleep (Bootzin et al., 1996). Stimulus control techniques are helpful for both the sleep onset and the sleep maintenance insomniac. The instructions for stimulus control are as follows (Bootzin, Epstein & Wood, 1991):

1. Do not use your bed or bedroom for anything but sleep (or sex).
2. Go to bed only when sleepy.
3. If you do not fall asleep with 15 to 20 minutes, leave the bed and do something in another room. Go back to bed only when you feel sleepy again.
4. If you do not fall asleep quickly on returning to bed, repeat step 3 as many times as necessary.
5. Use your alarm to leave your bed at the same time every morning.
6. Do not nap.

Sleep restriction techniques developed in response to the observation that insomniacs are inefficient sleepers (Spielman, Saskin & Thorpy, 1987). The goal of these interventions is to consolidate sleep by restricting the time in bed based on the actual number of hours an individual sleeps. For example, if a person spends eight hours in bed, but sleeps four and a half hours, he or she would be prescribed four and a half hours in bed only. In the beginning of treatment, it is common for the person to have increased daytime sleepiness, but as this treatment becomes effective, sleep becomes more efficient. Guidelines for using this technique with older persons recommend weekly increases to the amount of time prescribed (Spielman & Glovinsky, 1991).

Progressive muscle relaxation (PMR) is the systematic tensing and releasing of 16 major muscle groups throughout the body in order to decrease anxiety and arousal and promote sleep (Bernstein & Borkovec, 1973; see also Chapter 5 in this volume). PMR is a favourite intervention among sleep researchers (Lichstein & Fischer, 1985). Older adults with arthritis or other pain disorders may exacerbate physical symptoms and tension using PMR, which may ultimately inhibit sleep (Bootzin et al., 1996; Lichstein & Johnson, 1993). Instead, a passive form of relaxation has been designed: the older person is trained to identify and relax noticeable physical tension, while utilizing guided imagery to calm both ruminating thoughts and tense muscles (Bootzin et al., 1996). Relaxation techniques are also recommended to replace daytime napping for older adults in order to enhance sleep efficiency during the night (Engle-Friedman et al., 1992).

Worry, dysfunctional beliefs about sleep, and intrusive thoughts accompany insomnia (Hall et al., 2000; Morin et al., 1993). Typical dysfunctional beliefs that occur with insomnia include: (1) catastrophic consequences regarding the effects of sleep loss; (2) erroneous appraisal of the quantity of sleep obtained during the night; (3) misperceptions that sleep is out of one's control; and (4) erroneous beliefs about what constitutes good sleep behaviours (Morin et al., 1993). As with other disorders, cognitive restructuring is employed to identify these faulty beliefs and determine realistic information to challenge and ultimately substitute more helpful, sleep-promoting beliefs (Morin, 1993; Morin et al., 1993).

EFFICACY OF TREATMENTS FOR LATE-LIFE INSOMNIA

Behavioural and cognitive interventions are highly effective in treating late-life insomnia. The majority of treatment outcome research in late-life insomnia has focused on older adults suffering from primary insomnia. Early research tested the efficacy of utilizing an individual treatment modality for treating sleep onset insomnia, such as stimulus control (Davies et al., 1986; Puder et al., 1983) and sleep hygiene (Morin, Culbert & Schwartz, 1994). The majority of research has used combinations of behavioural techniques or created a CBT modality that incorporates cognitive restructuring techniques and one or more of the behavioural interventions described above. When combinations of behavioural interventions are employed, stimulus control interventions demonstrate the greatest effects for both the sleep maintenance insomnia (Morin et al., 1994; Morin & Azrin, 1988) and mixed sleep onset and sleep maintenance insomnia for older adults (Engle-Friedman et al., 1992). Follow-up data indicates that treatment effects from stimulus control techniques are maintained up to two years post-treatment (Engle-Friedman et al., 1992).

When cognitive interventions are added to the treatment package, outcome is augmented. Edinger and colleagues (1992) evaluated the efficacy of treating sleep maintenance insomnia in older adults with cognitive restructuring, stimulus control, sleep hygiene and relaxation training. These authors also reported strong effects when all modalities were used. Similar findings were reported in a larger study by Morin et al. (1993) who treated older adults with sleep maintenance insomnia with a treatment package combining sleep restriction and stimulus control methods, cognitive restructuring, and sleep hygiene procedures. When the CBT treatment 'package' is compared to the single modality of PMR, it is demonstrated to be the preferred treatment (Edinger et al., 2001a, 2001b). Research also suggests that CBT can enhance the efficacy of sleep medications in older adults (Epsie, Inglis & Harvey, 2001; Morin et al., 1999).

Until recently, older adults who presented with concurrent medical or psychiatric issues had been specifically excluded from early research as it was believed that the sleep disturbance attributed to other disorders would not respond well to treatment (Lichstein, Wilson & Johnson, 2000). Yet, Lichstein and colleagues (2000) demonstrated that older adults with secondary insomnia responded well to stimulus control treatment and a revised PMR designed not to exacerbate medical symptoms. In the first controlled trial addressing the treatment of insomnia secondary to chronic pain, Currie et al. (2000) demonstrated the efficacy of CBT as a promising treatment package for patients with this presentation.

CASE EXAMPLE

Mrs J is a 70-year-old widowed woman who has been living alone since her husband died two years ago. Mrs J worked as a librarian for 35 years until she retired three years ago to care for her husband when he was diagnosed with cancer. For the past 18 months, she has been complaining to her primary medical doctor of difficulty falling asleep and staying asleep. She reported that she often has to get up in the middle of the night to urinate, and at times never gets back to sleep. She additionally complained of lack of energy and lack of interest in activities that once gave her great joy. Since she presented with a subclinical picture of depression, her doctor attributed her anhedonia and reduced activity to lack of sleep. Initially, he prescribed medication to help initiate sleep. She reported that after one night's dose, she felt 'like a zombie' the next morning, slept off the side-effects through most of the next day, and ultimately had a disrupted night. The doctor ordered a sleep study to rule out the possibility of another sleep disorder such as sleep apnoea or muscular disorder.

The study showed that sleep onset did not occur for almost 40 minutes, and she had two awakenings. The first awakening occurred after three hours of sleep. She did not return to sleep for 45 minutes, and the second awakening occurred one hour later. Mrs J never returned to sleep for the rest of the study. She was diagnosed with a mixed presentation of both sleep onset and sleep maintenance insomnia. The sleep study was able to rule out the presence of both sleep apnoea and a muscular disorder related to her extremities. Mrs J was told that she had a treatable condition that was best handled in a brief course of psychotherapy specifically tailored to treating insomnia.

When she began treatment, Mrs J was asked to complete a sleep diary in order to assess her sleep behaviours (Figure 9.1). It was discovered that she had a cup of tea with dinner, as well as a glass of warm milk at her bedside before turning out the light. She also consistently read and watched TV in bed. Sleep hygiene information was immediately presented. Mrs J explained that she didn't believe tea had enough caffeine to affect her sleep, especially when she ate an early dinner and got into bed at 10 p.m. She also explained that she uses reading and TV to 'make her tired', and had never heard that these behaviours could have a detrimental effect.

Mrs J was given specific stimulus control instructions and several goals were targeted. Instead of believing that she 'must' go to bed at 10 p.m., she was to perform actions that would promote relaxation and sleepiness *outside of the bedroom* and then get into bed when she recognized that her body and mind were ready for sleep. It was also believed that the warm milk she drank immediately before turning out the light might contribute to her need to urinate in the middle of the night. She was given a guided relaxation tape that taught her to relax each part of her body systematically and clear her mind of distracting thoughts. With practice, Mrs J reported that this exercise created similar relaxation effects as the warm milk. She was also instructed not to turn on the TV or start reading in bed when she experienced her awakenings. She was told to get out of bed until sleepy again.

Mrs J's anhedonia was also addressed. As a result of her lack of interest in activities that once gave her pleasure, she reported being quite inactive during the day. This inactivity would increase daytime fatigue (and possibly napping) as well as prevent the onset of sleep later when she desired it. Encouraging her to re-engage in social activities would not only elevate her mood and structure her day, it would also assist in initiating fatigue and sleep at a more appropriate time at night.

Mrs J had very rigid beliefs about both the necessity of eight hours of sleep as well as the detrimental effects of sleep loss. She would report that during sleepless periods she would repeat over and over in her mind, 'My day is ruined if I do not sleep! I will get critically ill and no one will help me.' Mrs J was open to educational information about the realities of sleep loss and was open to challenging these catastrophic beliefs. Her daily activity log and mood ratings were integrated to provide evidence that even after a night of less satisfying sleep, she was able to be active and keep her mood at a comfortable level. She was eventually able to replace her faulty beliefs with self-statements of encouragement that she can 'cope' with less sleep. Likewise, she was taught thought-stopping techniques to combat the ruminations 'I will never return to sleep' once she was awakened in the middle of the night. This strategy, combined with relaxation techniques, eventually shortened her night-time awakenings and promoted faster returns to sleep. After 15 sessions Mrs J reported improved sleep, increased daytime activity and improved mood.

CONCLUSIONS

Complaints of poor sleep are a common occurrence when working with older adults. While inadequate sleep in later life may have numerous causes, cognitive and behavioural treatments have become a first-line choice of interventions regardless of the nature of the sleep difficulty. We are often challenged by the patients, however, who in their great discomfort of poor sleep, request medication as their first choice as it is perceived to provide the most immediate result. At this point, it becomes necessary that we offer a solid educational and therapeutic rationale to encourage our patients that agreeing to learn new sleep habits and beliefs about sleep are far more beneficial in the long run.

Chapter 10

PHYSICAL ILLNESS, DISABILITY AND DEPRESSION

INTRODUCTION

In this chapter, the challenge of applying cognitive behaviour therapy (CBT) with physically ill and sensory impaired older adults is discussed using clinical case examples. Haley (1996) points out that psychologists and psychotherapists are often biased against the possibility of good therapy outcome in the presence of significant physical conditions. Padesky (1998) also comments upon the potential impact on therapy outcome of a therapist's own beliefs. In the case of a heart condition, such as angina, therapists can often be quite reluctant to apply standard CBT procedures when treating comorbid anxiety. In this instance therapists often report being fearful of challenging and removing safety behaviours such as sitting or resting when patients report their heart racing for fear that the patient will have a heart attack.

This chapter sets out to equip the therapist with a set of skills and a knowledge base to develop innovative practices in CBT for the treatment of emotional disorder in the context of physical illness. Examples of how to apply CBT for depression and anxiety using macular degeneration and Parkinson's disease, as examples of comorbid physical conditions commonly found in older adults, are outlined below. Equally well, however, the concepts and practices discussed using the case examples in this chapter could be applied with a wide range of chronic and degenerative conditions commonly found in

Cognitive Behaviour Therapy with Older People.
Ken Laidlaw, Larry W. Thompson, Leah Dick-Siskin & Dolores Gallagher-Thompson.
© 2003 John Wiley & Sons Ltd.

later life, such as arthritis, chronic obstructive pulmonary disease and cardiovascular disease. Readers should also consult Chapter 11 dealing with post-stroke depression.

DISABILITY AND DEPRESSION

As Chapter 1 reminds us, the likelihood of limitations on activities because of chronic conditions increases with age. In the USA, the UK and most of Western Europe, death is commonly as a result of chronic medical conditions (non-communicable diseases or NCDs) such as heart disease, stroke and cancer (Sahyoun et al., 2001; Kinsella & Velkoff, 2001; WHO, 2001). Thus older people are more likely to experience some form of chronic illness as they age. Increasing longevity has resulted in relatively larger increases in the numbers of the oldest-old section of the population, precisely the section of the population at risk of disablement. Recently data from a number of sources (see WHO, 1999, for review) suggests a significant reduction in age-specific disability rates in many of the developed countries in the world (WHO, 2001). While levels of disability in developed countries in the world are declining, the number of years lived without disability is increasing in line with increasing longevity (Kinsella & Velkoff, 2001).

Often depression in the presence of medical illnesses is considered a reaction to the illness. Recently it has been realized that depression may in itself be an independent risk factor contributing to the development of illnesses. For instance, Roose, Glassman and Seidman (2001) review evidence that suggests that depression increases mortality and morbidity in ischaemic heart disease. Haley (1996) reviews evidence that supports the idea that depression maintains, prolongs and exacerbates the consequences of physical illnesses. Kemp, Corgiat and Gill (1991/2) comment that depression negatively affects the attributes of perseverance, optimism, stamina and motivation, and it is precisely these attributes that are required to cope with the demands of physical rehabilitation.

It is important to bear in mind that physical disability in late life does not automatically result in depression; disability or, more correctly, impairment does not equate with depression. As Zeiss et al. (1996) point out, functional impairment needs to be disentangled from physical disease. While functional impairment is the loss of the ability to meet one's needs independently and the likelihood of functional impairment is increased following physical illness, it is not inevitable as older people generally accommodate to chronic illness over very many years. Reviews of the association between physical illness and depression point out that the majority of people with physical illnesses do not meet criteria for depression (Zeiss et al., 1996; Cohen-Cole & Kaufman, 1993; Schulberg & McCleland, 1987). The important issue for consideration here is not whether the person has a medical condition but the functional impact of this illness, particularly on the ability to participate in meaningful and idiosyncratically significant activities (Champion & Power, 1995; Lewinsohn et al., 1985). Thus when working with a person with depression and anxiety who has been diagnosed with a medical condition that may limit physical independence, the crucial information is what has been the impact of the illness and what does the person believe may be responsible for his or her depression or anxiety. CBT adopts a collaborative stance and collaboration in this regard avoids making unhelpful and unwarranted assumptions about causality and maintenance. When seeking to understand the impact of a chronic medical condition on a person's life, the best way to achieve this is to ask the patient.

DEPRESSION, DISABILITY AND COGNITIVE THERAPY EFFICACY

Kemp, Corgiat and Gill (1991/2) showed that a 12-week course of group CBT was effective for individuals diagnosed with a range of chronic physical conditions such as heart disease, rheumatoid arthritis, pulmonary disease, etc. Following CBT for depression and anxiety, the non-disabled group and the disabled group achieved similar gains at the end of treatment. However, in comparison to the non-disabled group, the disabled group maintained treatment gains but did not achieve further treatment gains at six months follow-up assessment. Kemp, Corgiat and Gill (1991/2) provide a rationale for the use of CBT as a treatment for depression comorbid with a medical condition such that 'Disabling conditions cause psychological distress, decrements in enjoyable activities, loss of independence and lowered self-esteem. These factors are often the critical elements leading to a depressive disorder and they can be aided through psychotherapy.'

Kunik and colleagues (2001) provide evidence that one session of cognitive therapy for patients diagnosed with chronic obstructive pulmonary disease (COPD) was more effective than psycho-education in reducing depression and anxiety symptoms. In a number of other small psychological studies, cognitive and behavioural interventions have proved useful in increasing exercise compliance in COPD patients (Atkins et al., 1984), improving functional performance (Eiser et al., 1997) and reducing illness perception and impact (Lisanky & Clough, 1996).

Dreisig et al. (1999) recently carried out a pilot study of cognitive therapy for depression in Parkinson's disease (PD). Preliminary findings on a limited number of patients provide some optimism that cognitive therapy is relevant and efficacious. Treatment using CBT resulted in lowered levels of depression and anxiety in PD. Currently, there are no randomized-controlled trials of CBT for the treatment of depression in PD. While the efficacy of CBT for depression in PD has yet to be established, psychological treatment for depression is consistent with good clinical practice, as Manyam (1997) states: 'The primary goal in all stages [of Parkinson's disease] is to attain functional improvement in the patient's condition by using the fewest drugs as infrequently as possible.'

Hence it should be clear that while the evidence for CBT's efficacy as a treatment for depression and anxiety across a range of physical conditions is at an early stage, CBT's applicability and clinical utility appear promising. In reality, more studies are required to properly evaluate the efficacy of CBT as a treatment for depression and anxiety in disability. However, leaving depression untreated in physical illnesses, especially if depression is seen as reactive and therefore 'understandable', is to sentence older people to, at the very least, prolonged periods of illness morbidity. At the very worst, indications from the research literature suggest that untreated depression in later life can result in premature mortality. As such, the case for the treatment of depression in physical illness using psychological methods takes on a much stronger imperative.

WORLD HEALTH ORGANIZATION ICF SYSTEM

In 1980 the World Health Organization (WHO) developed a classification system for assessing the consequences of disease that used the terms 'impairment', 'disability' and 'handicap' (see Chapter 1 for further discussion of this model's applicability in psychotherapy with older adults). In 2001, the WHO extensively revised this classification system as it was felt that the emphasis ought to be less focused on morbidity and instead developed a 'components of health' classification, known as the International Classification of Functioning, Disability and Health (ICF).

The ICF (WHO, 2001b) is a flexible classification system that facilitates communication across disciplines and therefore can be used as a clinical, educational, research and social policy tool. The ICF is divided into two parts, each of which is further subdivided into two components. Thus, Part 1, *functioning and disability*, is subdivided into (1) body functions and body structures and (2) activity and participation components. In Part 2, *contextual factors*, the two components are (1) environmental factors and (2) personal factors. Each component has positive and negative aspects.

When developing psychotherapy interventions in depression or anxiety comorbid with physical illness, the ICF system specifies interrelations between functioning and disability that are compatible with the cognitive therapy model. For example, Mrs D, who lives alone, has over the last 10 years developed macular degeneration and now finds it difficult to manage many tasks independently. Age-related macular degeneration (AMD) is the leading cause of blindness in older people. AMD is so called because the disease

	Health Condition Macular degeneration	
Body Functions and Structure Visual impairment	**Activities** Loss of independence	**Participation** Social isolation
Environmental Factors Living alone with limited contact With family members Supportive housing		**Personal Factors** Depressed following death of dog I'm too old to get another dog

Figure 10.1 Applying the ICF system in practice

affects the central part of the retina, called the macular. Therefore central vision is primarily affected. Loss of vision occurs gradually and both eyes may be differentially affected. Peripheral vision is unaffected and the individual rarely becomes totally blind. Even when AMD is severe, most people retain the ability to move about independently and to benefit from the use of low vision aids. Mrs D developed depression following the death of her dog. AMD is important in understanding the development of depression in Mrs D's case. In this instance, AMD is only important in the respect that it disrupts activities of daily living and Mrs D's ability to participate in meaningful and idiosyncratically valuable daily activities (Zeiss et al., 1996; Lewinsohn et al., 1985). In this case example, functional impairment is quite significant as a result of late-stage AMD. Of equal and of additive importance for understanding the development of depression in this case example is the loss of Mrs D's dog. In losing her dog, Mrs D also lost access to the outside world and lost her sense of security outside her own immediate surroundings. Figure 10.1 outlines how the ICF system can be useful in thinking about psychotherapy with physically compromised older adults.

The ICF system (Figure 10.1) takes account of the fact that depression and its treatment are complicated by the presence of a significant deteriorating physical condition, but AMD here is only important insofar as it produces significant functional impairment in valued roles and goals (see CMOP, Figure 10.2). Personal factors are also taken account of, such as Mrs D's age. Mrs D considers that since she is 87 years of age there are too few 'good' years left to even try to get another dog (see Chapter 2 to deal with this common myth in working with older adults in psychotherapy). In this instance, a discussion with Mrs D allowed her to see that she was making age-related thinking errors in terms of 'fortune-telling', i.e. assuming that she knew how many (or how few) years she had left to live. With humour, the therapist pointed out that none of us know how long we have to live. There is no guarantee that the younger therapist would outlive her. Following this discussion, Mrs D decided to ask her daughter to accompany her to the local dog shelter where

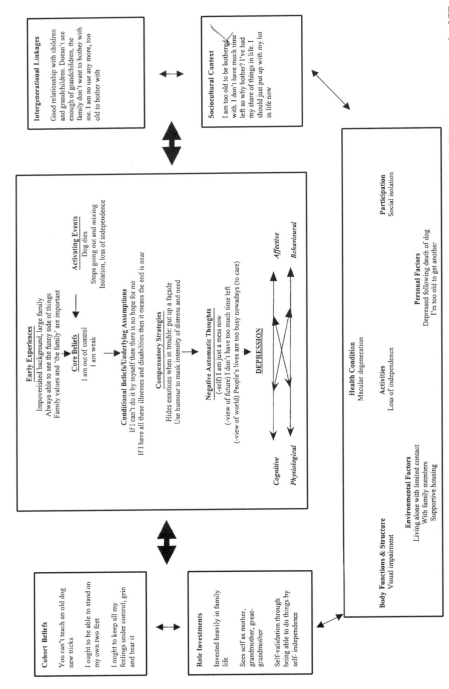

Cohort Beliefs

You can't teach an old dog new tricks

I ought to be able to stand on my own two feet

I ought to keep all my feelings under control, grin and bear it

Role Investments

Invested heavily in family life

Sees self as mother, grandmother, great-grandmother

Self-validation through being able to do things by self : independence

Early Experiences

Impoverished background, large family
Always able to see the funny side of things
Family values and 'the family are important

Activating Events

Dog dies
Stops going out and mixing
Isolation, loss of independence

Core Beliefs

I am out of control
I am weak

Conditional Beliefs/Underlying Assumptions

If I can't do it by myself then there is no hope for me
If I have all these illnesses and disabilities then it means the end is near

Compensatory Strategies

Hides emotions when in trouble: put up a façade
Use humour to mask intensity of distress and need

Negative Automatic Thoughts

(-self) I am just a mess now
(-view of future) I don't have too much time left
(-view of world) People's lives are too busy nowadays (to care)

DEPRESSION

Cognitive

Physiological

Affective

Behavioural

Intergenerational Linkages

Good relationship with children and grandchildren. Doesn't see enough of grandchildren, the family don't want to bother with me. I am no use any more, too old to bother with

Sociocultural Context

I am too old to be bothered with. I don't have much time left so why bother? I've had my share of things in life. I should just put up with my lot in life now

Body Functions & Structure

Visual impairment

Environmental Factors

Living alone with limited contact
With family members
Supportive housing

Health Condition

Macular degeneration

Activities

Loss of independence

Personal Factors

Depressed following death of dog
I'm too old to get another

Participation

Social isolation

Figure 10.2 Cognitive formulation for depression in AMD using cognitive model for older people (CMOP), incorporating the ICF (WHO, 2001)

she picked out an 'old dog' to take home with her (reinforcing the message to herself that old dogs can learn new tricks). Her independence and mood improved shortly thereafter. The ICF model can also accommodate a reciprocal negative relationship between depression and AMD in this instance whereby the individual loses the motivation to go out, and depression reduces the person's confidence in coping on her own. The result is that the individual becomes more and more isolated and hopelessness can easily set in, reducing the individual's sense that she can change her circumstances. Using the ICF it can be seen that this patient's problems can be addressed by focusing on the components of activity participation by changing aspects of the environmental and personal factors. Normally, activity levels and interpersonal participation are very amenable to improvement using cognitive-behavioural methods, however when a condition such as AMD is present, psychotherapists can often feel at a loss to suggest appropriate goals and aims for therapy. The ICF reminds us that important aspects of functioning are nonetheless amenable to change and that psychological interventions within the physical health domain are very important as they can positively impact upon a person's quality of life.

The ICF system is also compatible with the cognitive model for older people (CMOP) introduced in Chapter 3, and provides a further level of assessment and formulation within the health subcomponent of the CMOP. Figure 10.2 illustrates the interaction between the CMOP and the ICF using Mrs D as a case example. It can be seen that the health/illness domain of the CMOP is enhanced when formulating cases where physical illnesses become an important consideration in CBT treatment.

Importantly, the extra level of analysis in the cognitive model for older people (CMOP) provided by factors external to the traditional Beck model for cognitive therapy is useful to the clinician as it keeps him focused on the issues pertinent to understanding how depression may have developed in this case example and, importantly, the factors that maintain depression.

In Figure 10.2 it should be seen that causal and maintaining factors are quite different. The clinical usefulness of Figure 10.2 is that it allows the therapist to work with the patient to differentiate the impact of the disease condition (in this instance, AMD) in terms of its functional impact, and this leads to the development of treatment interventions. Without such a formulation, it is easy for the therapist to become de-skilled in the face of what appears to be a significant medical handicap producing 'understandable' depression. In this case example, there are clear reasons why Mrs D may have been particularly vulnerable at this time to developing depression, such as her beliefs that she is no longer needed by her family and that she has very few good years left in her life. It is also clear, when considering this case, that cohort beliefs are very important in considering socializing this lady into therapy work that would appear meaningful and relevant.

APPLYING CMOP AND ICF IN PRACTICE: DEPRESSION IN PARKINSON'S DISEASE

Approximately one hundred thousand people in the UK and one million people in the USA are diagnosed as having Parkinson's disease (PD). Like Alzheimer's disease, PD is a diagnosis only ever confirmed by post-mortem, with up to 25 per cent of cases of presumed PD apparently incorrectly diagnosed with PD (Tintner & Jankovic, 2001). PD is characterized by four core symptoms, such as tremor at rest, bradykinesia (slowed movements), rigidity, and impaired postural reflexes (Pentland, 1999), and can also be divided into three clinical stages: early, non-fluctuating and fluctuating (Manyam, 1997). In the early stage, PD symptoms may be mild and generally well controlled by medication. In the non-fluctuating stage, PD symptoms may not have progressed to the stage that medication such as levodopa carbamide (L-dopa) is required. L-dopa is used sparingly because of its side-effect profile and reduced efficiency after prolonged use. It is recommended that treatment with L-dopa is delayed for as long as possible (Brooks, 2000). Given too early in the disease, the individual is at great risk of developing dsykinesias (motoric dysfunction) and psychotic symptoms. In the later stages of this disease patients may be at the maximum level of medication and yet may still experience 'off-periods' lasting up to a number of hours in each day.

Prevalence rates for depression in PD have been reported in up to 50–60 per cent of people diagnosed with PD (Cummings & Masterman, 1999; Zesiewicz et al., 1999). The presence of depression in PD complicates diagnosis and pharmacological treatment (Cummings & Masterman, 1999) and depression may often remain undiagnosed and untreated (Poewe & Euginger, 1999). Depression in Parkinson's disease is not necessarily related to the level of impairment in the disease, as measured by stage of illness (Schrag, Jahanshahi & Quinn, 2001; Zesiewicz et al., 1999; MacCarthy & Brown, 1989). Brown and Jahanshahi (1995) note that the duration of illness appears to have little relationship with the development of depression. A more important consideration would appear to be the rate of progression of disability (Schrag, Jahanshahi & Quinn, 2001). More rapid onset and deterioration obviously allows less time to develop compensatory strategies for deficits consequent to Parkinson's disease and may be associated with higher levels of depression. Brown and Jahanshahi (1995) argue that depression may become more evident at different stages of the disease process, for example, during initial diagnosis where uncertainty and fear about the consequences of this neurodegenerative condition may result in elevated levels of distress. This distress may reduce as the individual enters the non-fluctuating stage of the illness. During the fluctuating stage of the condition, one might expect levels of distress to increase once again.

TREATING DEPRESSION IN PD USING CBT

The following case example highlights certain considerations when working with patients with a chronic illness, such as PD. Mr P was originally referred for CBT by his GP with a mixed picture of anxiety and depression following his diagnosis with PD the previous year. Mr P had a marked tremor in his right hand and was thought to have PD. Mr P himself stated that his main difficulty was coming to terms with his diagnosis of possible PD and described himself as feeling 'devastated' when the possibility of this diagnosis was shared with him. Over the course of 12 months (since it was first suggested that he may have PD) Mr P had gradually cut back on pleasurable activities. He stopped visiting music shops in the city, cycling, hill-walking or going out on his own and had not done so for about one year. A weekly activity schedule was given to the patient to complete as homework after session one, and confirmed the reported curtailment of activities.

Over the course of a year, Mr P's family doctor had tried a number of antidepressant medications but with little effect on his depressive symptoms. Significantly Mr P's life-long friend recently died after developing a short but rapidly deteriorating course of PD. During the early stage of therapy, Mr P and his therapist agreed upon three main targets and goals. These were: (1) to target depression and aim to provide symptomatic relief; (2) to target inactivity (excess disability) and increase activity levels; and (3) to target assumptions and beliefs about the meaning of the PD diagnosis and aim to reduce its impact on functioning. Treatment lasted for a total of 14 one-hour sessions, on a regular monthly basis (plus a routine three-month follow-up appointment). Nine months following the end of treatment, the patient agreed to be videotaped discussing his experiences of taking part in therapy. At this interview Mr P stated he was still feeling much improved and had been able to maintain the progress achieved during treatment.

Mr P's baseline activity schedule revealed that he had only gone out of the house for a total of 12 hours over the course of the previous week. When Mr P did go out, he was always accompanied by his wife and he rarely ventured further than his local shops. Over the course of CBT treatment, Mr P increased his activity level markedly in that he managed to take trips outwith his locality and was able to leave his home for a total of 29 hours. This represents an increase of 58 per cent in activity over his baseline level. While Mr P did exhibit improvements in depression and anxiety scores over the course of treatment, the largest gains in treatment were shown to be in terms of levels of functioning and activities. At the end of treatment Mr P felt confident enough to browse in music shops by himself in a busy city centre on a fairly regular basis. In addition, Mr P regularly went for walks by himself and regained a renewed sense of confidence and independence. At baseline, Mr P's activity schedule also revealed that he had experienced sleeplessness on five separate occasions. Mr P had previously described himself as a good sleeper and had

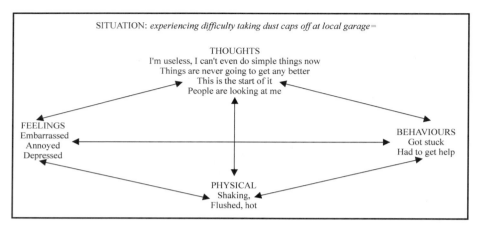

Figure 10.3 Using the CBT model to understanding the physical–psychological connection in Parkinson's disease

managed to improve his sleep to the extent that he experienced no episodes of sleeplessness over the previous weekly recording period.

INTEGRATING THE COGNITIVE MODEL AND THE ICF SYSTEM

In working with patients with physical illness it is extremely important to make sure that psychological understandings and interventions are relevant, valid and consistent with the patient's current difficulties. This is where the CBT model can be used to 'socialize' patients into treatment. The CBT model was presented to Mr P as a way to understand how his physical and psychological symptoms interact. Mr P tearfully relates an incident that he says shows how 'useless' he is nowadays (see Figure 10.3). He says that recently he went to the local garage to check on his car's tyre pressure. At this time he found it impossible to unscrew the dust caps and although he tried for a long time, '...I eventually had to give in and ask the young lads to do this simple thing for me'. He noted that after this incident his mood dropped markedly and he says he lost his confidence. He noted that his tremor appeared to get worse after this incident.

The important point in this example is to let the patients see the connections and reciprocal nature of these connections. It is important to point out to your patients that if they can change the way they think about things, they can change the way they behave. If these are also connected to their feelings and to their physical 'make-up' then these elements will change too. An alternative way to evaluate the same event is to use the ICF system (WHO, 2001), as indicated in Figure 10.4.

Figure 10.4 Using the ICF classification to understand the physical–psychological connection in Parkinson's disease

In developing psychotherapy for depression comorbid with a physical illness, the concept of 'excess disability' may be important. Excess disability is the proportion of disability a person experiences that is not determined by actual physical or cognitive impairments as a consequence of PD. For example, a person may withdraw from activities prematurely because of embarrassment at a tremor when around others. The cognitive model for older people (CMOP) can be supplemented by the ICF system of health (see Figure 10.5).

At the end of treatment, Mr P reported an increased ability to deal with current symptoms and a willingness to confront embarrassment induced by his tremor by staying in situations and using CT techniques to challenge thoughts. At the end of treatment, Mr P stated that he was feeling more optimistic about the future: 'I feel I have come to terms with things now.' CBT techniques appear to be relevant for treating depression in PD. It is important to recognize that, in this particular case, modifications to the CBT approach are slight.

CONCLUSION AND SUMMARY

In working with depressed or anxious older people who have significant medical comorbidity, much more emphasis is placed upon assessing the individual's adaptation to change in functional status than would be the case with relatively healthy older people. Working with older adults with comorbid physical illnesses requires that certain principles of CBT are adhered to, as outlined below.

- *Principle 1:* Collaborative empiricism—gather the information you need in order to determine with your client the extent of the difficulties facing him rather than allowing your own biases and preconceived notions to influence or determine the outcome.

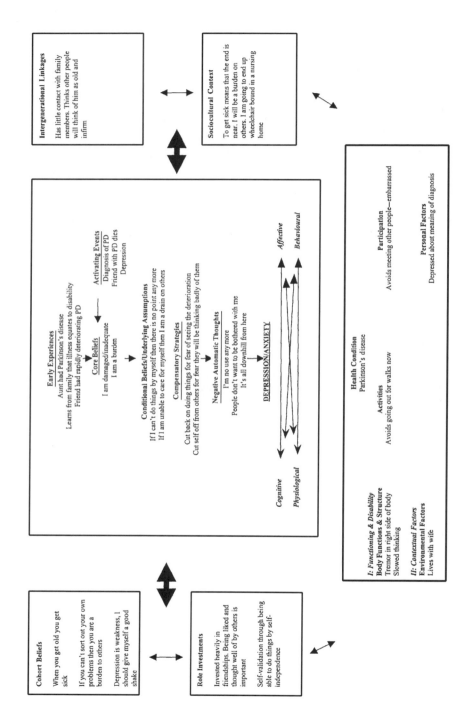

Figure 10.5 Depression in PD using cognitive model for older people, incorporating ICF (WHO, 2001)

- *Principle 2:* Use Socratic questioning to determine the meanings your client has developed following the onset of symptoms or illness. Use Socratic questions to explore ways of identifying and solving problems.
- *Principle 3:* Use agenda setting at the start of each meeting to structure all your sessions to make them as productive as possible. This is especially important when your client presents with a multiple level of problems.
- *Principle 4:* Always keep the discussion focused on specific aspects of your client's current difficulties following illness. Keep the focus on challenging and changing specific difficulties your client identifies. Problem-solve first and, if necessary, set aside time for discussions of predisposing any vulnerabilities your client may have.
- *Principle 5:* Always carry over session discussion into collaborative homework decisions. As a guide to planning homework tasks with a patient with physical problems, start small and build upwards, then you can really see how much or how little your client can do.

In addition to these principles, the CMOP provides further elements to treatment that may need to be taken into account in order to maximize treatment efficiency. As Chapter 3 has demonstrated, when working with older adults there are some modifications to CBT that may enhance the treatment outcome. The case for treatment modification is most probably strongest when working with physically compromised and depressed/anxious older adults. This chapter has shown that despite questions that may be raised about the biological basis of depression in conditions such as PD, the manifestation of the condition is clinically indistinguishable from depression that occurs without the accompaniment of a physical illness. In such circumstances the careful and skilled clinician is justified in applying CBT for depression and anxiety even if the existing empirical literature provides scant guidance since the evidence for the efficacy of CBT for late-life depression is strong. The ICF (WHO, 2001b) system also provides some justification and rationale for the use of psychological methods of treatment where depression and anxiety may be considered to have occurred after the development of a physical illness.

Chapter 11

POST-STROKE DEPRESSION

INTRODUCTION

This chapter outlines the main elements of cognitive behaviour therapy (CBT) for the treatment of post-stroke depression. Cerebrovascular accident (CVA), more commonly known as stroke, frequently results in emotional distress, particularly anxiety and depression (Robinson, 1998; House, 1987). For a person experiencing a stroke, or for that person's carer, a stroke can come as quite a shock, interrupting, disrupting and changing lives, and in many cases altering and foreshortening people's future plans. Treatment efforts following a stroke often concentrate on rehabilitation and, unfortunately in this process, psychological needs are often inadequately recognized, responded to, and managed. Although there is some evidence that antidepressants can be an effective treatment, CBT has much to offer in the treatment of depression following stroke (Kneebone & Dunsmore, 2000; Laidlaw & Thomson, 1999; Gordon & Hibbard, 1997; Hibbard et al., 1990). This chapter provides a guide to the application of CBT as a treatment for post-stroke depression.

STROKE AND DISABILITY

Stroke is the third leading cause of death in older people (WHO, 2002; Kinsella & Velkoff, 2001; Wood & Bain, 2001). Stroke affects approximately half a

Cognitive Behaviour Therapy with Older People.
Ken Laidlaw, Larry W. Thompson, Leah Dick-Siskin & Dolores Gallagher-Thompson.
© 2003 John Wiley & Sons Ltd.

million people a year in the USA (NINDS, 2002) and approximately 130 000 people a year in the UK. At any one time, 300 000 people are affected by stroke in the UK (TWG, 1999). Stroke affects mainly older people, with two-thirds of all strokes affecting people over the age of 65. After the age of 55, the risk of having a stroke doubles every 10 years. Survival rates following stroke have risen over the last decade, resulting in increased numbers of disabled individuals in need of stroke rehabilitation. As a result, stroke is now the number one cause of serious, long-term disability in older people (NINDS, 2002; Wood & Bain, 2001; TWG, 1999).

As a rough guide to prognosis following a stroke, Westcott (2000) states that approximately one-third of people who have a first stroke will die within one year, one-third will make a good recovery and one-third will be left with some type of disability. After a first stroke, about one-third of recurrent strokes take place within two years. The risk of recurrent stroke is roughly 12 per cent in the first year and 6 per cent in the second year (TWG, 1999). To put these figures into perspective, the risk of stroke in high-risk individuals (those who are overweight, smoke, have high blood pressure and take no exercise) is 8 per cent. Overall the rate of recurrence of a stroke is about 25 per cent over five years (NINDS, 2002). The risk of a stroke is greater for men, and since men generally have a stroke at a younger age they are more likely to survive, but with some form of disability as a result. As the risk of a stroke in women is generally greatest later in life, women are more likely to die from a stroke than men. With each recurrent stroke there is a greater risk of severe disability and death. Therefore many patients are understandably concerned about the risk of having another stroke with potentially fatal consequences. A rare complication of a stroke is the unawareness of deficits. This type of denial of illness is termed anosognosia (see Bisiach et al., 1986). Another complication that sometimes results from a stroke is misoplegia—an intense hatred and antipathy towards the person's affected limbs (see Bisiach, 1992).

POST-STROKE DEPRESSION

Severity of disability post-stroke is associated with higher levels of anxiety and depression (Bond et al., 1998). The prevalence of post-stroke depression ranges from 18 to 61 per cent (House, 1987). Post-stroke depression is often seen as an understandable psychological reaction to a catastrophic event and therefore this type of depression often goes untreated (Fiebel, Berk & Joynt, 1979).

Lack of treatment of depression after stroke may have serious consequences for the individual, as mortality rates after a stroke increase markedly if depression is left untreated (Everson et al., 1998). In a ten-year follow-up of people experiencing a stroke, Morris et al. (1993) reported that patients with post-stroke depression were 3.4 times more likely to have died during a ten-year follow-up period than were non-depressed stroke patients. This relationship between post-stroke depression and mortality was independent of other risk factors such as age, sex, social class, stroke type, lesion location, and level of social functioning. Of those patients with fewer social contacts the mortality rate was especially high as over 90 per cent of these patients had died at the ten-year follow-up point. In addition to risk of mortality post-stroke, there is also an increased risk of suicide. Kishi, Robinson & Kosler (1996) report that the development of suicidal plans among inpatient stroke survivors was strongly related to the existence of post-stroke depression.

Depression impairs the rehabilitation and recovery of individuals after a stroke (Chemerinski, Robinson & Kosier, 2001; Robinson, Murata & Shimoda, 1999; Robinson, 1998; Clark & Smith, 1998; Hibbard et al., 1990) and rehabilitation is compromised by the symptoms of depression, such as apathy and hopelessness, resulting in poorer responsiveness to rehabilitation, slower recovery rates, increased service utilization and increased burden of care (Gordon & Hibbard, 1997). The first 3–6 months are most important for recovery of function after a stroke, but recovery of some function can occur up to 18–24 months after a stroke. Generally psychological intervention is most effective at least 6 months after the onset of the stroke, for the reasons that the individual may have started to notice a slowing down in the extent and rate of recovery and this may be problematic and require adjustment. Also at this timepoint, the acute services will have started to withdraw and the rehabilitation services may also be reducing their active input.

TRAUMA DISORDER AFTER A STROKE (POST-STROKE TRAUMA)

Anxiety, as well as depression, is common following a stroke (Robinson, 1998; Sharpe et al., 1990). Recently the possibility of post-traumatic stress disorder (PTSD) occurring following acute medical procedures and medical events has been investigated (Bryant, 2001; Berry, 1998; Sembi et al., 1998; Shalev et al., 1993). The DSM-IV states that 'The essential feature of post-traumatic stress disorder is the development of characteristic symptoms following exposure to an extremely traumatic stressor involving direct personal experience of an event that involves actual or threatened death or serious injury, or other threat to one's physical integrity' (APA, 2002). In addition the person's response to the event must include intense fear. Some of the characteristic symptoms of PTSD also include avoidance of stimuli associated with the trauma and increased emotional arousal.

The issue of whether individuals experiencing an acute, intense and potentially fatal medical condition (such as a brain injury or a stroke) can develop trauma symptoms post-injury is complicated and controversial, not least because of the fact that impaired consciousness often accompanies brain injury (Bryant, 2001). It is arguable that stroke qualifies as an extremely traumatic stressor involving a direct threat to one's life and physical integrity (Sembi et al., 1998). Shalev et al. (1993) reported on the development of PTSD in patients following acute and traumatic medical and surgical events and noted that patients appeared to experience intrusive and distressing recollections of the medical event following surgery. Patients reported a persistent sense of danger or threat to life long after the acute period of danger had passed, thus Shalev et al. (1993) concluded that it was possible for patients undergoing emergency brain surgery to experience post-trauma effects. Sembi et al. (1998) assessed a number of people who had experienced a first stroke to see whether there was evidence for PTSD. Using the impact of events scale (Horowitz et al., 1979), one in five people experiencing a first stroke scored above cut-off on this measure for PTSD symptomatology. Sembi et al. (1998) note that PTSD case-ness appeared to be independent of physical severity of the stroke, thus idiosyncratic appraisal of events would seem to be important when working therapeutically with stroke survivors.

Laidlaw and Thomson (1999) proposed that post-trauma effects are important and are likely because of the nature of the onset of strokes. Strokes occur with no sense of warning. Often patients comment that the stroke occurred 'out of the blue' while they were engaged in normal everyday tasks. The person recognizes, perhaps for the first time, that unpredictable and uncontrollable events can happen without warning. This can leave stroke patients with an increased sense of physical vulnerability and, as a result, many patients become hypervigilant towards bodily symptoms in order to 'try and catch' the next stroke before it is too late. Stroke patients often become sensitized to the idea that their risk of recurrence is greater than for the public at large, and again this contributes to a sense of vulnerability.

Following a stroke, patients' views of life change. Premorbidly they may have viewed their lives as safe and their future as predictable and controllable. Following a stroke, patients are confronted with a loss of an anticipated and expected future. When working therapeutically with stroke survivors, the premorbid characteristics of patients and their response to challenges may be important. An important task of the early stage of therapy sessions is to get a sense from the patients of how they have responded to difficult situations in the past.

TREATMENT FOR POST-STROKE DEPRESSION

Research activity has generally focused on understanding the neuro-anatomical correlates of post-stroke depression (Sharpe et al., 1990), with relatively few reports in the literature focusing upon treatment of post-stroke depression. Evidence suggests that antidepressants are effective in treating post-stroke depression (Gainotti et al., 2001; Robinson, 1998); nevertheless, more randomized-controlled trials are required before a firm conclusion can be reached about whether, and of what type, antidepressants are efficacious and safe for the treatment of post-stroke depression.

In addition, many patients may not wish to take psychotropic medication when they may already be taking a number of prescribed medications following a stroke. Additionally there are patients who will not be able to tolerate antidepressant medication in combination with other medications prescribed to them. Thus there is an urgent need for the development and evaluation of a psychological treatment alternative to medication for post-stroke depression. A naturalistic series of single case studies by Lincoln et al. (1997) reported on the efficacy of cognitive-behavioural treatments for post-stroke depression. Treatment was delivered to 19 volunteers diagnosed with depression following a stroke. Treatment was delivered via a series of single case studies using standard AB design methods (each participant acted as his own control during baseline and within-treatment assessments). Over a three-month course of treatment, a significant decrease in depression severity, as measured by the BDI, was observed overall, although there were no changes in levels of functional disability. Overall, this study was flawed by the failure to have trained clinicians deliver the treatment. Nonetheless, results were broadly comparable to those reported for medication treatments.

USING CBT TO TREAT POST-STROKE DEPRESSION

Given concerns about the suitability of pharmacological treatment for post-stroke depression (Hibbard et al., 1990), CBT may constitute an alternative treatment of great potential (Kneebone & Dunsmore, 2000; Hibbard et al., 1990). As CBT sessions are structured, this is particularly appropriate for patients with neurological deficits. CBT develops individually tailored treatment interventions to target stereotypical beliefs and thoughts following a stroke that interfere with recovery, such as 'I'm a pathetic creature now', 'I ought to be able to do this by myself by now', 'I am no use to my family now', 'All my friends will pity me' or 'I'm going to have another stroke soon and die'.

The main focus for intervention in CBT for post-stroke depression is based around a number of similar themes:

- active problem solving to deal with disabilities and managing cognitive distortions and associated emotional and behavioural disturbances;
- education about strokes and depression;
- identifying the possibility of post-trauma effects of stroke and reducing anxiety associated with the 'inevitability' of having further strokes;
- evaluating the nature and quality of supports—utilizing caregiving education to prevent problems developing interpersonally;

- setting meaningful and manageable (realistic) goals;
- achieving meaning in life and adjusting to the new reality of life after a stroke (use of strategies based around selection, optimization and compensation).

CBT INTERVENTIONS IN POST-STROKE DEPRESSION

It is important to realize that CBT for post-stroke depression does not attempt to reverse any cognitive deterioration or to provide physical rehabilitation for the individual. The benefit of CBT is in recognizing that the physical nature of the difficulties following a stroke are not incompatible with psychological consequences. The concept of 'excess disability' may be an important issue in such instances (see Chapter 1). Excess disability is the proportion of a person's disability that is not determined by actual physical or cognitive impairments as a consequence of a stroke, e.g. a person may withdraw from activities prematurely because of embarrassment at a hemiparetic limb.

Laidlaw and Thomson (1999) identified a number of cognitive distortions that should be treated in post-stroke depression. Table 11.1 summarizes cognitive distortions, associated negative thoughts and suggested treatment strategies.

Following a stroke, it is not uncommon for people to experience anxiety if they are left alone for any extended periods of time, because they fear a further stroke is imminent. They seek reassurance by having someone close by to call in case a catastrophe happens. The net effect is that a person with a stroke is perpetually in fear of having a further stroke, and generally massively overestimates the likelihood of risk. Sleep very often becomes disturbed for both the person and his carer. The carer can very often become demoralized at the level of contact and dependency of the person with a stroke. Cognitive restructuring often helps the patient to make sense of his over-estimation of the likely danger. It is important to use psycho-education to give the patient reliable information about the real risk of stroke recurrence. It is also important to engage the patient in discussion about the effects of his thinking errors. Very often patients make fortune-telling errors (see Table 11.1; see also Chapter 6). A very useful intervention is to discuss with the patient that no one knows the future. Acting as if we do know the future generally results in increased anxiety and increased restriction of activities. In such cases, graded behavioural strategies can also be useful in helping the stroke patients to stretch the time they are unaccompanied by a specified number of minutes each day or week, until they become more comfortable about being on their own. Relaxation strategies and breathing techniques may also be helpful.

Psycho-education in post-stroke depression also involves examining a patient's own understanding of the process of recovery to set appropriate expectations. Unfortunately there is often the 'soap opera effect' that needs to

Table 11.1 Common cognitive distortions in post-stroke depression

Nature of distortion	Type of cognitive error	Negative thoughts	Treatment strategies
Symptom monitoring (overmonitoring and hypervigilance)	Catastrophic misinterpretation, fortune telling	I'm never going to get out of hospital. I've had one stroke, I'm certain to have another	Cognitive restructuring
Unrealistic, unhelpful and unfair comparisons	Dichotomous reasoning, baseline distortion	I'm a pathetic creature now. Everyone else in rehab is making faster progress than me	Set realistic goals—develop fairer baseline, progress charts, focus on discrepancy between actual loss and perceived loss
Hopelessness about the future	Fortune telling, arbitrary inference, selective abstraction	Is this going to be the quality of my life forever? What if I am never able to walk again	Graded task assignment; cognitive restructuring, worry management
Unrealistic expectations of the extent of recovery ('soap opera distortions')	Selective abstraction, dichotomous reasoning, magnification and minimization	I should be able to do this by now. Other people are looking at me and pitying me	Reality testing, exploration of the extent of disability following a stroke
Interpersonal relationships	Personalization, overgeneralization	I'm just a burden, I'm no use to my family any more. I'm disabled so people should do things for me. If I can't make progress my partner will leave me.	Involvement of partner in active treatment, psycho-education about caregiving; discuss premorbid nature of relationship; explore premorbid roles in relationship and how this may have changed now

Source: Laidlaw and Thompson (1999).

be taken into account in this condition. Many patients who suffer a head injury are completely ignorant of the nature and extent of recovery that can be expected. Often people base their expectations upon what they have gleaned from many sources, one of which would appear to be television dramas. In many soap operas injuries to the head that occur to characters are often the focus of short intense worry and drama and almost invariably the characters make a full recovery or occasionally die. Therefore, relatives and patients develop unrealistic expectations about the extent and rate of recovery from a brain injury such as a stroke, and these unrealistic expectations often interfere with recovery. Unfortunately, the data on the psychosocial impact of closed head injuries are much less optimistic than television dramas often suggest (for reviews, see Yasuda et al., 2001; Sherer, Madison & Hannay, 2000; Ounsworth & Oei, 1998).

In post-stroke depression people often make the cognitive error of baseline distortion. In post-stroke depression this type of thinking error is evident when people fail to give themselves credit for the extent of recovery they have made following the onset of their stroke. People often make the mistake of comparing their current level of functioning with their level of functioning prior to the onset of a stroke, but clearly this is biased thinking. The reality of the situation is that, following a stroke, levels of functioning are compromised and patients undermine what has been achieved by setting an inappropriate baseline: what they could do prior to their injury. A more appropriate and realistic baseline is the day after the stroke. How does their functioning compare to that level. Once this type of comparison is explained to patients, and graphs are drawn, they can quickly get the point.

COMPENSATING FOR POST-STROKE DISABILITY

An important element in the treatment of stroke-related difficulties is developing new and successful ways to adjust to changed circumstances. An analogy can be made with that of someone who needs to wear a plaster cast following a leg break. The individual in the plaster cast can try to do everything as before and ignore the plaster cast, but will actually make life very difficult for himself and will soon become demoralized at the lack of progress being made. If the patient considers how he might need to change things to cope with the plaster cast, he will get on a lot better. The theory of *selective optimization with compensation* (SOC: Baltes & Smith, 2002; Baltes, 1990, 1987) focuses on maintaining functioning in later life when limits of capacity are reached or even exceeded. The model suggests that older people cope with reduced or loss of capacity by compensating for these losses with the twin strategies of optimizing and selection. Baltes (1990) and Baltes and Smith (2002) illustrate the key elements of their model by reference to the pianist Arthur Rubinstein, who continued to perform at a high level late into life. When asked for the secrets of his success, Rubinstein mentioned three strategies: first he reduced the scope of his repertoire (an example of selection); secondly, he practised this repertoire more intensely than he would have done when he was younger (an example of optimization); and, finally, he used 'tricks' such as slowing down his speed of playing just immediately prior to playing the fast segments of his repertoire, thereby giving his audience the impression of faster play than was actually the case—an act that Baltes (1999) terms an example of compensation. Thus, for patients coping with the aftermath of a stroke the process of SOC can be extremely valuable if they are to adapt successfully to their disability.

Many people develop embarrassment and dislike of their affected limb and this can result in excess disability as the person may achieve less than one might expect given the extent of severity of stroke. In cases of excess disability, there are very often psychological rather than physical factors that limit recovery of function. For example, Mr J suffered a slight left-sided weakness following an ischaemic stroke, and was referred for psychological counselling as his progress was 'not as good as might be expected'. Mr J stated that although he had been told he had made a good recovery, he was frustrated with the extent of his recovery and at times struggled to come to terms with the nature of his difficulties. Mr J was also very embarrassed by any signs that he had experienced a stroke, and he tended to conceal his mild paralysis by keeping his hand in his pocket to prevent it 'waving' about. Mr J stated that he did not intend to return to his hobbies of playing golf, ballroom dancing and computers until he was satisfied that his limb function had returned to normal or near normal. In discussion with Mr J it became evident that his embarrassment at having a stroke was limiting his lifestyle far more than the actual stroke. A graded programme of exposure of the affected limb with friends was initiated and an exploration of the pros and cons of his strategy of waiting for full recovery of function was given as a homework task. It quickly became evident to Mr J that he had cut himself off from a number of enjoyable activities. Moreover, it was also apparent that by waiting for a recovery of function, Mr J's rehabilitation was paradoxically being held back. A process of selection, optimization and compensation was undertaken for a number of activities. For example, in ballroom dancing, Mr J selected a few dance partners who knew about his difficulties and his embarrassment, he optimized his enjoyment at dancing by only dancing for a few numbers, and compensated for his difficulties by taking long rests in between dances. Although there were restrictions that were not evident before the stroke, he was nonetheless able to participate where before he had not. When conceptualizing cases in CBT for post-stroke depression, the concept of compensation by selection and optimization can be usefully integrated into the physical health domain of the cognitive model for older people (CMOP. See Chapter 3).

If hemiplegia follows a stroke, then appetite can be affected as the person finds eating more challenging and there is the danger of food being 'trapped' in the side of the mouth that is affected by the paralysis. The person may not always be aware of this undigested food. Appetite can be affected by this experience as the person becomes wary of this. In some cases, taste sensations and sense of smell can also be disrupted after a stroke. The result is that often the person with stroke loses a sense of appetite. Weight loss often brings on responses from caregivers that are well intentioned, but counterproductive. In two very similar examples, both involving women who had experienced strokes that left them with left-sided weaknesses (hemiplegias), and resulted in appetite disturbance and subsequent weight loss, the husbands in each of these cases attempted to get their wives to eat more by making their favourite foods and serving food at more frequent intervals. As the ladies lost weight their husbands increased portion sizes that mirrored this weight loss, and a vicious cycle was set up. It became clear in each of these cases that as the amount of uneaten food increased, loss of morale was experienced by both sets of couples. This is a generation that has grown up with rationing of food after World War II and has family memories of the deprivations experienced during the great depression between 1919 and 1939. Thus 'wasting' food was seen as shameful. A simple yet effective intervention is to cut back not only on the size of food portions but to serve the food on smaller plates. The aim was to leave the person with the impression of having finished a meal. In both cases this intervention resulted in a reduction in anxiety and an increase in weight gain. Importantly, both couples gained a sense of mastery over their circumstances.

Reducing the types of food that can be eaten following a stroke resulting in a hemiplegia is an example of selection. Having a few set meals and snack times is an example of optimization. Eating from smaller plates and providing smaller portions is an example of compensation. This model deals with the reality of the situation and hence is very valuable when thinking about developing cognitive-behavioural interventions when working with people with post-stroke depression.

SUMMARY AND CONCLUSIONS

In summary, the structured, problem-focused, goal-oriented and individual-ized interventions that are routinely part of cognitive therapy suggest it as a natural psychosocial treatment for post-stroke depression. The usefulness of the CMOP as a way of conceptualizing cases becomes evident in post-stroke depression because of the importance of the physical health domain and the effect of cohort beliefs and the potential of previous role investments for the later development of depression post-stroke. CBT interventions for post-stroke depression are enhanced by the use of compensation, optimization and selection. These elements are considered to form the basis of successful ageing. Thus, to successfully age and adapt following a stroke, there are certain strategies that ought to be considered in individuals dealing with adjustment to life after stroke. Older people faced with the challenges of some of the illnesses more commonly associated with ageing have too frequently been underserved, and their needs have often been unmet. A challenge to all psychotherapists working with older people is to ensure that, even after a potentially severe disabling illness such as a stroke, older people are given the opportunity to achieve as much independence as they can. In closing this chapter one ought not to forget that the WHO definition of active ageing is based upon integration, participation and security. This definition does not only apply to healthy older people without disability, but ought to particularly apply to older people with disabilities. Stroke can remove security from older people as it can interfere with the ability to participate and integrate in society. Active ageing focuses on rights rather than needs, and in stroke the rights are to participate in society in as fully a way as possible. That is the challenge for CBT therapists working with older people.

Chapter 12

DEPRESSION IN DEMENTIA AND FAMILY CAREGIVING

INTRODUCTION

This chapter introduces readers to the application of CBT for people with depression or anxiety in mild to moderate dementia. With the advent of medications such as the so-called cognitive enhancers that aim to slow the progress of dementia, this has given rise to memory clinics in the UK and the USA. More memory clinics mean that older people are being diagnosed with dementia at an earlier stage in the disease process than ever before. This presents a challenge to psychotherapists working with older people, as there is the potential for an increase in the number of referrals for the treatment of depression and anxiety in early stages of dementia. Many therapists are uncertain how well the person with mild to moderately impaired dementia will be able to learn the CBT approach and question whether or not the person will be able to participate adequately in the therapeutic process. Other concerns relate to how much can be expected in terms of outcome, the use of homework techniques and the involvement of other family members. These and many more issues are addressed in this chapter.

Cognitive Behaviour Therapy with Older People.
Ken Laidlaw, Larry W. Thompson, Leah Dick-Siskin & Dolores Gallagher-Thompson.
© 2003 John Wiley & Sons Ltd.

DEMENTIA AND DEPRESSION

Approximately 30 per cent of older persons with dementia also meet criteria for major depressive disorder, and even higher prevalence rates are reported for individuals with subclinical levels of depression in dementia (Teri & Gallagher-Thompson, 1991). Dementia of the Alzheimer type (DAT) is the commonest type of dementia in older people, and is a syndrome characterized by gradual onset and progressive decline in global cognitive functioning, usually across a span of several years. Another common form of dementia is vascular dementia, also previously known as multi-infarct dementia. Vascular dementia is more common among older men and has a more stepwise deterioration in functioning. With the increase in the numbers of younger women who smoke, this gender difference may reduce or disappear as this cohort ages. According to the latest text revision of the DSM-IV (APA, 2000), the hallmark sign and symptom of DAT is a progressive impairment in memory function, accompanied by a decline in one or more cognitive processes, such as difficulties in language and word-finding abilities, impairment in visuospatial processing, constructional difficulties, and declines in abstract reasoning, executive functions or concentration.

There are numerous causes of dementia, including degenerative cerebral disease, cardiovascular and cerebrovascular disorders, head traumas, brain tumours, infectious diseases, long-term substance misuse, and severe metabolic disorders. Degenerative brain disorders, such as Alzheimer's disease or DAT, have an increasing prevalence rate with age, although even in the oldest-old (i.e. aged 80 years and above), only one person in five is likely to display signs of a dementia. Importantly, diagnosis of DAT is only ever confirmed at post-mortem. DAT is progressive with several cognitive abilities manifesting definitive changes across the later years of the lifespan. During the early stages of the disease, memory changes tend to be limited to poor recall, but as the disease progresses, there is a loss of ability to use cues for recall, along with loss of recognition memory. In the final stages of the disease, patients often show complete lack of recognition and disorientation even to person, as well as to place and time. Similarly, there are usually mild losses in verbal fluency during the early course of the disease, but in the later stages, patients may only be capable of using highly overlearned verbal expressions and finally may be completely mute. In the later stages they often are unable to complete even very simple tasks, such as putting mail in a mail slot or flushing the toilet. Executive and reasoning abilities typically show marked declines, with an inability to solve novel and abstract problems being the first to show impairment, but eventually the ability to solve highly overlearned and concrete problems is grossly diminished.

There are many other behavioural changes that may occur, such as notable lability in mood with loss of impulse control and judgement in social situations. Depression is frequently observed throughout the course of the disease, but it may manifest with different symptom profiles at different stages. In the early stages, when patients are keenly aware that changes are occurring, it is common to observe depression and anxiety accompanied by some frustration and agitation focused on the loss of functions, while in the later stages one may observe withdrawal, psychomotor retardation and mutism with minimal affective response to positive or negative environmental events. Finally, as the disease progresses, other behavioural problems become apparent, such as severe agitation, wandering, gait disturbances, incontinence, extremely constricted ambulation and rigidity (Corey-Bloom, 1996).

THE IMPORTANCE OF ASSESSMENT

A diagnostic issue facing psychotherapists is the careful disentanglement of symptoms attributable to dementia and those attributable to depression. The problem of accurate assessment is further complicated, because a decline in cognitive abilities is also seen in normal healthy individuals over the course of their later years. Without a comprehensive work-up, a false positive diagnosis may occur, thus resulting in a decision that dementia is present, when in reality the impairment may be related to a psychiatric problem, or may even be related to normal age changes that are compounded by the presence of milder forms of distress.

Kaszniak and Scogin (1995) offer guidelines to assist the clinician in the differential diagnosis of depression versus dementia in older people. For example, people with dementia are more likely to demonstrate impairments in recognition memory and delayed memory than people who are depressed. Patients experiencing depression are more likely to 'give-up' even on tasks that offer minimal challenges. Prompting is often more helpful for the depressed person than for the individual with dementia. With prompting, apparent impairment in function reduces to a level that is indistinguishable from non-depressed levels of functioning. Finally, individuals with dementia are more likely to be unaware that they have cognitive impairment, while depressed individuals are not only aware of their impairment, but often magnify the level of severity despite the presentation of evidence to the contrary.

A comprehensive assessment can also be extremely helpful when developing a treatment programme for patients with dementia and depression. If possible, information relevant to all of the following topics should be obtained: (a) general mental status, including evidence of bizarre ideation, delusions or hallucinations; (b) comprehensive assessment of cognitive abilities; (c) psychometric evaluation of level and type of emotional distress; (d) assessment of the pattern and adequacy of coping; (e) social, family and work history; (f) current work and social environment; (g) general health and physical functioning; and (h) adequacy of social, emotional and instrumental support systems. It is necessary to consult many sources within and across disciplines in order to complete such a comprehensive report. Optimally, this is done by an interdisciplinary team, which may then coordinate the delivery of services required. CBT can be a useful component of this team effort.

The pattern of cognitive capabilities will help to develop a therapy plan, both in terms of how to proceed in therapy sessions as well as how to modify the environment to maximize functioning. Knowing what the patient can and cannot do is of paramount importance in developing a suitable living situation that will be minimally stressful for both the depressed patient and the family or formal caregivers. A number of excellent publications are available that address problems and issues in assessing a wide range of topics pertaining to older people (Lichtenberg, 1999; Spreen & Strauss, 1998; Lawton & Teresi, 1994; Raskin & Niederehe, 1988).

EFFICACY OF CBT FOR DEPRESSION IN PATIENTS WITH DEMENTIA

A review of the literature completed in the 1980s (Thompson et al., 1989) revealed only clinical cases using cognitive and behavioural techniques, rather than randomized-controlled trial evaluations of psychotherapy for the treatment of depression in dementia. Teri and Gallagher-Thompson (1991) reported pilot data from their work using both cognitive and behavioural approaches with appropriate modifications, suited to the ability level of the patient. More recently, Cohen-Mansfield (2001) completed a comprehensive review of 83 studies describing non-pharmacological interventions for inappropriate behaviours in patients with dementia. However, there are still only a few controlled studies that have evaluated non-pharmacological techniques for treating depression in this patient group. Teri et al. (1997) reported that two behavioural treatments—one focused on increasing pleasant events and the other focused on problem-solving strategies—were more effective in reducing depression levels in the treatment-as-usual group than in the no-treatment group (wait list control). Beneficial effects of treatment were found not only in the dementia patients but also in their caregivers. Both treatments used the caregiver as an active agent in the therapy. The use of family caregivers as part of the treatment team in behavioural therapy has been repeatedly emphasized in past clinical studies (see Haley, 1983, for review).

An alternative treatment mode is the provision of psychologically oriented treatment primarily to the caregiver, with the underlying assumption that the alleviation of distress in the caregiver improves the quality of care that can be provided to the person with dementia, which in turn improves the level of depression in the care recipient. Over the past two decades a psycho-educational approach, based on cognitive-behavioural principles and presented in a small group format, has proved effective in alleviating caregiver depression, burden and other forms of psychological distress (Gallagher-Thompson et al., 2000; Gallagher-Thompson et al., 1998; Lovett & Gallagher, 1988). The basic concept is that caregivers can benefit from learning new coping skills to deal with their everyday distress. Such skills include: learning how to relax when dealing with stressful caregiving situations; learning to challenge effectively persistent negative views about current caregiving demands and fears about the future; and learning to increase the frequency of occurrence of everyday pleasant events—including building in pleasant activities with the cognitively impaired spouse or elder relative. Groups are held weekly, generally over three to four months, and include time for practice and discussion of skills taught. Role playing is frequently used to reinforce learning, home practice assignments are made each week, and small group discussion is encouraged so that caregivers can learn from one another's experience. Following this intensive phase of intervention, classes are typically held monthly, often for an additional 6 to 12 months, in order to reinforce what was learned and to encourage its continued application as new challenges arise in the caregiving situation.

Several variations of this approach are available in manual format (available from the authors, see Appendix 2) and while these approaches emphasize different cognitive and/or behavioural skills, they can be blended as needed. Manuals include: 'Increasing Life Satisfaction' (Thompson, Gallagher & Lovett, 1992), 'Controlling Your Frustration' (Gallagher-Thompson et al., 1992) and 'Coping with Caregiving' (Gallagher-Thompson, Ossinalde & Thompson, 1996a). In the 'Coping with Caregiving' manual, a section on learning how to be assertive with healthcare professionals and with family members in order to get additional assistance with caregiving is included. This manual also includes a section on planning for the future that encourages families to discuss end-of-life issues and to talk about the 'anticipatory grief' they may be experiencing. More detailed descriptions of these classes and other modifications of a CBT approach for caregivers are reported in Castleman, Gallagher-Thompson and Naythons (1999) and Coon, Thompson and Gallagher-Thompson (2002).

Recent demographic trends in the USA have focused interest on the development and implementation of interventions for culturally diverse caregivers. For example, individuals of Hispanic background from the various countries of Latin America, as well as Mexico, Cuba and South and Central America, constitute the fastest-growing segment of the US population over age 65 (US Census Bureau, 2000). Variations of the psycho-educational approach mentioned above have proved effective in working with Hispanic/Latino caregivers (Gallagher-Thompson et al., 2001 and in press). However, much more remains to be learned about the combination of skills that will prove most effective in assisting them to cope with caregiving with less stress. Similarly, other ethnic and cultural minority groups have received little attention in the caregiving research literature to date; it is anticipated that this will change dramatically in the decade ahead, as population-based demographic trends result in more and more ethnic and culturally diverse caregivers seeking help for themselves and their loved ones.

RECOMMENDATIONS FOR TREATING THE COGNITIVELY IMPAIRED ELDER

One might question how a person with dementia could be treated with CBT when cognitive skills suffer the greatest impairment. However, variations of CBT are frequently the treatment of choice. The reasoning behind this can be made clearer by referring to the CBT model depicted in Figure 3.1, which emphasizes the potential role that external factors, such as intergenerational linkages, support systems, sociocultural context, etc., may play in the development and treatment of affective disorders. These factors can be particularly important to consider when treating patients suffering from both dementia and depression. For example, during the earlier stages of dementia, psychological distress may often occur because the patient has the perception of incompetence in attempting to complete routine daily tasks. Changes within the environment can often minimize such confrontations, either by simplifying the challenges for the patients, or by reinforcing sociocultural values that allow patients to feel comfortable as they are being relieved of responsibility for carrying out their customary vocational and domestic duties. Several points to keep in mind when conducting therapy with dementia patients are listed below:

1. *Become familiar with the older person's strengths and weaknesses.* Knowledge of the older person's cognitive strengths and weaknesses is critical to setting appropriate and realistic goals. Objective information about capabilities can also provide a useful framework for family members and caregivers, which enables them to develop and maintain interaction patterns with patients that minimize stress. For example, if family members are provided with evidence that the patient can no longer comprehend complex information, but can still understand and execute one-step or two-step commands, this can help them to develop a rational basis for simplifying communications, so that ideas or requests are presented to the patient in stages.

   Attributions that family members make about a patient's behaviour is another source of distress to both themselves and the patient. Family members often view memory lapses on the part of the patient as lack of concern for others, and disruptive behaviours as being intentionally contrary. Objective evidence showing that the patient's overlearned social reasoning and verbal functioning may be reasonably intact—which is frequently the index used by lay persons to determine competence, while memory and the ability to solve novel problems are clearly shattered—can help family members to reframe troublesome behaviours as being due to the patient's disorder. This eases frustration, resulting in more strategic and productive interactions with the patient, which in turn minimize the stress experienced by both parties.

2. *Keep sessions structured*. CBT calls for the therapist to take an active role to maximize the older person's strengths and facilitate learning. A well-formulated agenda to enhance structured skill building can reduce the depression and anxiety that overwhelms the older patient. This structure is additionally advantageous to teach the family and other significant persons new ways of approaching situations based on the responses achieved in therapy. Agendas also provide a consistent structure across sessions that make therapy sessions easier for cognitively impaired persons to follow.

3. *Keep goals realistic and simple*. The overall treatment goal is to reduce depression and optimize the patient's level of functioning. The therapist's focus is on setting appropriate primary goals for the patient and the family. It is generally helpful to remind the family that therapy cannot alter the course of the dementia, yet it is possible to observe some minor improvements in cognitive functioning with improvement in depression.

4. *Utilize all available tools to enhance learning*. CBT is known for utilizing a variety of modalities to maximize a patient's understanding. These tools become exponentially useful when working with a patient whose ability to learn has become impaired. The use of audiotapes, notebooks and index cards are examples of strategies for reviewing material and keeping track of homework assignments. Offering shorter, more frequent sessions and more frequent summarizations by the patient in each session is recommended. A key strategy is to reduce the complexity of steps when designing interventions. Likewise, the creation of 'cue cards' to capture more helpful cognitions or state positive affirmations simplifies the process of cognitive restructuring that is often too complex for the cognitively impaired older person. An important principle when working therapeutically with people with dementia is to be creative.

5. *Be mindful of the role of loss and grief*. The progressive nature of dementia is an overwhelming process that leaves no family member untouched. Spouses lose their life-long partners, children lose a parent, and the patient loses his or her sense of self. This process is a painful one that progresses over an extended period of time, and these realities must be addressed in therapy for both the patient and the family.

CASE EXAMPLE

Mr M is a 71-year-old married man who was diagnosed with dementia two years ago. During the past few months, his family has observed increased isolation, tearfulness, anxiety, poor appetite, poor sleep, as well as decreased motivation to participate in any family events. Mr M was diagnosed as experiencing a major depressive episode and referred to a psychologist. The psychologist obtained Mr M's most recent assessment report and reviewed the findings with the family to obtain greater clarification of his cognitive abilities.

The psychologist observed Mr M to be oriented to person, place and time. He could perform simple tasks, such as a three-stage command, but demonstrated greater difficulty with more complex tasks. He became tearful easily and gave up when frustrated. He was able to benefit from prompting and encouragement in performing complex tasks. At the initial session, his level of depression was in the moderate to severe range according to behavioural ratings. Mr M agreed to treatment and set the following goals: increase daily pleasant activities, try to do more independent tasks, and talk about fears of losing independence.

Educating the Family

Family sessions covered the following topics: (1) the recent marked decrease in Mr M's abilities was probably attributable to the depression, and (2) while his dementia could not be 'cured', depression was a treatable disorder. Thus, the purpose of therapy was to improve the depression and his level of functioning. It was reported that Mr M was a retired music teacher and a composer. The family explained that after they observed him getting frustrated at the piano, and in an effort to not 'make things worse' for him, they packed away many of his musical recordings, music sheets and photographs of him with his students.

Behavioural Interventions

Relaxation training was utilized to assist Mr M with both his anxiety and his frustration. He was given a relaxation tape that had a brief guided imagery, positive affirmations and calming music. He was instructed to use this intervention daily, and the family was informed that they could offer him the tape when they observe him becoming anxious or frustrated. Similarly, the therapist learned that Mr M utilized music to soothe his tension, and he was able to actively discuss his favourite pieces. At a family session, the therapist helped Mr M to negotiate the return of his musical recordings to serve this purpose.

The therapist enrolled his spouse as a sort of informal co-therapist in order to help Mr M to complete a daily mood rating form as well as the Pleasant Events Schedule–AD, a specialized measure for patients with dementia (Teri & Logsdon, 1991). The daily mood rating served to educate his wife (who was the primary caregiver) that Mr M's mood was at its lowest when he was inactive, and higher when he found a way to be around music or to help around the house. Mr M made a list of pleasant activities for himself, and he and his wife also developed a list of shared pleasant events to do together.

Cognitive Interventions

Mr M believed that he was a burden to his family and was 'treated like a baby'. Examining the evidence helped him to understand that he was supported and loved. In order to reinforce these beliefs, the therapist helped him to create affirming statements on index cards that he could carry with him to read if he began to feel worthless. His wife was asked to encourage this activity periodically. Mr M also wished to be more helpful around the house. He knew that he could carry out certain tasks once he had all of the instructions, but he often would forget the instructions along the way. Together with his wife they made a list of household tasks he was capable of doing and they created a step-by-step card for each one. The therapist taught the family to utilize direct, gentle prompting in order to facilitate his involvement in the task.

Mr M also explored his sadness regarding his illness worsening in the future. With the assistance of therapy, he discussed his wishes for his end-of-life care should he become medically ill and was not able to communicate with his family. Likewise, he put together individual collections of mementos, photographs and letters that he presented to his wife and each of his children so that he could express what they meant to him. During this work, Mr M was able to develop a renewed positive impression of himself as a husband, father and teacher.

Mr M's depression was reduced after several weeks, and his functioning improved. Family members also reported improved mood, in part due to Mr M's responsiveness to CBT. For Mrs M, learning to challenge her own negative thoughts about her husband's condition and to appraise his strengths more realistically (not just focusing on his weaknesses) led to a definite improvement in her mood and her sense of well-being. Mrs M also reported that she felt better knowing that she was doing her best to maximize her husband's functioning—compared to the sense of helplessness that she had experienced at the beginning of treatment.

SUMMARY

Although there are only a handful of controlled studies, the evidence in the literature supports the argument that non-pharmacological interventions using CBT techniques can be effective in alleviating depression in patients with dementia. In most studies the importance of family members or formal caregivers in institutional settings as instrumental in treatment delivery has been emphasized. Where practical, therapists working in this area, whether as a member of an interdisciplinary team or alone, should formulate treatment programmes that involve family members and other relevant personnel.

Section Four

FINAL THOUGHTS

Chapter 13

WHAT TO DO WHEN YOUR PATIENT SAYS...

INTRODUCTION

In therapy it is not uncommon to experience difficulties with patients; either in terms of relating to the patients or in the types of issues that patients present. Often in therapy a number of issues arise during therapy that may initially challenge therapists, and if dealt with effectively can result in significant improvements in therapy outcome. In this chapter, we look at the issues that commonly (and sometimes not so commonly) occur when working with older people in CBT. Many of these problems can be anticipated from your therapy formulation or from the sorts of interactions you have with your patient in your sessions. For example, a person who is difficult to engage in therapy will often experience difficulties in establishing close intimate relationships outside of therapy. Safran and Segal (1990) comprehensively review aspects of the interpersonal relationship in cognitive therapy and interested readers are encouraged to consult their text for an in-depth examination of the therapeutic relationship in a way that goes beyond the scope of this book. Outlined below are several challenges that we have experienced, along with a range of possible options. Each challenge is identified in no particular order of merit or severity.

Cognitive Behaviour Therapy with Older People.
Ken Laidlaw, Larry W. Thompson, Leah Dick-Siskin & Dolores Gallagher-Thompson.
© 2003 John Wiley & Sons Ltd.

I DON'T HAVE ANY NEGATIVE AUTOMATIC THOUGHTS...

During the early phase of therapy when the concept of automatic thoughts is being explained to patients, it is not uncommon for depressed and/or anxious patients to believe that their mood has changed for no apparent reason. They may find it difficult to identify an automatic thought associated with (or preceding) a negative shift in mood. We offer several suggestions to address this situation.

Imagery

Have your patient try to report images or pictures in his head just immediately prior to the deterioration in mood state. If your patient still experiences difficulty identifying a thought or image, you can use guided discovery to help him to identify what he was doing exactly before his mood changed. Here the strategy is to ask the patient to specify the circumstances prior to his mood change in as much detail as possible. It is important that the patient is encouraged to elaborate on the images of where he was and what he was doing. Sometimes it is helpful to find out if someone else was there. Imaginal elaboration increases the likelihood of being able to access the thoughts that may be important in determining how moods change in depression and anxiety. It is important when working with anxiety patients to check out fears they may hold about 'bringing' on a panic attack by putting themselves back into a situation in which they may have experienced intense discomfort. In anxiety the inability to identify and recall anxiogenic type thoughts may be a form of cognitive avoidance. Finally, it is important to check that your patient is able to use imagery in this situation as this aids mood state recall. This recall is used as a basis for establishing mood changes. This skill may take the patient some time to master, so we recommend guidance and encouragement in the early stages of the use of this procedure.

Distinguishing between 'Primary' and 'Secondary' Cognitions

It may be that your patient has difficulty identifying thoughts that occur just as his/her mood changes for the worse. These types of negative thoughts are referred to as 'primary negative cognitions' and are generally more difficult to identify and report than negative thoughts that occur when a person's low mood has become established. These thoughts are called 'secondary negative cognitions' and are generally easier to identify and report verbatim. The secondary negative cognitions serve to maintain and prolong negative mood. A good way to educate patients about negative automatic thoughts is to initially identify secondary negative cognitions and discuss their role in determining effect and subsequent behaviour. The skills learned in the process of identifying and challenging secondary negative cognitions can then be transferred to identifying and challenging primary negative cognitions. It is arguable that primary negative cognitions reflect themes that are much more personally meaningful to the individual as they may have more of a direct role in changing a person's mood. An example of a primary negative cognition is 'I'm a failure'. This thought may occur when someone makes a mistake thus precipitating the subsequent development of low mood. One could argue that primary negative cognitions share many characteristics with the patient's core beliefs, as they are global, rigid and internal. Likewise, it may be more difficult for the person to provide alternative explanations or supply contradictory evidence for this thought. When dealing with primary negative cognitions, patients may find it easier to learn to identify and challenge these once they have mastered cognitive restructuring skills in dealing with secondary negative cognitions. An example of a secondary negative cognition is 'I can't stand feeling like this for much longer'. In this instance it can be pointed out to the patient that this thought, while patently false, actually maintains the depressed mood for much longer. This secondary negative cognition can induce quite a degree of short-term hopelessness but it doesn't have the same amount of personally relevant meaning that characterizing oneself as a failure does. In short, the secondary negative cognitions are the most efficient route to take when educating patients about thought monitoring and challenging.

Using Behavioural Interventions

The integration of behavioural interventions such as mood ratings in diaries such as the weekly activity schedule can challenge a patient's hypothesis that his or her mood is constant. A useful strategy is to recommend that patients rate their mood at different times each day, e.g. morning, afternoon and evening. Thus, the patient brings to the session evidence of fluctuations in mood, which can open the door for a more detailed investigation into the precipitating cognitions. It is often helpful to use behavioural interventions expressly for the purpose of generating cognitions. For example, an older depressed woman may state that she is no longer very interested in seeing friends or in doing things that used to be enjoyable, but when asked, she may not be able to identify any associated thoughts. However, by suggesting a behavioural assignment (such as calling an old friend to set up a lunch or shopping trip together), and evaluating what the person gained by this assignment, may lead to the identification of certain cognitive and behavioural barriers to the alteration of depression in this individual.

I DON'T THINK THOUGHT CHALLENGING IS MAKING A DIFFERENCE . . .

If cognitive restructuring techniques have met with limited success it may be that the negative automatic thought may actually be better understood as a core belief and strategies adjusted accordingly (see Chapter 7). In some cases reframing certain 'thoughts' as core beliefs may result in a restructuring of your conceptualization and understanding of your patient's problems. It is also important to understand that anxiety about change may prevent a person from making the changes that are necessary. In interpersonal psychotherapy, this sort of behaviour is considered as 'security operations' (Safran & Segal, 1996). In this instance the patient may fall back on old habits of doing things when the anxiety generated by expectation for change becomes too over-whelming. Here it is important to try to investigate the patient's under-standings of what change would mean. It may be necessary to start to investigate the use of anxiety management strategies, especially worry management strategies, if you suspect your patient is engaging in 'security operations'. In cases such as these, it is important to work with the individual to identify the pros and cons of leaving this position of safety and comfort. It may be that a hierarchical approach is needed to help the individual to make changes at a pace that feels comfortable.

Patients in this stage also need a good deal of encouragement to 'hang in there' with the work, as they are taking on faith that an adapted core belief will eventually develop. In essence, patients are secure in what they *believe* to be true, despite its painful emotions and maladaptive behaviours. It is important that as therapists we do not forget that we are asking our patients to work through a process where the outcome is unknown to them, and often frightening.

IT'S ALL SO HOPELESS, IT'S NOT GOING TO GET BETTER SO WHY TRY...

It is very common for people to develop 'blinkers' when trying to think in new ways about their situation and themselves. In many cases, patients will have been dealing with their distress for far longer than they will have been working in therapy, and in these circumstances it is easy to see that patients' expectations can quickly become quite hopeless. It is helpful to discuss with patients their expectations of how things will change, and how rapidly they will change. A small piece of research by Laidlaw and Bailey (1997) investigated the reasons that patients discontinued psychological treatment early. A random series of patients who attended for at least three sessions of psychological treatment provided by a large clinical psychology department were invited to complete an anonymous questionnaire about their experiences of treatment. Two of the main reasons stated by ex-patients for premature discontinuation were (a) that therapy did not result in the rapid change that they expected and (b) that therapy was more painful than they had expected. In short, all pain and very little gain. Thus, at the start of therapy it may be useful to explore the expectations your patient holds, and it is also helpful to discuss mood congruent memory bias with your patient.

In depression people typically find it harder to recall pleasant memories, with selective recall for mood congruent memories. Thus, people find it harder to see things improving for themselves as they look back over a perceived catalogue of failures. Their memories are in fact coloured by their mood and may not be entirely accurate. It is also helpful to use the cognitions related to this hopelessness as an issue to work on immediately in the session. In our work, if a patient states that the current interventions are 'useless', we recommend stopping the current agenda and addressing these statements as an 'event' unto themselves. For example, the use of a thought record in this case would summarize the antecedent ('A' column) as, 'Facing a hopeless situation, etc.'

Sometimes the issue is not what your patients say, but what they do in and out of therapy that causes concern. This subsection of the chapter is appropriately entitled, *What to do when . . .*

. . . YOUR PATIENT COMPLIES BUT ONLY MINIMALLY

Often therapists experience difficulties in ensuring that their patients comply with therapeutic procedures. One part of cognitive therapy that carries the highest risk of non-compliance is homework. Therapists can sometimes feel at a loss as to how to proceed in terms of 'setting a homework task'. Sometimes therapists will try to think of tasks in advance of the therapy session. This strategy rarely produces a homework task that is congruent with the patient's current difficulties. Non-compliance is very high with this particular strategy. The idea that a homework task must be set rather than agreed upon runs counter to the collaborative nature of CBT. It is a common mistake to leave the agreement of a task until the last few minutes of therapy as, often, homework is inadequately agreed upon and there is a high risk that the task agreed has been misunderstood, or that the patient has agreed with the therapist's suggestion because he does not wish to make the therapist late for the next patient. It is little wonder that when homework in CBT is assigned in this manner, it is likely to be poorly complied with.

Persons (1989) states that therapists may have a number of fears and negative predictions about the compliance with meaningful homework assignments. The following examples of therapists' fears are examined below. Each fear is identified and then countered by a realistic appraisal of the situation.

- *If I suggest some homework my patient will feel coerced and controlled*
  I am not coercing my patient. We are working together to find out more about the sorts of difficulties she has been experiencing. We can work

together to come up with a relevant task. I can ask my patient how she feels about doing tasks.

- *If I suggest a homework task, I'm only increasing the demands on my patient and she already feels overwhelmed!*
  I'm being pessimistic about treatment. I'm also being overprotective and this will not help my patient in the long run. In order for things to have a possibility of changing, my patient must work on her difficulties outside of our therapy hour. If my patient tries tasks set at a manageable level, her confidence that things will change will increase.
- *What if I suggest a homework task and my patient doesn't do it?*
  What if I suggest a homework task and it is successful! The only way to find out is to try it. I can suggest to my patient that we can look at the results of this 'experiment' whether it works out or not. If my patient doesn't do the homework we can put this on the next agenda and try to learn more about what prevents her from completing tasks.

GUIDELINES FOR HOMEWORK ASSIGNMENTS

- *Homework should arise from discussions within the session* (therefore you may actually decide upon a homework task midway through the session). You might say to your patient, 'What do you think would be a good way to take our discussion further?' as a way of collaboratively agreeing upon a homework task.
- *Homework should be personally important and relevant to the individual.* It should take topics further. It is central to the presenting problems
- *Homework should be manageable and time-limited.* Make assignments small, especially at first. Do not ask the person to do something you would be unwilling to do yourself. Be flexible in how assignments are done: if the person has difficulty writing things down, ask her to record into a tape recorder, or call you at a certain time during the day to leave her homework as a phone message. For some types of homework, such as doing a thought record, these kinds of alternatives can prove to be just as effective as the traditional method of actually writing it out in full.
- *Homework should be specific.* You and your patient should be clear about what is to be done and the reason for agreeing upon this. You might ask your patient her understanding about this. 'What is the reason for doing this, what do you think you might gain?'
- *Homework should be realistic.* You might try to help the person to problem solve in advance. 'Are there any problems you foresee which might make this task difficult for you to complete?'
- *Homework is a learning process.* It is not necessary that the person has to do everything successfully. The purpose of homework is to find out more. If things do not work out as predicted then a lot can be learned from this

experience. Try to set tasks as a 'no-lose' situation. Even if the person has not completed her homework, this can be used as a fruitful topic for discussion within the session.

If your patient is not complying despite clearly understanding the rationale for aspects of your therapeutic work together, you need to raise this as an issue in therapy. It is a common mistake among some therapists that homework is not properly addressed during sessions. Set this on the agenda for your next session and spend time exploring what it is that prevents your patient from fully participating in therapy. This will ensure that the task is given adequate attention. This is validating to your patient as she will see that her efforts do not go unnoticed. It is also good practice because giving homework such a prominent place within each therapy session tends to increase compliance.

In discussing with your patient the results of her homework task, it is helpful to try to use Socratic questioning to work through what your patient has learned. Useful questions to ask are: What did you learn from doing this— What does this tell you?; Were you surprised by anything following your completion of this task?; What do you think would be a step forward here?

The discussion about incomplete homework should include such questions as: Does your patient have any fears or expectations about the outcome? Does your patient fear that you will have less regard for her if she reveals herself more openly. In these scenarios, you may need to open up a discussion about trust and risk. Perhaps your patient needs to risk something in order for her old habits to change.

The therapist can ask the patient if the homework task seemed unconnected to her current difficulties. Common reasons for non-compliance with homework are a lack of clarity of assignment; lack of time on patient's part; lack of motivation; no real belief in the outcome or relevance, etc. Homework can be set up as a 'no-lose' experiment: If it is beneficial then the patient obviously reaps the benefits, if it is not beneficial then spending time exploring reasons why this is so can be very helpful to the patient in the longer run.

Remember that many older adults come to therapy with specific beliefs about the 'kind of patient' they *should* be. Be mindful that this cohort was socialized to be patients within a medical model that does not encourage collaboration. We find that many older adults need encouragement and practice to be able to articulate feedback to the therapist about homework (or any other element of the session) that they may perceive as negative.

Likewise, the term 'homework' can either be a foreign or an antiquated term for many older patients. If so, a short discussion with your patients can usually result in an acceptable term. Here the use of humour can make this process very enjoyable and informative for your patients. In an important sense your patients are seeing at first hand that their point of view matters in the therapy setting. In working collaboratively with your patients, discuss how homework can be referred to and how these tasks will be decided.

Further factors that may need consideration are the sensory and cognitive functioning (and limitations) of your patients. For example, are the handouts you provide to be read for homework in a print that is large enough and can be easily read? If not, you need to correct that situation rather than expect your patients to do so. Have you considered whether your patients are still able to write? Many older adults with such conditions as moderate to severe arthritis find it very difficult to write things down; in those instances an alternative method of recording homework is needed. Another pertinent area of enquiry with older adults involves their ability to remember the assignments. In order to facilitate accurate recall of homework, they can write it down in a notebook that they can bring to every session. A written record reduces confusion and reinforces that you, as the therapist, view this aspect of treatment as important enough to spend time in the session recording it properly for or with the patients.

These factors also need to be considered when working in the session to ensure that the patient understands, sees and hears the material that forms the basis of the homework assignments. Again, modelling the collaborative process provides a forum for the patient to be able to state specific needs that can enhance his or her learning process. In our experience, it is at times appropriate to involve family members so that home practice is encouraged outside the sessions. In some instances, a spouse or other concerned family member may become part of the actual homework (with the patient's permission, of course). For example, a depressed older gentleman may need encouragement to talk about his lack of pleasure in life with his adult son or daughter; if they are 'coached' by the therapist, the entire experience can be much more fulfilling and reinforcing for the patient, thus encouraging further exchanges with the adult child in the future.

I DO NOT FEEL ANY BETTER...

Sometimes patients become discouraged when they 'have a bad day' after experiencing some improvement. Patients often hold the belief that if they had a good day on Monday but a bad day on Tuesday, it means that therapy is not effective, or that their depression will never get any better. We find it is necessary to educate patients on the process of change. In an ideal world, there would be a direct, smooth relationship between setting our goals and attaining them. Yet, change rarely happens in this fashion. Instead, change occurs similar to the phrase, 'two steps forward, one step backward'. If one were to make a graph of this process, a saw-toothed line connecting the place where patients start therapy and the final outcome would be the result. The jagged line of change across therapy sessions represents the natural process of having good days and bad days, but the critical piece is what is happening *in the long run*. In order for our patients to become less distressed when they experience a negative event once starting treatment, we must educate them regarding the point of origin to make the comparison. A bad Tuesday should not be compared to Monday, but rather to the point where therapy began. In all likelihood, despite its saw-toothed appearance, the overall slope of the line of progress will indicate steady improvement. It is recommended that this rationale is explained to patients in the very beginning of therapy to help them put a framework on the more uncomfortable moments that are a feature of many therapeutic treatment courses.

YOU DON'T LIKE, OR ARE UNCOMFORTABLE WITH, YOUR PATIENT

Either of these reactions can occur when working with older adults and it may come as quite a shock to therapists who are used to being able to offer their patients positive unconditional regard. For example, many older adults grew up in an era when prejudice against different racial or ethnic groups was tolerated or perhaps even encouraged. If you happen to be a member of one of these groups, you may hear what you view as prejudicial comments or labelling from the older patient that might be contrary to your personal beliefs and standards for relating to others. However, this can be 'grist for the therapeutic mill' as it is likely that the patient engenders the same kinds of responses in others as well. Often if you reflect honestly on your feelings about your patient you may be able to use this productively to bring about change. If there are no issues of ethnicity or clashes of personal beliefs, then you may wish to reflect when you first started to experience such feelings towards your patient. Your patient's behaviour in sessions may provide important clues to the way he or she relates to others outside therapy. You may want to raise this as an issue with your patient. If you adopt a supportive stance on this issue this can promote important change for your patient. It may also feel uncomfortable if the strong feelings that are being engendered are ignored. Therapy is always better when it is conducted in a spirit of openness and acceptance. It may be difficult to raise such issues with patients but with warmth and acceptance offered by the therapist this may prove to be extremely important for a positive outcome in therapy.

YOU CAN'T TEACH AN OLD DOG NEW TRICKS...

This can be a common viewpoint early on in therapy. After all, societies are generally ageist and since older people are members of society they are not immune to the endorsement of societal attitudes. It is very common to find that older people are rather ageist in their beliefs and orientations, and you may wish to tackle this in a number of ways. First, ask your patients what age they were when they stopped learning things. You can use humour to point out the lack of reality in this global statement. You might also wish to take an educational stance here and ask the patients whether they learned anything from listening to the news or reading a book or magazine recently. If they say 'yes', which is highly likely, then you have empirically demonstrated to them that they are able to learn in the present. You can also help the patients to understand that learning will go at their own pace and that you will do your best not to give out too much information at once. Another strategy is to encourage the patients to do the experiment of participating in therapy for several sessions and then reassess whether or not they are capable of learning anything. This is often effective with highly sceptical individuals.

In other societies it is recognized that age does not have to be seen negatively. For example, in many Asian cultures, older adults are not only respected but revered, and ancestor worship is commonly practised even to this day. For those patients who feel particularly devalued, you can point out that research evidence shows that older people can be trained to improve their memory and actually can become better at remembering than untrained younger people. If your patients think all their problems are due to their age, you could ask them to complete a timeline and trace the antecedents of their current difficulties. Often the roots of current problems can be found in years past. This can be a helpful exercise to reinforce the concept that each age or stage in life brings its own challenges and its own rewards.

Alternatively, if your patient has an age-related physical illness (e.g. osteoarthritis, heart disease, any of the common forms of cancer, etc.) we recommend that you work with your patient to assess the main nature of his difficulties. Is the current depression due to the health problem itself? Is it compounded by age? (and, if so, in what way?), or does the problem result in consequences that your patient finds intolerable? (for example, chronic pain, or limitations in mobility, or dependence on others for assistance in daily life). If it is the latter, ask your patient 'Would these difficulties have been easier to cope with at a younger age?' This is a fertile area for using Socratic questions to really understand your patient's perspective. We have found that virtually all older patients have had prior stressful experiences with which they have coped quite effectively. It is useful, therefore, to enquire about these prior experiences and, in particular, to ask about the coping strategies that were used at that time, and whether or not they could be brought to bear now, in the current situation? Often this inspires hope, since the patient can honestly discuss successful coping and can think about how to use strategies that were helpful in the past to deal with his current stressors. While the situations may not be identical (past and present), there is often enough similarity so that the same kinds of cognitive and behavioural coping strategies will, in fact, apply.

AND DON'T FORGET...

In addition to the importance of understanding various patient factors that can make CBT difficult to implement with older adults, it is imperative to recognize the contribution of your own thoughts, beliefs and attitudes, as these may have the effect of limiting what can be achieved both within sessions and over the course of treatment. Padesky (1998) suggests that the ultimate efficacy of cognitive therapy is enhanced or limited by the beliefs of the therapist involved. It is probable that skilled therapists who believe that cognitive interventions are potentially beneficial to the patients they serve will be more inclined to adopt a 'try it and see' approach. This approach arguably enhances rather than limits therapy options that potentially have an effect on outcome.

Chapter 14

FUTURE DIRECTIONS AND INNOVATIONS IN PRACTICE

INTRODUCTION

In this final chapter, a little bit of crystal ball-gazing is undertaken in the full knowledge that the unforeseen frequently does occur (much more often than the apparently 'foreseen') and predictions often seem to shine as brightly as fool's gold and often turn out to be as worthless! Therefore, indulgence is requested of the readers and we caution that these speculative thoughts are attempted in the spirit of being a guide to what might take place given the varieties of experience and knowledge that the current authors possess.

A LITTLE BIT OF PSYCHOLOGY CAN GO A LONG WAY...

An important potential future direction for cognitive therapy with older people is the move into medical comorbidity. This book reflects the increasing potential for CBT to be useful within medical settings with a range of conditions. Going beyond Parkinson's disease and post-stroke depression, one can see that CBT may find increasing acceptance as a technique to enhance compliance with rehabilitative strategies following other types of illness. CBT can also enhance our understandings of the motivations of people coping with medical illnesses. While health psychologists have advanced our understandings

Cognitive Behaviour Therapy with Older People.
Ken Laidlaw, Larry W. Thompson, Leah Dick-Siskin & Dolores Gallagher-Thompson.
© 2003 John Wiley & Sons Ltd.

of the models of illness that may help to understand individual response to illness, the usefulness of CBT with medical populations has only now begun to be explored. It is hoped that this approach with medical patients will open new and exciting ways for therapists to enhance the care and treatment of older people who for so long have been underserved.

An important future direction for CBT with older people is the need to adapt this model for those patients who present with high symptom acuity, fractured social relationships, marginal social functioning, and a chronic history of multiple psychiatric episodes and hospitalizations. The Partial Hospital Program is an innovative programme that is specialized for older adults and is a brief (approximately six weeks), intensive (five days per week) multidisciplinary outpatient programme designed to prevent psychiatric hospitalization or reduce the need for a lengthy inpatient stay. The following discussion is based on the treatment model found at the Hillside Hospital, North Shore–Long Island Jewish Health System in New York. Interventions include medication management, case management, individual and group therapy, family work, and brief neuropsychological screening. The bulk of the patient's day is spent in group therapy and in the treatment milieu. Group therapy includes such themes as family issues, discharge planning, symptom management, medication management, goal setting, self-esteem, and a CBT group focusing on the teaching of specific cognitive and behavioural strategies to manage symptoms. The short-term nature of the programme, the need for rapid change, and the practical focus of teaching strategies to manage patients' immediate discomfort, make CBT a perfect fit within this programme.

While the staff of such a programme can attest to its efficacy from our day-to-day clinical data, no outcome data exist to support our enthusiasm or experience. Furthermore, we are aware that these types of patients exist in all settings, even if no such service is available. It is easy to assume that any presence of psychosis would preclude the utility of cognitive strategies, yet there is a growing body of data to support the efficacy of CBT for psychosis (Kuipers et al., 1998, 1997; Garety et al., 1997).

Until very recently CBT therapists have given scant attention to the treatment of personality disorder in older adults. Treatment obstacles often include establishing a collaborative relationship, convincing these patients to complete homework, or even obtaining reliable information regarding their history and symptoms. It is also observed that these acute, socially impaired patients demonstrate a low frequency of self-reflection that is inherently imperative for CBT. Studies comparing the efficacy of treatment for depressed older adults with and without personality disorder report poor response rates and early drop-out rates for older adults with personality disorder (Gradman, Thompson & Gallagher-Thompson, 1999). Research in this area is at a very early stage; nonetheless, the recommendation for research would serve to help all providers who see such difficult patients regardless of treatment setting.

USING GERONTOLOGY TO ENHANCE THE APPLICATION OF CBT

CBT can be further developed as a treatment approach for older people by taking account of research in gerontology, particularly research looking at successful ageing (Rowe & Kahn, 1998; Baltes, 1991) as this provides good evidence for challenging negative views of growing old. A pioneer in the field of gerontology and successful ageing is Paul Baltes, who has developed the concept of selection, optimization and compensation as a response to the changes evident in normal ageing. This simple conceptualization of successful adaptation to the challenges of growing old can be used within CBT and could be the beginnings of the development of a whole new series of cognitive and behavioural treatment strategies for use with older adults.

Another important and useful concept is one that has recently been developed by the World Health Organization (WHO, 2002). Active ageing is the process of optimizing health, participation and security, with the goal to enhance quality of life. Active ageing requires a shift in thinking away from seeing older people as passive recipients of care and instead considers that older people have 'rights' to equality of opportunity, participation and integration as valued members of society. Active ageing as a philosophy is entirely compatible with CBT for older people, stressing, as it does, collaboration and active teamwork. The data and evidence generated by gerontology contain a whole set of rationales for challenging ageist notions of growing old that can be used within CBT programmes.

USING INFORMATION TECHNOLOGY IN CBT

A recent on-line survey by the American Association of Retired Persons (AARP, 2000) has shown that older people are interested in keeping up to date with new developments in multimedia technologies such as the internet. CBT with older people may also benefit from treatment innovations using video technology. Telemedicine is where audio-visual and telecommunications technology is used to provide healthcare where a distance prevents people from participating in face-to-face meetings. This innovation may also allow greater numbers of older people to benefit from psychological treatment, as the relatively small numbers of professionals who work with older people can use this technology to reach far greater numbers of people in need. In 1996 the NIH established a telemedicine programme for biomedical research and recently convened a national meeting to discuss the applicability of telemedicine. Thus, while we are at the beginning of the application of this type of intervention, the interest and investment shown by the NIH shows the great promise of this innovation. In the case of working with older people, frail and housebound older people in psychological distress can receive psychological care and support without having to attend outpatient clinics.

This innovation in practice is particularly useful when treating the oldest-old section of the population who may be very frail. As will be remembered from the review of demographic changes, this is the section of the population experiencing the most rapid growth. It is also important to recognize that the majority of survivors of oldest age are women, and often as they age they will become more isolated, impoverished and disabled (Baltes & Smith, 2002). Telemedicine allows CBT psychotherapists the potential of reaching out to sections of society that have previously been ill-served. Many psychothera-pists have given telemedicine scant attention and have some reservations about this approach. In a recent review of the uses of teleconsultation in psychology with older people, Tyrrell et al. (2001) state that fears about problems in establishing alliance and rapport are generally unfounded. Tyrrell and colleagues also state that patients often favour this method for its convenience and privacy. Importantly the success of this method relies less on acceptance by older adults and more on the skills and technical preparedness of clinicians. The success of this type of intervention can be enhanced if an assistant is seated with the patient to deal with any technical difficulties. As technology increases and becomes easier to use, older people can be successfully and easily given skills that will enable them to benefit from telemedicine. In short, telemedicine holds a lot of promise as a potential for therapists working with older people.

ETHNIC MINORITIES AND CBT

A very exciting new direction for working with older people is the increasing access of ethnic older persons to the CBT approach. In the UK, the Asian and South East Asian communities very rarely present to therapists with psychological difficulties. Most ethnic older people do not seek psychological services, due to such factors as: cultural prohibitions, fear of 'the system', language barriers, and lack of available trained mental health personnel who are culturally sensitive (Miles, 1999; Yeo & Gallagher-Thompson, 1996). This, however, does not mean that they experience less psychological distress; rather, it reflects the fact that most mental health providers are not trained in basic cultural competence and therefore find themselves hard pressed not only to understand the problems of ethnic older people but also to provide the necessary therapeutic services. Yet research with younger non-white persons in the USA in recent years has highlighted their general acceptance of CBT approaches, along with CBT's effectiveness (overall) to treat affective disorders such as depression and anxiety (Organista, 2000). This should also encourage the use of CBT with ethnic older people. Reasons for CBT's success with younger non-white patients include the fact that it empowers clients through teaching them self-change skills. CBT also focuses on conscious processes and specific behaviours and uses a problem-centred approach that is action oriented and geared towards symptom relief.

Despite these encouraging prospects, it should be noted that there are a number of barriers that make it more difficult for ethnic older people (compared to their younger counterparts) to participate in therapy. These include issues such as: lack of reliable transportation to get to and from clinic visits on time; feelings of discomfort with professionals who are not of the same linguistic and/or cultural background; and belief that many of their symptoms are just part and parcel of 'normal ageing' and thus do not warrant the use of a professional person's time (Arean & Gallagher-Thompson, 1996).

CBT therapists should also be aware of, and address (so that they can develop trust and rapport with ethnic older people), the problem of expressing oneself in English (particularly with regard to emotionally laden material) when that is not the patient's first language. Many ethnic older people must first translate the words into their native language, and form their thoughts into their type of English before they can reply to the therapist. This is a complex and often difficult process. In addition, many ethnic older people practise and follow religious or folk remedies and beliefs regarding their illness and its treatment (Morales, 1999). Belief in spirits, jinxes, and other unseen forces and events are common with regard to mental illnesses like depression, resulting in ethnic older people seeking treatment from folk healers using folk remedies (e.g. herbs and teas). For these reasons, it is usually necessary first to educate the ethnic elder about CBT—what it is and is not, and what it can and cannot do—so that they can understand more fully what therapy will involve and can participate in it more effectively.

Finally, it is crucial that cognitive-behavioural therapists recognize and respect the value and power of the family (often over and above that of the individual) when it comes to decision making and to dealing with mental illness. According to traditional family values, endorsed by most ethnic minority groups, care for emotional distress should be provided first and foremost by members of the immediate family—not by 'outsiders'. This is particularly true regarding care for one's elder relatives: filial piety (duty) requires that the family 'take care of its own'. A related value for many Asian groups is the importance of 'saving face', meaning that mental illnesses are regarded as disgracing the family if they are known about; so much energy is expended minimizing problems and denying that help is needed. Concretely, this means that Asian older people will rarely, if ever, seek mental health assistance on their own initiative. Rather, the adult son or daughter will typically be the person in the family who recognizes that there is a problem and who will seek out assistance. These and other issues of importance when working with ethnic older people are discussed in more depth in Morales (1999) and Kitano and Maki (1996). In summary, working with ethnic older people within a CBT perspective is both challenging and rewarding, as our own clinical work with primarily Hispanic/Latino and Asian (Chinese and Japanese) older people has shown. Clearly, there is a great deal more to learn before most practitioners can describe themselves as 'culturally competent'. Yet the obviously increasing diversity of the population in both the USA and the UK will result in increased demand for mental healthcare by these groups. It is our hope that most CBT practitioners will become culturally competent so that they are able to work effectively with ethnic older people in the decades ahead.

MARKETING CBT

Another issue requiring attention from future practitioners of CBT is the need to market and promote this approach directly to consumers and healthcare providers. This is important so that they can be well informed about their treatment options, much as is done currently with antidepressant medications, which are heavily marketed in the media—often with advertisements that are pointedly directed at older adults. A recent study in the *Journal of the American Medical Association* (Olfson et al., 2002), based on data from 67 000 patients, found that the rate of outpatient treatment for depression increased from 0.73 per 100 individuals to 2.33 per 100 individuals between 1987 and 1997. The proportion of patients receiving antidepressant medications to treat their depression jumped from 37 per cent to 74 per cent in the same period, whereas the proportion of patients receiving any form of psychotherapy for their depression declined from 71 per cent to 60 per cent. On the one hand, it is impressive to find that more individuals are seeking treatment for depression now compared to a decade ago, suggesting that the stigma associated with seeking psychiatric care may be declining. On the other hand, we are concerned that patients are not availing themselves of treatments like CBT which are just as effective as medication (in some studies with older adults, CBT is more effective; cf. Thompson et al., 2001) and which have lower side-effect rates and reduced risk of relapse. Unfortunately, CBT is not viewed at present as a first-line treatment for depression at any age, despite the ever-increasing empirical literature demonstrating its effectiveness. For older people this is an especially important topic due to the decreased tolerance of older people to medications and the medical contra-indications that exist for some older people who are depressed. In the future, CBT psychotherapists may need to adopt a stronger role as advocates in collaboration with their older clients.

To address this point, we think that there needs to be both greater consumer awareness of the benefits of CBT and increased physician awareness of its value (either alone or in combination with medication). This involves several steps, such as: education of the general public (including older adults and their families) about CBT and its usefulness, as well as its acceptability, for most older adults; education of medical students and primary care physicians about the excellent 'risk/benefit ratio' of CBT—particularly for older adults who may be unable to take antidepressant medication due to the complex medical regimens they require for their overall health; and, finally, education of insurance carriers about the mounting empirical support for CBT which should result in CBT being a reimbursable treatment option for later-life depression. In short, we will need to become advocates for this approach if we are to see it thrive and flourish with older adults and their families.

CONCLUSION AND SUMMARY

It should be evident that there is still much work that needs to be done in the application of CBT with older people. The boundaries of this approach are still beyond the horizon when it comes to developing effective treatments for the sorts of difficulties older people commonly experience. This book has, of necessity, been selective in it choice of topics, and many more could have been included such as interventions for psychosis, depression and heart disease, managing elder abuse, and so on.

It is heartening that the field of older adult psychotherapy appears so dynamic and our future with regard to the extent of the application of CBT is thankfully uncertain. Uncertainty in this regard lets us know that we are still alive!

Appendix 1

BLANK FORMS

WEEKLY ACTIVITY SCHEDULE

	Mon .../.../...	Tues .../.../...	Wed .../.../...	Thurs .../.../...	Fri .../.../...	Sat .../.../...	Sun .../.../...
7.00 – 8.00							
8.00 – 9.00							
9.00 – 10.00							
10.00 – 11.00							
11.00 – 12.00							
12.00 – 1 p.m.							
1 p.m. – 2 p.m.							
2 p.m. – 3 p.m.							
3 p.m. – 4 p.m.							
4 p.m. – 5 p.m.							
5 p.m. – 6 p.m.							
6 p.m. – 7 p.m.							
7 p.m. – 8 p.m.							
8 p.m. onwards							

Note: Simply write down what you do in the times marked each day. One or two words are enough to describe what you do. For example, if you were doing housework at 10 a.m.–11 a.m. on Monday morning you would only need to write housework in the space provided. Please remember to bring this sheet with you at your next appointment. Your next appointment is scheduled for ..../......./....... at ....a.m./p.m.

DAILY MOOD-MONITORING FORM

1. Please rate your mood for each day, i.e. how good or bad you felt, using the 9-point scale shown below. If you felt good, put a higher number on the chart below. If you felt 'so-so', mark a 5. And if you felt low or depressed, mark a lower number

	1	2	3	4	5	6	7	8	9	
	Very depressed				'So-so'				Very happy	

2. On the two lines next to your mood rating for each day, please briefly give two major reasons that might have had an influence on your feelings. Try to be as specific as possible.

Time of day	Mood score	Reasons why I felt this way	
Average for the day			

PROBLEM-SOLVING WORKSHEET

My problem is:
My possible solution/strategy is:
In order to put my strategy into action I need to:

Advantages of strategy	Disadvantages of strategy

Identifiable obstacles

Step 1: *What was the problem? What did you need to solve?*

Step 2: *Brainstorm solutions. Remember, do not worry about the quality of each solution. Just write down whatever comes to mind.*

Step 3: *Evaluate and rank your choices. Start by picking out the most realistic, then the second, then the third, and so on.*

Step 4: *Choose an alternative.*

- What happened?
- What thoughts do you have about the way you solved your problem?
- How are you feeling about your problem now?

Step 5: *Choose another alternative, if needed.*

- What happened?
- What thoughts do you have about the way you solved your problem?
- How are you feeling about your problem now?

TENSION DIARY

Directions: For each day, rate your average tension score. Indicate your least relaxed and most relaxed situations, as well as any physical symptoms that you experience.

Tension rating: 1=Least tense you have ever been
10=Most tense you have even been

	MONDAY	TUESDAY	WEDNESDAY
Average Score for the day			
Most Tense Score			
When & Where?			
What was the situation?			
Physical Signs i.e. headache, stomachache, restless sleep			
Least Tense Score			
When & Where?			
What was the situation?			

RELAXATION PRACTICE LOG

Directions: Rate your level of tension from '1', least tense, to '9', most tense before and after the relaxation exercise (circle the number that best applies). Record the time of day that you did the exercise and some comments regarding the prior stressful situation and whether the relaxation helped you. Do this each day.

DATE	TIME	RELAXATION SCORE	COMMENTS
		Before: 1 2 3 4 5 6 7 8 9 After: 1 2 3 4 5 6 7 8 9	
		Before: 1 2 3 4 5 6 7 8 9 After: 1 2 3 4 5 6 7 8 9	
		Before: 1 2 3 4 5 6 7 8 9 After: 1 2 3 4 5 6 7 8 9	
		Before: 1 2 3 4 5 6 7 8 9 After: 1 2 3 4 5 6 7 8 9	
		Before: 1 2 3 4 5 6 7 8 9 After: 1 2 3 4 5 6 7 8 9	
		Before: 1 2 3 4 5 6 7 8 9 After: 1 2 3 4 5 6 7 8 9	
		Before: 1 2 3 4 5 6 7 8 9 After: 1 2 3 4 5 6 7 8 9	

DYSFUNCTIONAL THOUGHT RECORD: 5 COLUMNS

A: Situation	B: Beliefs	C: Emotions	D: Adaptive Thoughts	E: Outcomes
Describe the events that led to your unpleasant feelings: Where were you, what were you doing, who else was there?	As your mood changed what thought was in your mind?	What are you feeling (sad, angry, anxious, etc.)? How bad do you feel? 0–100% good?	(What is a more helpful way to think about this situation?)	(Re-rate the strength of the negative beliefs and feelings now)

DYSFUNCTIONAL THOUGHT RECORD: 6 COLUMNS

A: Situation	B: Beliefs	C: Emotions	D: Adaptive Thoughts	E: Outcomes	F: Functioning
Describe the events that led to your unpleasant feelings: Where were you, what were you doing, who else was there?	As your mood changed what thought was in your mind?	What are you feeling (sad, angry, anxious, etc.)? How bad do you feel? 0–100% good?	(What is a more helpful way to think about this situation?)	(Re-rate the strength of the negative beliefs and feelings now)	(How will changing your thoughts help you?)

SLEEP DIARY

TO COMPLETE SLEEP DIARY: Use these symbols

● Lights out or in bed trying to sleep   I Asleep   X Lights on or out of bed for the night   C Coffee, tea, soda with caffeine

	PM			MIDNIGHT						AM						NOON						PM			Day	**Fill out in the morning**			**Fill out in the evening**
	6	7	8	9	10	11	12	1	2	3	4	5	6	7	8	9	10	11	12	1	2	3	4	5	6		How much sleep?	Sleeping aid Time, type amount	Sleep quality?	Daytime fatigue
M																													Hi med lo	Hi med lo
T																													Hi med lo	Hi med lo
W																													Hi med lo	Hi med lo
Th																													Hi med lo	Hi med lo
F																													Hi med lo	Hi med lo
Sa																													Hi med lo	Hi med lo
Su																													Hi med lo	Hi med lo

Adapted from Spielman and Glovinsky (1991)

COGNITIVE FORMULATION WORKSHEET FOR DEPRESSION IN LATER LIFE

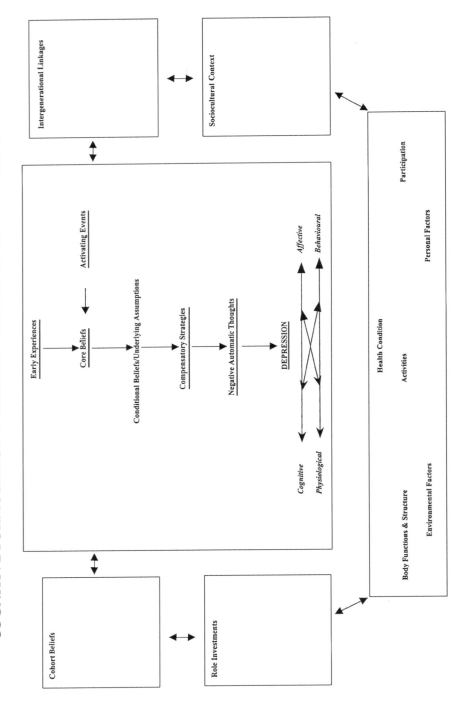

DAT SHEET

Situation: _____

_____

Thought: _____

Just for argument's sake, if this thought were true what would this mean to you? In what way would this be upsetting for you?

_____

If this were true what would this mean to you? In what way would this be upsetting for you? What would this say about you?

_____

If this were true what would this mean to you? In what way would this be upsetting for you? What would this say about you?

_____

If this were true what would this mean to you? In what way would this be upsetting for you? What would this say about you?

_____

If this were true what would this mean to you? In what way would this be upsetting for you? What would this say about you?

_____

Conclusions

I appear to believe that _____

The effect of holding this belief

is: _____

RISK ASSESSMENT

What are you worrying about? _____

_____

Rate your anxiety about this event (0–100%) _____

Rate degree of conviction, i.e that the feared event will come true (0–100%)

_____

What is the worst that could happen? _____

_____

If this did happen what thoughts might help you cope?_____

_____

If this did happen what actions/behaviours might help you cope better?

_____

What is an alternative way to think about this? _____

_____

Now:

Re-rate anxiety about this event (0–100%) _____

Re-rate how likely it is that fear will come true (0–100%) _____

Appendix 2

USEFUL REFERENCE MATERIAL

TREATMENT MANUALS

Dick, L.P., Gallagher-Thompson, D.G., Coon, D.W., Powers, D.V. & Thompson, L.W. (1995) *Cognitive Behavioral Therapy for Late Life Depression: A Client Manual*. Palo Alto, CA: VA Palo Alto Health Care System.

Gallagher-Thompson, D., Ossinalde, C. & Thompson, L.W. (1996a) *Coping with Caregiving: A Class for Family Caregivers*. Palo Alto, CA: VA Palo Alto Health Care System.

Gallagher-Thompson, D., Ossinalde, C. & Thompson, L.W. (1996b) *Como Mantener Su Bienestar*. Palo Alto, CA: VA Palo Alto Health Care System (Spanish Language manual).

Gallagher-Thompson, D., Rose, J., Florsheim, M., Jacome, P., DelMaestro, S., Peters, L., Gantz, F., Arguello, D., Johnson, C., Mooreland, R.S., Polich, T.M., Chesney, M. & Thompson, L.W. (1992) *Controlling your Frustration: A Class for Caregivers*. Palo Alto, CA: VA Palo Alto Health Care System.

Thompson, L., Gallagher, D. & Lovett, S. (1992) *Increasing Life Satisfaction Class: Leaders' and Participant Manuals*. Palo Alto, CA: Dept of Veterans Affairs Medical Center and Stanford University.

Thompson, L.W., Gallagher, D., Laidlaw, K. & Dick, L.P. (2000) *Cognitive-Behavioural Therapy for Late Life Depression: A Therapist Manual. UK Version*. Edinburgh, UK: University of Edinburgh, Dept of Psychiatry.*

Thompson, L.W., Gallagher-Thompson, D. & Dick, L.P. (1995) *Cognitive-Behavioral Therapy for Late Life Depression: A Therapist Manual*. Palo Alto, CA:

---

*A copy of this manual is available on request by writing to Ken Laidlaw, University of Edinburgh, Department of Psychiatry, Kennedy Tower, Royal Edinburgh Hospital, Morningside Park, Edinburgh, EH10 5HF. For all other manuals, please write to: Dr Dolores Gallagher-Thompson, Professor of Research, Department of Psychiatry and Behavioral Sciences, Stanford University School of Medicine, California.

Older Adult and Family Center, Veterans Affairs Palo Alto Health Care System.

SUGGESTED FURTHER READING FOR THERAPISTS

Kinsella, K. & Velkoff, V.A. (2001) US Census Bureau, Series P95/01-1, *An Aging World: 2001*. Washington, DC: US Government Printing Office. [Available free by writing to the authors at the Census Bureau in Washington, DC. Contains an amazing amount of detailed useful information about changing demographics currently and future projections, fascinating.]

Persons, J.B. (1989) *Cognitive Therapy in Practice: A Case Formulation Approach*. New York: W.W. Norton & Co. [Although this book may be getting a bit dated, it provides an excellent insight into applying cognitive therapy in the real world. Still a worthwhile investment.]

Rowe, J.W. & Kahn, R.L. (1998) *Successful Aging*. New York: Pantheon Books. [Essential reading for anyone with an interest in working with older people. This is a first-rate introduction to gerontology.]

Wood, R.T. (Ed.) (1996) *Handbook of the Clinical Psychology of Ageing*. Chichester: John Wiley & Sons. [This comprehensive handbook is an invaluable reference guide. Often the first stop when researching the background to a topic when working with older people.]

Zarit, S.H. & Knight, B.G. (Eds) (1996) *A Guide to Psychotherapy and Aging: Effective Clinical Interventions in a Life-Stage Context*. Washington, DC: American Psychological Association. [A mine of useful and thought-provoking chapters covering areas of great concern to therapists working with older people.]

Appendix 3

USEFUL WEBSITES

http://www.ageconcern.org.uk   This British-based charity has an extremely informative and useful website. There is lots of information that older people in the UK can use. For people working with older adults there are lots of resources at this site. This site has some excellent links to other older adult websites. Highly recommended.

http://www.aoa.dhhs.gov/   The Administration on Aging is an American website that has lots of information for clinicians and for older people. It is extremely useful as there are self-help materials available via this website.

http://www.nia.nih.gov/   The National Institute on Aging is an American Website with useful information on research. It is also a good general resource as it is linked to the National Institute of Health.

http://www.suicidology.org/index.html   This is a website that is dedicated to providing resources about suicide. Although it is not specific to older people this site contains a lot of useful information about suicide and it is a useful resource for anyone working with depressed clients.

http://www.un.org/esa/socdev/ageing/   This is a United Nations website that contains information generated for the second world assembly on ageing. There are lots of useful documents available at this site and good links to other useful sites. Another good UN site to consult on ageing demographics is http://www.un.org/popin/

http://www.who.int/whosis/menu.cfm   This is a statistical website developed by the World Health Organization and contains a lot of very useful information about population ageing.

http://www.who.dk/healthtopics HEALTHELDERLY   This WHO website is the main site for the healthy ageing programme. Online policy documents and research information is contained here.

http://www.oafc-menlo.com   This website was developed and is currently maintained by Drs Thompson and Gallagher-Thompson and describes their research projects at the Older Adults and Family Center in California. This website provides many links to other websites that focus on information pertinent to caregivers of frail older people.

REFERENCES

AARP (2000) *AARP Survey on Lifelong Learning: Learning Never Ends, Education in the 50+ Years.* New York: Harris Interactive, inc.

Abrams, R.C., Teresi, J.A. & Butin, D.N. (1992) Depression in nursing home residents. *Clinics in Geriatric Medicine*, **8**, 309–312.

Administration on Aging (2000) *Profile of Older Americans: 2000.* Washington, DC: National Institute of Mental Health.

Alexopoulos, G.S., Abrams, R.C., Young, R.C. & Shamoian, C.A. (1988) Cornell Scale for Depression in Dementia. *Biological Psychiatry*, **23**, 271–284.

American Association of Geriatric Psychiatry (1997) Recommendations for primary care physicians: When to refer depressed elderly patients to a geriatric psychiatrist. AAGP online.org.

Ames, D. & Allen, N. (1991) The prognosis of depression in old age: Good, bad, or indifferent? *International Journal of Geriatric Psychiatry*, **6**, 477–481.

Anderson, R. (2002) *Human resource measures in favour of an ageing workforce.* Paper presented at the Valencia Forum, Researchers, Educators and Providers contribution to the Second World Assembly on Ageing, Valencia, Spain.

Andrews, G., Crino, R., Hunt, C., Lampe, L. & Page, A. (1994) *The Treatment of Anxiety Disorders: Clinician's Guides and Patient Manuals.* Cambridge: Cambridge University Press.

Antonucci, D.O. (1998) The coping with depression course: A behavioural treatment for depression. *The Clinical Psychologist*, **51**, 3–5.

APA (1994) *Diagnostic and Statistical Manual of Mental Disorders, Fourth Edition.* Washington, DC: American Psychiatric Association.

APA (2000) *Diagnostic and Statistical Manual of Mental Disorders, Fourth Edition, Text Revision* (DSM-IV-TR). Washington, DC: American Psychiatric Association.

Arean, P.A., Perri, M.G., Nezu, A.M., Schein, R.L., Christopher, F. & Joseph, T.X. (1993) Comparative effectiveness of social problem-solving therapy and reminiscence therapy as treatments for depression in older adults. *Journal of Consulting and Clinical Psychology*, **61**, 1003–1010.

Arean, P. & Gallagher-Thompson, D. (1996) Issues and recommendations for the recruitment and retention of older ethnic minority adults into clinical research. *Journal of Consulting and Clinical Psychology*, **64**, 875–880.

Atkins, C.J., Kaplan, R.M., Timms, R.M., Reinish, S. & Lofback, K. (1984) Behavioral exercise programs in the management of chronic obstructive pulmonary disease. *Journal of Consulting and Clinical Psychology*, **52**, 591–603.

Baltes, P.B. (1987) Theoretical propositions of lifespan developmental psychology: On the dynamics between growth and decline. *Developmental Psychology*, **23**, 611–626.

Baltes, P.B. (1991) The many faces of human aging: Toward a psychological culture of old age. *Psychological Medicine*, **21**, 837–854.

Baltes, P.B. & Smith, J. (2002) *New frontiers in the future of aging: From successful ageing of the young old to the dilemmas of the fourth age.* Paper presented at the Valencia Forum, Researchers, Educators and Providers contribution to the Second World Assembly on Ageing, Valencia, Spain.

Barber, J.P., Connolly, M.B., Crits-Christoph, P., Gladis, L. & Siqueland, L. (2000) Alliance predicts patients' outcome beyond in-treatment change in symptoms. *Journal of Consulting and Clinical Psychology*, **68**, 1027–1032.

Barker, A., Carter, C. & Jones, R. (1994) Memory performance, self-reported memory loss and depressive symptoms in attenders at a GP-referral and a self-referral memory clinic. *International Journal of Geriatric Psychiatry*, **9**, 305–311.

Basevitz, P., Pushkar, D., Conway, M. & Chaikelson, J. (2000) *Life reflections and worry in older adults.* Poster presented at the 53rd Annual Scientific Meeting of the Gerontological Society of America, Washington, DC.

Beck, A.T. (1983) Cognitive therapy of depression: New perspectives. In P.J. Clayton & J.E. Barrett (Eds), *Treatment of Depression: Old Controversies and New Approaches* (pp. 265–290). New York: Raven Press.

Beck, A.T. (1987) Cognitive models of depression. *Journal of Cognitive Psychotherapy: An International Quarterly*, **1**, 5–37.

Beck, A.T., Emery, G. & Greenberg, R.L. (1996) *Handbook of the Treatment of the Anxiety Disorders* (2nd edn). Northvale, NJ: Aronson.

Beck, A.T., Epstein, N., Brown, G.K. & Steer, R.A. (1988) An inventory for measuring clinical anxiety: Psychometric properties. *Journal of Consulting and Clinical Psychology*, **56**, 893–897.

Beck, A.T., Rush, A.J., Shaw, B.F. & Emery, G. (1979) *Cognitive Therapy of Depression.* New York: Guilford Press.

Beck, A.T., Steer, R.A. & Brown, G.K. (1996) *The Beck Depression Inventory—II.* San Antonio, TX: Psychological Corporation.

Beck, A.T., Ward, C.H., Mendelsohn, M., Mock, J. & Erbaugh, J. (1961) An inventory for measuring depression. *Archives of General Psychiatry*, **4**, 561–567.

Beck, A.T., Emery, G. & Greenberg, R.L. (1985) *Anxiety Disorders and Phobias: A Cognitive Perspective.* Basic Books: New York.

Beck, J.G. & Stanley, M.A. (1997) Anxiety disorders in the elderly: The emerging role of behavior therapy. *Behavior Therapy*, **28**, 83–100.

Beck, J.G., Stanley, M.A. & Zebb, B.J. (1999) Effectiveness of the Hamilton Anxiety Scale with older Generalized Anxiety Disorder. *Journal of Clinical Geropsychology*, **5**, 281–290.

Beck, J.S. (1995) *Cognitive Therapy: Basics and Beyond.* New York: Guilford Press.

Beekman, A.T., Copeland, J.R.M. & Prince, M.J. (1999) Review of community prevalence of depression in later life. *British Journal of Psychiatry*, **174**, 307–311.

Bengston, V.L. (2001) Beyond the nuclear family: The increasing importance of multigenerational bonds. *Journal of Marriage and the Family*, **63**, 1–16.

Bengston, V.L. & Boss, P. (2000) What living longer means to families. In NCFR (Eds), *Public Policy through a Family Lens: Sustaining Families in the 21st Century.* Minnesota: NCFR.

Bengston, V.L., Blblarz, T., Clarke, E., Giarusso, R., Roberts, R. & Richlin-Klonsky, J. (2000) Intergenerational relationships and aging: Families, cohorts, and social change. In J.M. Clair & R. Allman (Eds), *The Gerontological Prism: Developing Interdisciplinary Bridges.* New York: Baywood Publishing Co.

Bernstein, D.A. & Borkovec, T.D. (1973) *Progressive Relaxation Training: A Manual for the Helping Professions.* Champaign, IL: Research Press.

Berry, E. (1998) Post-traumatic stress disorder after subarachnoid haemorrhage. *British Journal of Clinical Psychology*, **37**, 365–367.

Beutler, L.E., Scogin, F., Kirkish, P., Schretlen, D., Corbishley, A., Hamblin, D., Meredith, K., Potter, R., Bamford, C.R. & Levenson, A.I. (1987) Group cognitive therapy and Alprazolam in the treatment of depression in older adults. *Journal of Consulting and Clinical Psychology*, **55**, 550–556.

Bisiach, E. (1992) Understanding consciousness: Clues from unilateral neglect and related disorders. In A.D. Milner & M.D. Rugg (Eds), *The Neuropsychology of Consciousness* (pp. 113–138). London: Academic Press Limited.

Bisiach, E., Vallar, G., Perani, D., Papagno, C. & Berti, A. (1986) Unawareness of disease following lesions of the right hemisphere: Anosognosia for hemiplegia and anosognosia for hemianopia. *Neuropsychologia*, **24**, 471–482.

Blanchard, M. (1992) The elderly. *International Review of Psychiatry*, **4** (3–4), 251–256.

Blazer, D. (1997) Generalized anxiety disorder and panic disorder in the elderly: A review. *Harvard Review of Psychiatry*, **5**, 18–27.

Blazer, D. (1998) *Emotional Problems in Later Life: Intervention Strategies for Professional Caregivers* (2nd edn). New York: Springer.

Blazer, D.G. (1994) Epidemiology. In J.R.M. Copeland, M.T. Abou-Saleh & D.G. Blazer (Eds), *Principles and Practice of Geriatric Psychiatry.* Chichester, UK: John Wiley & Sons.

Blazer, D.G. (1998) *Emotional Problems in Later Life: Intervention Strategies for Professional Caregivers.* New York: Springer Publishing.

Blazer, D.G. (2002) The prevalence of depressive symptoms. *Journals of Gerontology— Biological Sciences and Medical Sciences*, **57**, 155–161.

Bond, J.G.B., Smith, M., Rousseau, N., Lecouturier, J. & Rodgers, H. (1998) Outcomes following acute hospital care for stroke or hip fracture: How useful is an assessment of anxiety or depression for older people? *International Journal of Geriatric Psychiatry*, **13**, 601–610.

Bootzin, R.R., Epstein, D., Engle-Friedman, M. & Salvio, M. (1996) Sleep disturbances. In L. Carstensen, B. Edelstein & L. Dornbrand (Eds), *The Practical Handbook of Clinical Gerontology* (pp. 398–420). Thousand Oaks, CA: Sage Publications.

Bootzin, R.R., Epstein, D. & Wood, J.M. (1991) Stimulus control instructions. In P. Hauri (Ed.), *Case Studies in Insomnia* (pp. 19–28). New York, NY: Plenum Publishing Corp.

Borkovec, T.D. & Newman, D.G. (1999) Worry and generalized anxiety disorder. In P. Salkovskis (Ed.), *Comprehensive Clinical Psychology, Vol. 6: Adults: Clinical Formulation and Treatment.* Oxford, UK: Elsevier Press.

Borkovec, T.D. & Ruscio, A.M. (2001) Psychotherapy for generalized anxiety disorder. *Journal of Clinical Psychiatry*, **62**, 37–42.

Borkovec, T.D., Ray, W.J. & Stober, J. (1998) Worry: A cognitive phenomenon intimately linked to affective, physiological, and interpersonal behavioral process. *Behavioral Research and Therapy*, **22**, 561–576.

Brawman-Mintzer, O. (2001) Pharmacologic treatment of generalized anxiety disorder. *Psychiatric Clinics of North America*, **24**, 119–137.

Brokaw, T. (1998) *The Greatest Generation.* New York: Random House Publishing.

Brooks, D.J. (2000) Dopamine agonists: Their role in the treatment of Parkinson's disease. *Journal of Neurology, Neurosurgery and Psychiatry*, **68**, 685–689.

Brown, R. & Jahanshahi, M. (1995) Depression in Parkinson's disease: A psychosocial viewpoint. *Advances in Neurology*, **65**, 61–84.

Bryant, R.A. (2001) Post-traumatic stress disorder and traumatic brain injury: Can they co-exist? *Clinical Psychology Review*, **21**, 931–948.

Burns, D.D. (1980) *Feeling Good: The New Mood Therapy.* New York: Avon Books.

Burvill, P.W. & Hall, W.D. (1994) Predictors of increased mortality in elderly depressed patients. *International Journal of Geriatric Psychiatry*, **9**, 219–227.

Butler, G. & Hope, T. (1997) *Managing Your Mind: The Mental Fitness Guide*. Oxford, UK: Oxford University Press.

Butler, R.N., Lewis, M.I. & Sunderland, T. (1998) *Ageing and Mental Health* (5th edn). Boston: Allyn & Bacon.

Caine, E., Lyness, J. & Conwell, Y. (1996) Diagnosis of late life depression: Preliminary studies in primary care settings. *American Journal of Geriatric Psychiatry*, **4**, S45–S50.

Castleman, M., Gallagher-Thompson, D. & Naythons, M. (1999) *There's Still a Person in There: The Complete Guide to Treating and Coping with Alzheimer's*. New York: Putnam.

Chambless, D.L., Sanderson, W.C., Shoham, V., Johnson, S.B., Pope, K.S., Crits-Cristoph, P., Baker, M., Johnson, B., Woody, S.R., Sue, S., Beutler, L., Williams, D.A. & McCurry, S. (1996) An update on empirically validated therapies. *The Clinical Psychologist*, **49**, 5–18.

Champion, L.A. & Power, M.J. (1995) Social and cognitive approaches to depression: Towards a new synthesis. *British Journal of Clinical Psychology*, **34**, 485–503.

Chemerinski, E., Robinson, R.G. & Kosier, J.T. (2001) Improved recovery in activities of daily living associated with remission of post-stroke depression. *Stroke*, **32**, 113–117.

Church, M. (1983) Psychological therapy with elderly people. *Bulletin of the British Psychological Society*, **36**, 110–112.

Clark, D.M. (1986) A cognitive approach to panic. *Behaviour Research & Therapy*, **24**, 461–470.

Clark, D.M. (1989) Anxiety states: Panic and generalized anxiety. In K. Hawton, P. Salkovskis, J. Kirk & D.M. Clark (Eds), *Cognitive Behaviour Therapy for Psychiatric Problems: A Practical Guide*. Oxford: Oxford University Press.

Clark, D.M. (1999) Anxiety disorders: Why they persist and how to treat them. *Behaviour Research and Therapy*, **37**, S5–S27.

Clark, D.M. & Ehlers, A. (1993) An overview of the cognitive theory and treatment of panic disorder. *Applied and Preventive Psychology*, **2**, 131–139.

Clark, M.S. & Smith, D.S. (1998) The effects of depression and abnormal illness behaviour on outcome following rehabilitation from stroke. *Clinical Rehab*, **12**, 73–80.

Cohen-Cole, S.A. & Kaufman, K.G. (1993) Major depression in physical illness: Diagnosis, prevalence, and antidepressant treatment (a ten year review: 1982–1992). *Depression*, **1**, 181–204.

Cohen-Mansfield, J. (2001) Nonpharmacologic interventions for inappropriate behaviors in dementia: A review, summary, and critique. *American Journal of Geriatric Psychiatry*, **9**, 316–381.

Conwell, Y., Duberstein, P.R., Cox, C., Herrmann, J., Forbes, N. & Caine, E. (1996) Relationships of age and Axis I diagnoses in victims of completed suicide: A psychological autopsy study. *American Journal of Psychiatry*, **153**, 1001–1008.

Coon, D., Rider, K., Gallagher-Thompson, D. & Thompson, L. (1999) Cognitive-behavioral therapy for the treatment of late-life distress. In M. Duffy (Ed.), *Handbook of Counseling and Psychotherapy with Older Adults* (pp. 487–510). New York: John Wiley & Sons Ltd.

Coon, D., Thompson, L.W. & Gallagher-Thompson, D. (2002) *Intervention for Distressed Caregivers: From Research to Practice*. Springer Publishing Co.

Corey-Bloom, J., Wiederholt, W.C., Edelstein, S., Salmon, D.P., Cahn, D. & Barrett-Connor, E. (1996) Cognitive and functional status of the oldest old. *Journal of the American Geriatrics Society*, **44**, 671–674.

Crawford, M., Prince, M., Menezs, P. & Mann, A. (1998) The recognition and treatment of depression in older people in primary care. *International Journal of Geriatric Psychiatry*, **13**, 172–176.

Cuijpers, P. (1998) Psychological outreach programmes for the depressed elderly: A meta-analysis of effects and dropout. *International Journal of Geriatric Psychiatry*, **13**, 41–48.

Cummings, J.L. & Masterman, D.L. (1999) Depression in patients with Parkinson's disease. *International Journal of Geriatric Psychiatry*, **14**, 711–718.

Currie, S.R., Wilson, K.G., Pontefract, A.J. & deLaplante, L. (2000) Cognitive-behavioral treatment of insomnia secondary to chronic pain. *Journal of Consulting & Clinical Psychology*, **68** (3), 407–416.

Dada, F., Sethi, S. & Grossberg, G.T. (2001) Generalized anxiety disorder in the elderly. *Psychiatric Clinics of North America*, **24**, 155–164.

Davies, K.N., Burn, W.K., McKenzie, F.R., Bothwell, J.A. & Wattis, J.P. (1993) Evaluation of the Hospital Anxiety and Depression Scale as a screening instrument in geriatric medical inpatients. *International Journal of Geriatric Psychiatry*, **8**, 165–169.

Davies, R., Lacks, P., Storandt, M. & Bertelson, A.D. (1986) Counter-control treatment of sleep-maintenance insomnia in relation to age. *Psychology of Aging*, **1**, 233–238.

de Beurs, E., Beekman, A.T., Deeg, D.J., van Dyck, R. & van Tilburg, W. (2000) Predictors of change in anxiety symptoms of older persons: Results from the Longitudinal Aging Study Amsterdam. *Psychological Medicine*, **30**, 515–527.

de Beurs, E., Beekman, A.T., van Balkom, A.J., Deeg, D.J., van Dyck, R. & van Tilburg, W. (1999) Consequences of anxiety in older persons: Its effect on disability, well-being and use of health services. *Psychological Medicine*, **29**, 583–593.

Denman, C. (1995) What is the point of a formulation? In C. Mace (Ed.), *The Art and Science of Assessment in Psychotherapy*. London: Routledge.

DeRubeis, R.J. & Crits-Christoph, P. (1998) Empirically supported individual and group psychological treatment for adult mental disorders. *Journal of Consulting and Clinical Psychology*, **66**, 37–521.

Dick, L.P. & Gallagher-Thompson, D. (1995) Cognitive therapy with the core beliefs of a distressed lonely caregiver. *Journal of Cognitive Psychotherapy: An International Quarterly*, **9**, 215–227.

Dick, L.P., Gallagher-Thompson, D. & Thompson, L.W. (1996) Cognitive-behavioural therapy. In R.T. Woods (Ed.), *Handbook of the Clinical Psychology of Ageing*. Chichester, UK: John Wiley & Sons.

Draper, B. (1996) Attempted suicide in old age. *International Journal of Geriatric Psychiatry*, **11**, 577–587.

Dreisig, H., Beckmann, J., Wermuth, L., Skovlund, S. & Bech, P. (1999) Psychologic effects of structured cognitive psychotherapy in young patients with Parkinson disease: A pilot study. *Nordic Journal of Psychiatry*, **53**, 217–221.

Edinger, J.D., Wohlgemuth, W.K., Radtke, R.A., Marsh, G.R. & Quillian, R.E. (2001a) Cognitive behavioral therapy for treatment of chronic primary insomnia: A randomized controlled trial. *Journal of the American Medical Association*, **285** (14), 1856–1864.

Edinger, J.D., Wohlgemuth, W.K., Radtke, R.A., Marsh, G.R. & Quillian, R.E. (2001b) Does cognitive-behavioral insomnia therapy alter dysfunctional beliefs about sleep? *Sleep*, **24** (5), 591–599.

Edinger, J.D., Hoelscher, T.J., Marsh, G.R., Lipper, S. & Ionescu-Pioggia, M. (1992) A cognitive-behavioral therapy for sleep-maintenance insomnia in older adults. *Psychology and Aging*, **7** (2), 282–289.

Eells, T.D. (1997) Psychotherapy case formulation: History and current status. In T.D. Eells (Ed.), *Handbook of Psychotherapy Case Formulation*. New York: Guilford Press.

Eiser, N., West, C., Evans, S., Jeffers, A. & Quirk, F. (1997) Effects of psychotherapy in moderately severe COPD: A pilot study. *European Respiratory Journal*, **10**, 1581–1584.

Emery, G. (1981) Cognitive therapy with the elderly. In G. Emery, S. Hollon & R. Bedrosian (Eds), *New Directions in Cognitive Therapy* (pp. 84–98). New York: Guilford Press.

Engels, G.I. & Verney, M. (1997) Efficacy of nonmedical treatments of depression in elders: A quantitative analysis. *Journal of Clinical Geropsychology*, **3**, 17–35.

Engle-Friedman, M., Bootzin, R.R., Hazlewood, L. & Tsao, C. (1992) An evaluation of behavioral treatments for insomnia in the older adult. *Journal of Clinical Psychology*, **48**, 77–90.

Epsie, C.A., Inglis, S.J. & Harvey, L. (2001) Predicting clinically significant response to cognitive behavior therapy for chronic insomnia in general medical practice: Analyses of outcome data at 12 months posttreatment. *Journal of Consulting and Clinical Psychology*, **69** (1), 58–66.

Everson, S.A., Roberts, R.E., Goldberg, D.E. & Kaplan, G.E. (1998) Depressive symptoms and increased risk of stroke mortality over a 29 year period. *Archives of Internal Medicine*, **158**, 1133–1138.

Feibel, J.H., Berk, S. & Joynt, R.J. (1979) The unmet needs of stroke survivors. *Neurology*, **29**, 592–594.

Fennell, M.J.V. (1997) Low self-esteem: A cognitive perspective. *Behavioural and Cognitive Psychotherapy*, **25**, 1–25.

Flint, A.J. (1994) Epidemiology and comorbidity of anxiety disorders in the elderly. *American Journal of Psychiatry*, **151**, 640–649.

Flint, A.J. (1999) Anxiety disorders in late life. *Canadian Family Physicican*, **11**, 2672–2679.

Flint, A.J. & Rifat, S.L. (1996) Validation of the Hospital Anxiety and Depression Scale as a measure of severity of geriatric depression. *International Journal of Geriatric Psychiatry*, **11**, 991–994.

Freund, A.M. & Baltes, P.B. (1999) Selection, optimization, and compensation as strategies of life management: correlations with subjective indicators of successful aging. (Erratum appears in *Psychology & Aging*, **14**, 700–702). *Psychology & Aging*, **13**, 531–543.

Fry, P.S. (1984) Cognitive training and cognitive-behavioral variables in the treatment of depression in the elderly. *Clinical Gerontologist*, **3**, 25–45.

Fuentes, K. & Cox, B. (2000) Assessment of anxiety in older adults: A community-based survey and comparison with younger adults. *Behaviour Research and Therapy*, **38**, 297–309.

Futterman, A., Thompson, L.W., Gallagher-Thompson, D. & Ferris, R. (1995) Depression in later life: Epidemiology, assessment, etiology, and treatment. In E.E. Beckham & W.R. Leber (Eds), *Handbook of Depression* (2nd edn). New York: Guilford Press.

Gainotti, G., Antonucci, G., Marra, C. & Paolucci, S. (2001) Relation between depression after stroke, antidepressant therapy, and functional recovery. *Journal of Neurology, Neurosurgery and Psychiatry*, **71**, 258–261.

Gallagher, D.G. & Steffen, A. (1994) Comparative effects of cognitive/behavioral and brief psychodynamic psychotherapies for depressed family caregivers. *Journal of Consulting and Clinical Psychology*, **62**, 543–549.

Gallagher, D. & Thompson, L.W. (1981) *Depression in the Elderly: A Behavioral Treatment Manual*. Los Angeles: University of Southern California Press.

Gallagher, D. & Thompson, L.W. (1982) Treatment of major depressive disorder in older adult outpatients with brief psychotherapies. *Psychotherapy: Theory, Research, and Practice*, **19**, 482–490.

Gallagher, D. & Thompson, L.W. (1983) Effectiveness of psychotherapy for both endogenous and nonendogenous depression in older adults outpatients. *Journal of Gerontology: Psychological Sciences*, **38**, 707–712.

Gallagher-Thompson, D.E., Coon, D.W., Rivera, P., Powers, D. & Zeiss, A.M. (1998) Family caregiving: Stress, coping, and intervention. In M. Hersen & V.B. van Hasselt (Eds), *Handbook of Clinical Geropsychology. The Plenum Series in Adult Development and Aging* (pp. 469–493). New York, NY: Plenum Press.

Gallagher-Thompson, D., Hanley-Peterson, P. & Thompson, L.W. (1990) Maintenance of gains versus relapse following brief psychotherapy for depression. *Journal of Consulting and Clinical Psychology*, **58**, 371–374.

Gallagher-Thompson, D., Coon, D., Solano, N., Ambler, C., Rabinowitz, R. & Thompson, L.W. (in press). Change in indices of distress among Latina and Anglo female caregivers of elderly relatives with dementia: Site specific results from the REACH national collaborative study. *The Gerontologist*.

Gallagher-Thompson, D. & Osgood, N. (1997) Suicide in late life. *Behavior Therapy*, **28**, 23–41.

Gallagher-Thompson, D. & Steffen, A. (1994) Comparative effectives of cognitive-behavioral and brief psychodynamic psychotherapies for depressed family caregivers. *Journal of Consulting and Clinical Psychology*, **62**, 543–549.

Gallagher-Thompson, D. & Thompson, L.W. (1996) Applying cognitive-behavioral therapy to the psychological problems of later life. In S.H. Zarit & B.G. Knight (Eds), *A Guide to Psychotherapy and Aging: Effective Clinical Interventions in a Life-Stage Context*. Washington, DC: American Psychological Association.

Gallagher-Thompson, D., Arean, P., Rivera, P. & Thompson, L.W. (2001) A psychoeducational intervention to reduce distress in Hispanic family caregivers: Results of a pilot study. *Clinical Gerontologist*, **23**, 17–32.

Gallagher-Thompson, D., Lovett, A., Rose, J., McKibbin, C., Coon, D., Futterman, A. & Thompson, L.W. (2000) Impact of psychoeducational interventions on distressed family caregivers. *Journal of Clinical Geropsychology*, **6**, 91–110.

Gallagher-Thompson, D., Ossinalde, C. & Thompson, L.W. (1996a) *Coping with Caregiving: A Class for Family Caregivers*. Palo Alto, CA: VA Palo Alto Health Care System.

Gallagher-Thompson, D., Rose, J., Florsheim, M., Jacome, P., DelMaestro, S., Peters, L., Gantz, F., Arguello, D., Johnson, C., Mooreland, R.S., Polich, T.M., Chesney, M. & Thompson, L.W. (1992) *Controlling your Frustration: A Class for Caregivers*. Palo Alto, CA: VA Palo Alto Health Care System.

Gallo, J.J. & Rabins, P.V. (1999) Depression without sadness: Alternative presentations of depression in late life. *American Family Physician*, **60**, 820–826.

Gallo, J.J., Rabins, P.V., Lyketsos, C.G., Tien, A.Y. & Anthony, J.C. (1997) Depression without sadness: Functional outcomes of nondysphoric depression in later life. *Journal of the American Geriatrics Society*, **45**, 570–578.

Garety, P., Fowler, D., Kuipers, E., Freeman, D., Dunn, G., Bebbington, P., Hadley, C. & Jones, S. (1997) London–East Anglia randomised controlled trial of cognitive-behavioural therapy for psychosis. II: Predictors of outcome. *British Journal of Psychiatry*, **171**, 420–426.

Gatz, M. & Pearson, C.G. (1988) Ageism revised and the provision of psychological services. *American Psychologist*, **43**, 184–188.

Gatz, M., Fiske, A., Fox, L.S., Kaskie, B., Kasl-Godley, J.E. & McCullum, T.J. (1998) Empirically validated psychological treatments for older adults. *Journal of Mental Health and Aging*, **4**, 9–46.

Gauthier, A.H. & Smeeding, T.M. (2000) *Time Use at Older Ages: Cross National Differences*. New York: Organisation for Economic Cooperation and Development.

Gerson, S., Belin, T.R., Kaufman, M.S., Mintz, J. & Jarvik, L. (1999) Pharmacological and psychological treatments for depressed older patients: A meta-analysis and overview of recent findings. *Harvard Review of Psychiatry*, **7**, 1–28.

Gordon, W. & Hibbard, M.R. (1997) Post-stroke depression: An examination of the literature. *Archives Physical Medicine and Rehabilitation*, **78**, 658–653.

Gorenstein, E.E., Papp, L.A. & Kleber, M.S. (1999) Cognitive behavioral treatment of anxiety in late life. *Cognitive and Behavioral Practice*, **6**, 305–320.

Gotlib, I.H. & Hammen, C.L. (1992) *Psychological Aspects of Depression: Towards a Cognitive Interpersonal Integration*. Chichester: John Wiley & Sons Ltd.

Gould, R.A., Otto, M.W., Pollack, M.H. & Yap, L. (1997) Cognitive behavioral and pharmacological treatment of generalized anxiety disorder: A preliminary meta-analysis. *Behavior Therapy*, **28**, 285–305.

Gradman, T.J., Thompson, L.W. & Gallagher-Thompson, D. (1999) Personality disorders and treatment outcome. In E. Rosowsky, R. Abrams & R. Zweig (Eds), *Personality Disorders in Older Adults* (pp. 69–94). New Jersey: Lawrence Erlbaum.

Grant, R.W. & Casey, D.A. (1995) Adapting cognitive behavioral therapy for the frail elderly. *International Psychogeriatrics*, **7**, 561–571.

Greenberger, D. & Padesky, C.A. (1995) *Manage your Mood*. New York: Guilford Press.

Gurland, B.J., Teresi, J., Smith, W.M., Black, D., Hughes, G. & Edlavitch, S. (1988) Effects of treatment for isolated systolic hypertension on cognitive status and depression in the elderly. *Journal of the American Geriatrics Society*, **36**, 1015–1022.

Haley, W.E. (1983) A family-behavioral approach to the treatment of the cognitively impaired elderly. *Gerontologist*, **23**, 18–20.

Haley, W.E. (1996) The medical context of psychotherapy with the elderly. In B.G. Knight & S.H. Zarit (Eds), *A Guide to Psychotherapy and Aging: Effective Clinical Interventions in a Life-Stage Context*. Washington, DC: American Psychological Association.

Hall, M., Buysse, D.J., Nowell, P.D., Nofzinger, E.A., Houck, P., Reynolds, C.F. III & Kupfer, D.J. (2000) Symptoms of stress and depression as correlates of sleep in primary insomnia. *Psychosomatic Medicine*, **62** (2), 227–230.

Hamilton, M. (1959) The assessment of anxiety states by rating. *British Journal of Medical Psychology*, **32**, 50–55.

Hamilton, M. (1960) A rating scale for depression. *Journal of Neurology, Neurosurgery and Psychiatry*, **23**, 56–62.

Haythornthwaite, J.A., Hegel, M.T. & Kerns, R.D. (1991) Development of a sleep diary for chronic pain patients. *Journal of Pain and Symptom Management*, **6**, 65–72.

Help the Aged (2000) *Background Briefings: The older population*. Online at www.helptheaged.org.uk.

HelpAge International (2002) *State of the World's Older People 2002*. London: HelpAge International.

Hepple, J. & Quinton, C. (1997) One hundred cases of attempted suicide in the elderly. *British Journal of Psychiatry; the Journal of Mental Science*, **171**, 42–46.

Hersen, M., van Hesselt, V.B. & Goreczny, A.J. (1993) Behavioral assessment of anxiety in older adults. *Behavioral Modification*, **17**, 99–112.

Hibbard, M.R.G., Grober, S.E., Gordon, W., Aletta, E.G. & Freeman, A. (1990) Cognitive therapy and the treatment of post-stroke depression. *Topics in Geriatric Rehabilitation*, **5**, 43–55.

Hopko, D.R., Bourland, S.L., Stanley, M.A., Beck, J.G., Novy, D.M., Averill, P.M. & Swann, A.C. (2000) Generalized anxiety disorder in older adults: Examining the relation between clinician severity ratings and patient self-report measures. *Depression and Anxiety*, **12**, 217–225.

Horowitz, M., Wilner, N. & Alvarez, W. (1979) Impact of event scale: A measure of subjective stress. *Psychosomatic Medicine*, **41**, 309–318.

Horvath, A.O. & Luborsky, L. (1993) The role of the therapeutic alliance in psychotherapy. *Journal of Consulting and Clinical Psychology*, **61**, 561–573.

House, A. (1987) Mood disorders after stroke: A review of the evidence. *International Journal of Geriatric Psychiatry*, **2**, 211–221.

Jacobsen, N.S. (1989) The therapist–client relationship in cognitive-behavioral therapy: Implications for treatment depression. *Journal of Cognitive Psychotherapy*, **3**, 85–96.

James, J.W. & Haley, W.E. (1995) Age and health bias in practicing clinical psychologists. *Psychology and Aging*, **10**, 610–616.

Jarvik, L.F., Mintz, J., Steuer, J. & Gerner, R. (1982) Treating geriatric depression: A 26-week interim analysis. *Journal of the American Geriatrics Society*, **30**, 713–717.

Kaplan, C.P. & Gallagher-Thompson, D. (1995) Treatment of clinical depression in caregivers of spouses with dementia. *Journal of Cognitive Psychotherapy: An International Quarterly*, **9**, 35–44.

Karel, M.J. & Hinrichsen, G. (2000) Treatment of depression in late life: Psychotherapeutic interventions. *Clinical Psychology Review*, **20**, 707–729.

Karel, M.J., Ogland-Hand, S., Gatz, M. & Unuetzer, J. (2002) *Assessing and Treating Late-Life Depression: A Casebook and Resource Guide.* New York, NY: Basic Books, Inc.

Kaszniak, A.W. & Scogin, F.R. (1995) Assessing for dementia and depression in older adults. *The Clinical Psychologist*, **48** (2), 17–24.

Katona, C., Manela, M.V. & Livingston, G. (1997) Comorbidity with depression in older people: The Islington study. *Ageing & Mental Health*, **1**, 57–61.

Katz, I.R., Lesher, E., Kleban, M., Jethanandani, V. & Parmalee, P. (1989) Clinical features of depression in the nursing home. *International Psychogeriatrics*, **1**, 5–15.

Kemp, B.J., Corgiat, M. & Gill, C. (1991/2) Effects of brief cognitive-behavioral group psychotherapy on older persons with and without disabling illness. *Behavior, Health, and Aging*, **2**, 21–28.

Kenn, C., Wood, H., Kucyj, M., Wattis, J. & Cunane, J. (1987) Validation of the Hospital Anxiety and Depression Rating Scale (HADS) in an elderly psychiatric population. *International Journal of Geriatric Psychiatry*, **2**, 189–193.

King, P. & Barrowclough, C. (1991) A clinical pilot study of cognitive-behavioural therapy for anxiety disorders in the elderly. *Behavioral Psychotherapy*, **19**, 337–345.

Kinsella, K. & Velkoff, V.A. (2001) US Census Bureau, Series P95/01-1, *An Aging World*. Washington, DC: US Government Printing Office.

Kirby, M., Denihan, A., Bruce, I., Radic, A., Croakley, D. & Lawlor, B. (1999) Benzodiazepine use among the elderly in the community. *International Journal of Geriatric Psychiatry*, **14**, 280–284.

Kishi, Y., Robinson, R.G. & Kosier, J.T. (1996) Suicidal plans in patients with stroke: comparison between acute-onset and delayed-onset suicidal plans. *International Psychogeriatrics*, **8**, 623–634.

Kitano, H.H.L. & Maki, M.T. (1996) Continuity, change, and diversity: Counseling Asian Americans. In P.B. Pedersen & J.G. Draguns (Eds), *Counseling Across Cultures* (4th edn). Thousand Oaks, CA: Sage Publications, Inc.

Kneebone, I. & Dunsmore, E. (2000) Psychological management of post-stroke depression. *British Journal of Clinical Psychology*, **39**, 53–65.

Knight, B.G. (1996a) *Psychotherapy with older adults* (2nd edn). London, UK: Sage Publications.

Knight, B.G. (1996b) Overview of psychotherapy with the elderly: The contextual, cohort-based, maturing-specific-challenge model. In S.H. Zarit & B.G. Knight (Eds), *A Guide to Psychotherapy and Aging: Effective Clinical Interventions in a Life-Stage Context.* Washington, DC: American Psychological Association.

Knight, B.G. (1999) Scientific bias for psychotherapeutic interventions with older adults: An overview. *Journal of Clinical Psychology*, **55**, 927–934.

Knight, B.G. & McCallum, T.J. (1998) Adapting psychotherapeutic practice for older clients: Implications of the contextual, cohort-based, maturity, specific challenge model. *Professional Psychology: Research and Practice*, **29**, 15–22.

Knight, B.G. & Satre, D.D. (1999) Cognitive behavioral psychotherapy with older adults. *Clinical Psychology*, **6**, 188–203.

Koder, D.A., Brodaty, H. & Anstey, K.J. (1996) Cognitive therapy for depression in the elderly. *International Journal of Geriatric Psychiatry*, **11**, 97–107.

Kogan, J.N., Edelstein, B.A. & McKee, D.R. (2000) Anxiety in older adults: Current status. *Journal of Anxiety Disorders*, **14**, 109–132.

Kovacs, M. & Beck, A.T. (1978) Maladaptive cognitive structures in depression. *American Journal of Psychiatry*, **135**, 525–533.

Kramer, A.M., Fox, P.D. & Morgenstern, N. (1992) Geriatric care approaches in health maintenance organizations. *Journal of the American Geriatrics Society*, **40**, 1055–1067.

Kuipers, E., Garety, P., Fowler, D., Dunn, G., Bebbington P., Freeman, D. & Hadley, C. (1997) London–East Anglia randomised controlled trial of cognitive-behavioural therapy for psychosis. I: Effects of the treatment phase. *British Journal of Psychiatry*, **171**, 319–327.

Kuipers, E., Fowler, D., Garety, P., Chisholm, D., Freeman, D., Dunn, G., Bebbington, P. & Hadley, C. (1998) London–East Anglia randomised controlled trial of cognitive-behavioural therapy for psychosis. III: Follow-up and economic evaluation at 18 months. *British Journal of Psychiatry*, **173**, 61–68.

Kunik, M.E., Braun, U., Stanley, M.A., Wristers, K., Molinari, V., Stoebner, D. & Orgengo, C.A. (2001) One session cognitive behavioural therapy for elderly patients with chronic obstructive pulmonary disease. *Psychological Medicine*, **31**, 717–723.

Laidlaw, K. (2002) Depression in older adults. In M.J. Power (Ed.), *Mood Disorders: A Handbook of Science and Practice*. Chichester: John Wiley & Sons.

Laidlaw, K. (2003) Impact of mental health and illness on successful ageing. In Kovacs, M. (Ed.), *Late Life Depression and Anxiety*. Budapest: Springer.

Laidlaw, K. (in press) Depression in older adults. In Power, M.J. (Ed.), *Mood Disorders: A Handbook of Science and Practice*. Chichester: John Wiley & Sons, Ltd.

Laidlaw, K. & Bailey, S. (1997) Psychology out-patient treatment satisfaction and investigation into premature therapeutic termination. *British Psychological Society Annual Conference*, Edinburgh, 3–6 April 1997.

Laidlaw, K. (2001) An empirical review of cognitive therapy for late life depression: Does research evidence suggest adaptations are necessary for cognitive therapy with older adults? *Clinical Psychology & Psychotherapy*, **8**, 1–14.

Laidlaw, K. & Thomson, A.S. (1999) *Psychological consequences of stroke: The management of depression and anxiety following stroke*. Paper presented at the Stanford University Medical School Veterans Affairs Palo Alto Health Care System, Palo Alto, CA, USA.

Landreville, P., Landry, J., Baillargeon, L., Guerette, A. & Matteau, E. (2001) Older adults' acceptance of psychological and pharmacological treatments for depression. *Journal of Gerontology; Psychological Sciences*, **50B**, 285–291.

Lau, A.W., Edelstein, B.A. & Larkin, K.T. (2001) Psychophysiological arousal in older adults: A critical review. *Clinical Psychology Review*, **21**, 609–630.

Lawton, M.P. & Teresi, J.A. (1994) *Annual Review of Gerontology and Geriatrics: Focus on Assessment Techniques* (Vol. 14). New York, NY: Springer Publishing Co., Inc.

Lebowitz, B.D. & Niederehe, G. (1992) Concepts and issues in mental health and aging. In J.E. Birren, R.B. Sloane & G.D. Cohen (Eds), *Handbook of Mental Health and Aging* (2nd edn). San Diego: Academic Press.

Lebowitz, B.D., Pearson, J.L., Schneider, L.S., Reynolds, C.F., Alexopoulos, G.S. & Bruce, M.L. (1997) Diagnosis and treatment of depression in late life: Consensus statement update. *Journal of American Medical Association*, **278**, 1186–1190.

Lenze, E.J., Mulsant, B.H., Shear, M.K., Alexopoulos, G.S., Frank, E. & Reynolds, C.F. (2001) Comorbidity of depression and anxiety disorders in later life. *Depression and Anxiety*, **14**, 86–93.

Leung, S.N. & Orrell, M.W. (1993) A brief cognitive behavioural therapy group for the elderly: Who benefits? *International Journal of Geriatric Psychiatry*, **8**, 593–598.

Lewinsohn, P.M. & Gotlib, I.H. (1995) Behavioral theory and treatment of depression. In E.E. Beckham & W. Leber (Eds), *Handbook of Depression* (2nd edn). New York: Guilford Press.

Lewinsohn, P.M. & Hoberman, H.M. (1982) Behavioural and cognitive approaches to treatment. In E.G. Paykel (Ed.), *Handbook of Affective Disorders*. Edinburgh: Churchill-Livingstone.

Lewinsohn, P.M., Hoberman, H., Teri, L. & Hautzinger, M. (1985) An integrative theory of depression. In S.B. Reiss (Ed.), *Theoretical Issues in Behaviour Therapy*. San Diego: Academic Press Inc.

Lewinsohn, P.M., Munoz, R.F., Youngren, M.A. & Zeiss, A.M. (1986) *Control your Depression. Revised and Updated*. New York: Prentice Hall.

Lewinsohn, P.M., Sullivan, J.M. & Grosscup, S.J. (1980) Changing reinforcing events: An approach to the treatment of depression. *Psychotherapy: Theory, Research and Practice*, **17**, 322–324.

Lichstein, K.L. & Morin, C.M. (Eds) (2000) *Treatment of Late-Life Insomnia*. Thousand Oaks, CA: Sage.

Lichstein, K.L. & Fischer, S.M. (1985) Insomnia. In M. Hersen & A.S. Bellack (Eds), *Handbook of Clinical Behavior Therapy with Adults* (pp. 319–352). New York: Plenum Press.

Lichstein, K.L. & Johnson, R.S. (1993) Relaxation for insomnia and hypnotic use in older women. *Psychology of Aging*, **8**, 103–111.

Lichstein, K.L. & Morin, C.M. (2000) Treatment overview. In K.L. Lichstein & C.M. Morin (Eds), *Treatment of Late-Life Insomnia* (pp. 111–124). Thousand Oaks: Sage Publications.

Lichstein, K.L., Wilson, N.M. & Johnson, C.T. (2000) Psychological treatment of secondary insomnia. *Psychology and Aging*, **15** (2), 232–240.

Lichtenberg, P.A. (1999) Psychotherapy in geriatric long-term care. *Journal of Clinical Psychology*, **55**, 1005–1014.

Lincoln, N.B., Flanagan, T., Sutcliffe, L. & Rother, L. (1997) Evaluation of cognitive behavioural treatment for depression after stroke: A pilot study. *Clinical Rehabilitation*, **11**, 114–122.

Lindesay, J. (1991) Phobic disorders in the elderly. *British Journal of Psychiatry*, **159**, 531–541.

Lindesay, J., Brigs, K. & Murphy, E. (1989) The Guys/Age concern survey: Prevalence rates of cognitive impairment, depression and anxiety in an urban elderly community. *British Journal of Psychiatry*, **155**, 317–329.

Lisanky, D.P. & Clough, D.H. (1996) A cognitive-behavioral self-help educational program for patients with COPD: A pilot study. *Psychotherapy & Psychosomatics*, **65**, 97–101.

Livingston, G., Hawkins, A., Graham, N., Blizard, B. & Mann, A. (1990) The Gospel Oak study: Prevalence rates of dementia, depression, and activity limitation among elderly residents in inner London. *Psychological Medicine*, **20**, 137–146.

Lovestone, S. (1983) Cognitive therapy with the elderly depressed: A rational and efficacious approach? In R. Levy & A. Burns (Eds), *Treatment and Care in Old Age Psychiatry*. New York: Biomedical Publishing Inc.

Lovett, S. & Gallagher, D. (1988) Psychoeducational interventions for family caregivers: Preliminary efficacy data. *Behavior Therapy*, **19**, 321–330.

MacCarthy, B. & Brown, R. (1989) Psychosocial factors in Parkinson's disease. *British Journal of Clinical Psychology*, **28**, 41–52.

Madan, S. & Bodagh, I.Y.O. (2002) Dedicated to elderly care: Geriatric medicine on the internet. *Age & Ageing*, **31**, 70–74.

Manyam, B.V. (1997) Practical guidelines for management of Parkinson disease. *Journal of the American Board of Family Practice*, **10**, 412–424.

McKay, M., Davis, M. & Fanning, P. (1997) *Taking Control of your Moods and your Life: A Thoughts and Feelings Workbook*. New York: MJF Books.

Mellinger, G.D., Balter, M.B. & Uhlenhuth, E.H. (1985) Insomnia and its treatment: Prevalence and correlates. *Archives of General Psychiatry*, **42**, 225–232.

Meyer, T.J., Miller, M.L., Metzger, R.L. & Borkovec, T.D. (1990) Development and validation of the Penn State Worry Questionnaire. *Behaviour Research and Therapy*, **28**, 487–495.

Midwinter, E. (1991) *Attitudes to Ageing*. Reading, UK: British Gas Reports.

Miles, L.E. & Dement, W.C. (1980) Sleep and aging. *Sleep*, **3**, 119–120.

Miles, Toni P. (1999) Living with chronic disease and the policies that bind. In Toni P. Miles (Ed.), *Full-color Aging: Facts, Goals, and Recommendation for America's Diverse Elders* (pp. 53–63). Washington, D.C.: Gerontological Society of America.

Miranda, J. & Persons, J.B. (1988) Dysfunctional attitudes are mood-state dependent. *Journal of Abnormal Psychology*, **97**, 76–79.

Miranda, J., Persons, J.B. & Nix Byers, C. (1990) Endorsement of dysfunctional beliefs depend on current mood state. *Journal of Abnormal Psychology*, **99**, 237–241.

Morales, P. (1999) The impact of cultural differences in psychotherapy with older clients: Sensitive issues and strategies. In M. Duffy (Ed.), *Handbook of Counseling and Psychotherapy with Older Adults* (pp. 132–153). New York, NY: John Wiley & Sons Inc.

Morin, C.M. & Azrin, N.H. (1988) Behavioral and cognitive treatments of geriatric insomnia. *Journal of Consulting and Clinical Psychology*, **56** (5), 748–753.

Morin, C.M. (1993) *Insomnia: Psychological Assessment and Management*. New York, NY: Guilford Press.

Morin, C.M., Colecchi, C., Stone, J., Sood, R. & Brink, D. (1999a) Behavioral and pharmacological therapies for late-life insomnia. *Journal of the American Medical Association*, **281**, 991–999.

Morin, C.M., Culbert, J.P. & Schwartz, S.M. (1994) Nonpharmacological interventions for insomnia: A meta-analysis of treatment efficacy. *American Journal of Psychiatry*, **151**, 1172–1180.

Morin, C.M., Hauri P.J., Espie, C.A., Spielman, A.J., Buysse, D.J. & Bootzin, R.R. (1999b) Nonpharmacologic treatment of chronic insomnia. *Sleep*, **22**, 1134–1156.

Morin, C.M., Kowatch, R.A., Barry, T. & Walton, E. (1993) Cognitive-behavior therapy for late-life insomnia. *Journal of Consulting and Clinical Psychology*, **61**, 137–147.

Morin, C.M., Stone, J., Trinkle, D., Mercer, J. & Remsberg, S. (1993) Dysfunctional beliefs and attitudes about sleep among older adults with and without insomnia complaints. *Psychology and Aging*, **8** (3), 463–467.

Morris, P.L., Robinson, R.G., Andrzejewski, P., Samuels, J. & Price, T.R. (1993) Association of depression with 10-year post-stroke mortality. *American Journal of Psychiatry*, **150**, 124–129.

Morris, R.G. & Morris, L.W. (1991) Cognitive and behavioural approaches with the depressed elderly. *International Journal of Geriatric Psychiatry*, **6**, 407–413.

Muran, J.C., Samstag, L.J., Ventur, E.D., Segal, Z.V. & Winston, A. (2001) A cognitive-interpersonal case study of a self. *Journal of Clinical Psychology*, **57**, 307–330.

Nicholson, A.N. (1994) Hypnotics: clinical pharmacology and therapeutics. In M.H. Kryger, T. Roth & W.C. Dement (Eds), *Principles and Practice of Sleep Medicine* (2nd edn, pp. 355–363). Philadelphia: W.B. Saunders.

NIH (1991) *Diagnosis and Treatment of Depression in Later Life*. National Institute of Health Consensus Statement.

NINDS (2002) *Stroke: Hope Through Research*. Washington, DC: National Institute of Neurological Disorders and Stroke.

O'Carroll, P.W. (1989) A consideration of the validity and reliability of suicide mortality data. *Suicide and Life Threatening Behavior*, **19**, 1–16.

Olfson, M., Marcus, S.C., Druss, B., Elinson, L., Tanielian, T. & Pincus, H.A. (2002) National trends in the outpatient treatment of depression. *Journal of the American Medical Association*, **287**, 203–209.

ONS (2000) Social Trends, No. 30. London: The Stationery Office.

ONS (2001) Social Trends, No. 31. London: The Stationery Office.

ONS (2002) Social Trends, No. 32. London: The Stationery Office.

Organista, K.C. (2000) Latinos. In J.R. White & A.S. Freeman (Eds), *Cognitive-Behavioral Group Therapy: For Specific Problems and Populations*. Washington, DC: American Psychological Association.

Ounsworth, T.L. & Oei, T.P. (1998) Depression after traumatic brain injury: Conceptualization and treatment considerations. *Brain Injury*, **12**, 735–751.

Pachana, N.A., Gallagher-Thompson, D. & Thompson, L.W. (1994) Assessment of depression. In M.P. Lawton & J.A. Teresi (Eds), *Annual Review of Gerontology and Geriatrics: Focus on Assessment Techniques*. New York, NY: Springer Publishing Co., Inc.

Padesky, C.A. (1998) *Protocols and personalities: The therapist in cognitive therapy*. Keynote address at the European Association for Behavioural and Cognitive Therapies (EABCT), Annual Conference, Cork, Ireland.

Padesky, C.A. (1993a) *Socratic questioning: Changing minds or guided discovery?* Paper presented at the European Congress of Behavioural and Cognitive Therapies, London.

Padesky, C.A. (1993b) Schema as self-prejudice. *International Cognitive Therapy Newsletter*, **5/6**, 16–17.

Padesky, C.A. (1994) Schema change processes in cognitive therapy. *Clinical Psychology and Psychotherapy: An International Journal of Theory and Practice*, **1**, 267–278.

Padesky, C.A. & Greenberger, D. (1995) *Mind over Mood*. New York: Guilford Press.

Parrott, T.M., Mills, T.L. & Bengston, V.L. (2000) The United States: Population demographics, changes in the family, and social policy challenges. In V.L. Bengston, K.D. Kim, G.C. Myers & K.S. Eun (Eds), *Aging in the East and West: Families, States, and the Elderly*. New York: Springer.

Pearson, J.L. (1998) Research in late life anxiety: Summary of a National Institute of Mental Health workshop on late life anxiety. *Psychopharmacology Bulletin*, **34**, 127–138.

Pentland, B. (1999) The nature and course of Parkinson's disease. In R.H. Percival (Ed.), *Parkinson's disease: Studies in Psychological and Social Care* (pp. 1–13). Leicester: British Psychological Society.

Persons, J.B. (1991) Psychotherapy outcome studies do not accurately represent current models of psychotherapy. *American Psychologist*, **46**, 99–106.

Persons, J.B. (1989) *Cognitive Therapy in Practice: A Case Formulation Approach*. New York: W.W. Norton & Co.

Persons, J.B. (1993) Case conceptualization in cognitive-behavioral therapy. In K. Kuehlwein & H. Rosen (Eds), *Cognitive Therapy in Action: Evolving Innovative Practice*. San Francisco: Josey-Bass.

Persons, J.B. (1995) Why practicing psychologists are slow to adopt empirically-validated treatments. In S.C. Hayes & V.M. Follette (Eds), *Scientific Standards of Psychological Practice: Issues and Recommendations*. Reno, NV: Context Press.

Persons, J.B. & Miranda, J. (1991) Treating dysfunctional beliefs: Implications of the mood-state hypothesis. *Journal of Cognitive Psychotherapy: An International Quarterly*, **5**, 15–25.

Persons, J.B. & Miranda, J. (1992) Cognitive theories of vulnerability to depression: Reconciling negative evidence. *Cognitive Therapy and Research*, **16**, 485–502.

Persons, J.B. & Tompkins, M.A. (1997) Cognitive-behavioral case formulation. In T.D. Eells (Ed.), *Handbook of Psychotherapy Case Formulation*. New York, NY: The Guilford Press.

Poewe, W. & Euginger, E. (1999) Depression in Parkinson's disease: Impediments to recognition and treatment options. *Neurology*, **52**, S2–S6.

Powell, D.H. (1998) *The Nine Myths of Aging: Maximizing the Quality of Later Life*. New York: W.H. Freeman & Co.

Powers, D.V., Thompson, L.W., Futterman, A. & Gallagher-Thompson, D. (2002) Depression in later life: Epidemiology, assessment, impact and treatment. In I.H. Gotlib & C.L. Hammen (Eds), *Handbook of Depression* (pp. 560–580). New York: Guilford Press.

Puder, R., Lacks, P., Bertelson, A.D. & Storandt, M. (1983) Short-term stimulus control treatment of insomnia in older adults. *Behavior Therapy*, **14** (3), 424–429.

Radloff, L.S. (1977) The CES-D Scale: A self-report depression scale for research in the general population. *Applied Psychological Measurement*, **1**, 385–401.

Raskin, A. & Niederehe, G. (1988) Assessment in diagnosis and treatment of geropsychiatric patients. *Psychopharmacology Bulletin, Special Feature*, **24**, 501–828.

Regier, D.A., Boyd, J.H., Burke, J.D. & Rae, D.S. (1988) One-month prevalence of mental disorders in the United States: Based on five epidemiologic catchment area sites. *Archives of General Psychiatry*, **45**, 977–986.

Rehm, L.P. (1977) A self-control model of depression. *Behavior Therapy*, **8**, 787–804.

Reidel, B.W. & Lichstein, K.L. (2000) Insomnia in older adults. In S.K. Whitbourne (Ed.), *Psychopathology in Later Adulthood* (pp. 299–322). New York: John Wiley & Sons Inc.

Robinson, L.A., Berman, J.S. & Neimeyer, R.A. (1990) Psychotherapy for the treatment of depression: A comprehensive review of controlled outcome research. *Psychological Bulletin*, **108**, 30–49.

Robinson, R.G. (1998) Treatment issues in post-stroke depression. *Depression and Anxiety*, **8**, 85–90.

Robinson, R.G., Murata, Y. & Shimoda, K. (1999) Dimensions of social impairment and their effect on depression and recovery following stroke. *International Psychogeriatrics*, **11**, 375–384.

Rogers, A.E., Caruso, C.C. & Aldrich, M.S. (1993) Reliability of sleep diaries for assessment of sleep/wake patterns. *Nursing Research*, **42** (6), 368–372.

Rokke, P.D. & Scogin, F. (1995) Depression treatment preferences in younger and older adults. *Journal of Clinical Geropsychology*, **1**, 243–258.

Rokke, P.D., Tomhave, J.A. & Jocic, Z. (2000) Self-management therapy and educational group therapy for depressed elders. *Cognitive Therapy and Research*, **24**, 99–119.

Roose, S.P., Glassman, A.H. & Seidman, S.N. (2001) Relationship between depression and other medical illnesses. *JAMA*, **286**, 1687–1690.

Rowe, J.W. & Kahn, R.L. (1998) *Successful Aging*. New York: Pantheon Books.

Safran, J.D. & Muran, J.C. (1996) The resolution of ruptures in the therapeutic alliance. *Journal of Consulting and Clinical Psychology*, **64**, 447–458.

Safran, J.D. & Segal, Z.V. (1996) *Interpersonal Process in Cognitive Therapy*. Northvale, NJ: Jason Aronson, Inc.

Safran, J.D., Segal, Z.V., Hill, C. & Whiffen, V. (1990) Refining strategies for research on self-representations in emotional disorders. *Cognitive Therapy and Research*, **14**, 143–160.

Sahyoun, N.R., Lentzner, H., Hoyert, D. & Robinson, K.N. (2001) Trends in causes of death among the elderly. *Aging Trends, No. 1*. Hyattsville, MD: National Center for Health Statistics.

Schaub, R.T. & Linden, M. (2000) Anxiety and anxiety disorders in the old and very old—Results from the Berlin Aging Study (BASE). *Comprehensive Psychiatry*, **41**, 48–54.

Schrag, A., Jahanshahi, M. & Quinn, N.P. (2001) What contributes to depression in Parkinson's disease? *Psychological Medicine*, **31**, 65–73.

Schulberg, H.C. & McClelland, M. (1987) Depression and physical illness: The prevalence, causation and diagnosis of comorbidity. *Clinical Psychology Review*, **7**, 145–167.

Schwab, M., Roder, F., Aleker, T., Ammon, S., Thon, K. & Eichelbaum, M. (2000) Psychotropic drug use, falls and hip fracture in the elderly. *Aging*, **12**, 234–239.

Scogin, F. & McElreath, L. (1994) Efficacy of psychosocial treatments for geriatric depression: A quantitative review. *Journal of Consulting and Clinical Psychology*, **62**, 69–74.

Segal, Z.V. & Ingram, R.E. (1994) Mood priming and construct activation in tests of cognitive vulnerability to unipolar depression. *Clinical Psychology Review*, **14**, 663–695.

Sembi, S., Tarrier, N., O'Neill, P., Burns, A. & Faragher, B. (1998) Does post-traumatic stress disorder occur after stroke: A preliminary study. *International Journal of Geriatric Psychiatry*, **13**, 355–362.

Shalev, A.Y., Schreiber, S., Galai, T. & McImed, R. (1993) Post-traumatic stress disorder following medical events. *British Journal of Clinical Psychology*, **32**, 247–253.

Shapiro, A.M., Roberts, J.E. & Beck, J.G. (1999) Differentiating symptoms of anxiety and depression in older adults: Distinct cognitive and affective profiles? *Cognitive Therapy and Research*, **23**, 53–74.

Sharpe, M., Hawton, K., House, A., Molyneux, A., Sandercock, P., Bamford, J. & Warlow, C. (1990) Mood disorders in long term survivors of stroke: Associations with brain lesion location and volume. *Psychological Medicine*, **20**, 815–828.

Sheikh, J. & Cassidy, E. (2000) Treatment of anxiety disorders in the elderly: Issues and strategies. *Journal of Anxiety Disorders*, **14**, 173–190.

Sherer, M., Madison, C.F. & Hannay, H.J. (2000) A review of outcome after moderate and severe closed head injury with an introduction to life care planning. *Journal of Head Trauma Rehabilitation*, **15**, 767–782.

Silverstein, M. & Bengston, V. (2001) Intergenerational solidarity and the structure of adult child–parent relationships in American families. In A. Walker (Ed.), *Families in Later Life: Connections and Transitions*. Thousand Oaks, CA: Pine Forge Press.

Sinoff, G., Ore, L., Zlotogorosky, D. & Tamir, A. (1999) Short anxiety screening test: A brief instrument for detecting anxiety in the elderly. *International Journal of Geriatric Psychiatry*, **14**, 1062–1071.

Small, G.W. (1997) Recognizing and treating anxiety in the elderly. *Journal of Clinical Psychiatry*, **58** (Suppl 3), 41–50.

Smyer, M.A. & Qualls, S.H. (1999) *Aging and Mental Health*. Oxford, UK: Blackwell Publishers.

Speilberger, C.D., Gorsuch, R.C., Lushene, R.E., Vagg, P.R. & Jacobs, G.A. (1983) *Manual for the State-Trait Anxiety Inventory*. Palo Alto, CA: Consulting Psychologists Press.

Spielman, A.J. & Glovinsky, P.B. (1991) The varied nature of insomnia. In P.J. Hauri (Ed.), *Case Studies in Insomnia* (pp. 1–15). New York: Plenum.

Spielman, A.J., Saskin, P. & Thorpy, M.J. (1987) Treatment of chronic insomnia by restriction of time in bed. *Sleep*, **10**, 45–55.

Spreen, O. & Strauss, E. (1998) *A Compendium of Neuropsychological Tests: Administration, Norms, and Commentary*. New York: Oxford University Press.

Stanley, M.A., Beck, J.G. & Zebb, B.J. (1996) Psychometric properties of four anxiety measures in older adults. *Behaviour Research and Therapy*, **34**, 827–838.

Stanley, M.A. & Averill, P.M. (1999) Strategies for treating generalized anxiety in the elderly. In. M. Duffy (Ed.), *Handbook of Counseling and Psychotherapy with Older Adults* (pp. 511–525). New York: John Wiley & Sons.

Stanley, M.A. & Beck, J.G. (2000) Anxiety disorders. *Clinical Psychology Review*, **20**, 731–754.

Stanley, M.A. & Novy, D.M. (2000) Cognitive-behavior therapy for generalized anxiety in late life: An evaluative overview. *Journal of Anxiety Disorders*, **14**, 191–207.

Stanley, M.A., Beck, J.G. & Glassco, J.D. (1996) Treatment of generalized anxiety in older adults: A preliminary comparison of cognitive-behavioral and supportive approaches. *Behavior Therapy*, **27**, 565–581.

Stanley, M.A., Novy, D.M., Bourland, S.L., Beck, J.G. & Averill, P.M. (2001) Assessing older adults with generalized anxiety: A replication and extension. *Behaviour Research and Therapy*, **39**, 221–235.

Steer, R.A., Willman, M., Kay, P.A.J. & Beck, A.T. (1994) Differentiating elderly medical and psychiatric outpatients with the Beck Anxiety Inventory. *Assessment*, **1**, 345–351.

Steuer, J.L. & Hammen, C.L. (1983) Cognitive-behavioral group therapy for the depressed elderly: Issues and adaptations. *Cognitive Therapy and Research*, **7**, 285–296.

Steuer, J.L., Mintz, J., Hammen, C.L., Hill, M.A., Jarvik, L.F. & McCarley, T. (1984) Cognitive-behavioral and psychodynamic group psychotherapy in the treatment of geriatric depression. *Journal of Consulting and Clinical Psychology*, **52**, 180–189.

Taylor, S., McCraken, C.F., Wilson, K.C. & Copeland, J.R. (1998) Extent and appropriateness of benzodiazepine use: Results from an elderly urban community. *British Journal of Psychiatry*, **173**, 433–438.

Teasdale, J.D. (1985) Psychological treatments for depression: how do they work? *Behaviour Research & Therapy*, **23**, 157–165.

Teri, L. & Lewinsohn, P.M. (1986) Individual treatment of unipolar depression: Comparison of treatment outcome and identification of predictors of successful treatment outcome. *Behavior Therapy*, **17**, 215–228.

Teri, L. & Gallagher-Thompson, D. (1991) Cognitive behavioural interventions for the treatment of depression in Alzheimer patients. *The Gerontologist*, **31**, 413–416.

Teri, L. & Logsdon, R.G. (1991) Identifying pleasant activities for Alzheimer's disease patients: The pleasant events schedule—AD. *The Gerontologist*, **31**, 124–127.

Teri, L., Logsdon, R.G., Uomoto, J. & McCury, S.M. (1997) Behavioral treatment of depression in dementia patients: A controlled clinical trial. *Journal of Gerontology: Psychological Sciences*, **52B**, 159–166.

Thompson, L.W. (1996) Cognitive-behavioral therapy and treatment for later life depression. *Journal of Clinical Psychiatry*, **57** (Suppl. 5), 29–37.

Thompson, L.W., Coon, D.W., Gallagher-Thompson, D., Sommer, B.R. & Koin, D. (2001) Comparison of desipramine and cognitive/behavioral therapy in the treatment of elderly outpatients with mild-to-moderate depression. *American Journal of Geriatric Psychiatry*, **9**, 225–240.

Thompson, L.W., Gallagher, D. & Breckenridge, J.S. (1987) Comparative effectiveness of psychotherapies for depressed elders. *Journal of Consulting and Clinical Psychology*, **55**, 385–390.

Thompson, L.W., Gallagher, D., Laidlaw, K. & Dick, L.P. (2000) *Cognitive-Behavioural Therapy for Late Life Depression: A Therapist Manual. UK Version*. Edinburgh, UK: University of Edinburgh, Dept. of Psychiatry.

Thompson, L.W., Gallagher-Thompson, D. & Dick, L.P. (1995) *Cognitive-Behavioral Therapy for Late Life Depression: A Therapist Manual*. Palo Alto, CA: Older Adult and Family Center, Veterans Affairs Palo Alto Health Care System.

Thompson, L.W., Kaye, J.L., Tang, P.C.Y. & Gallagher-Thompson, D. (2002) Bereavement and adjustment disorders: Theories and clinical implications. In D. Blazer & E.W. Busse (Eds), *Geriatric Psychiatry* (2nd edn). Washington, DC: American Psychiatric Association.

Thompson, L.W., Wagner, B., Zeiss, A. & Gallagher, D. (1989) Cognitive-behavioral therapy with early stage Alzheimer's patients: An exploratory view of the utility of this approach. In E. Light & B.D. Lebowitz (Eds), *Alzheimer's Disease Treatment and Family Stress: Directions for Research* (pp. 383–397). Rockville, MD: US Department of Health & Human Services.

Thompson, L., Gallagher, D. & Lovett, S. (1992) *Increasing Life Satisfaction: Class Leaders' and Participant Manuals*. Palo Alto, CA: Dept of Veterans Affairs Medical Center and Stanford University.

Tintner, R. & Jankovic, J. (2001) Assessment and treatment of Parkinson's disease. *Clinical Geriatrics*, **9**, 62–74.

TWG (1999) *NHS R&D Strategic Review; Coronary Heart Disease and Stroke: A report of the Topic Working Group*. London: Department of Health.

Tyrrell, J., Couterier, P., Montani, C. & Franco, A. (2001) Teleconsultation in psychology: The use of videolinks for interviewing and assessing elderly patients. *Age and Ageing*, **30**, 191–195.

United Nations (2001) *World Population Prospects: The 2000 Revision, Highlights*. New York: UN Population Division, Department of Economic and Social Affairs.

Unutzer, J., Katon, W., Sullivan, M. & Miranda, J. (1999) Treatment depressed older adults in primary care: Narrowing the gap between efficacy and effectiveness. *Midbank Quarterly*, **77**, 225–256.

Warwick, H.M.C. (1995) Assessment of hypochondriasis. *Behaviour Research and Therapy*, **33**, 845–853.

Wells, A. (1997) *Cognitive Therapy of Anxiety Disorders: A Practice Manual and Conceptual Guide*. Chichester: John Wiley & Sons.

Westcott, P. (2000) *Stroke: Questions and Answers*. London: Stroke Association.

Wetherell, J.L. & Arean, P.A. (1997) Psychometric evaluation of the Beck Anxiety Inventory with older medical patients. *Psychological Assessment*, **9**, 136–144.

WHO (1999) *Ageing: Exploding the Myths*. Geneva: World Health Organization.

WHO (2001) *Men, Ageing and Health: Achieving Health Across the Life Span*. Geneva: World Health Organization.

WHO (2001b) *International Classification of Functioning, Disability and Health*. Geneva: World Health Organisation.

WHO (2002) *Active Ageing: A Policy Framework*. Geneva: World Health Organization.

Wilkinson, P. (1997) Cognitive therapy with elderly people. *Age and Ageing*, **26**, 53–59.

Wisocki, P. (1988) Worry as a phenomenon relevant to the elderly. *Behavior Therapy*, **19**, 369–379.

Wisocki, P.A. (1986) The Worry Scale as a measure of anxiety among the elderly: A clinical comment. *Clinical Gerontologist*, **4**, 50–52.

Wisocki, P.A. (1998) The experience of bereavement by older adults. In M. Hersen & V.B. van Hasselt (Eds), *Handbook of Clinical Geropsychology. The Plenum Series in Adult Development and Aging* (Vol. xii, pp. 431–448). New York: Plenum Press.

Wolpe, J. (1958) *Psychotherapy by Reciprocal Inhibition*. Stanford: Stanford University Press.

Wood, R. & Bain, M. (2001) *The Health and Well-Being of Older People in Scotland: Insights from National Data*. Edinburgh: Information & Statistics Division, NHS Scotland.

Woods, R.T. (1995) Psychological treatments I: Behavioural and cognitive approaches. In J. Lindsay (Ed.), *Neurotic Disorders in the Elderly*. Oxford: Oxford University Press.

Yasuda, S., Wehman, P., Targett, P., Cifu, D. & West, M. (2001) Return to work for persons with traumatic brain injury. *American Journal of Physical Medicine and Rehabilitation*, **80**, 852–864.

Yeo, G. & Gallagher-Thompson, D. (1996) *Ethnicity and the dementias*. Washington, DC: Taylor & Francis.

Yesavage, J.A., Brink, T.L., Rose, T.L., Lum, O., Huang, V., Adey, M.B. & Leirer, V.O. (1983) Development and validation of a geriatric depression screening scale. *Journal of Psychiatric Research*, **39**, 37–49.

Yost, E.B., Beutler, L.E., Corbishley, M.A. & Allender, J.R. (1986) *Group Cognitive Therapy: A Treatment Approach for Depressed Older Adults*. New York: Pergamon Press.

Young, J.E. (1990) *Cognitive Therapy for Personality Disorders: A Schema Focused Approach*. Sarasota, FL: Professional Resource Exchange.

Zeiss, A. & Breckenridge, J. (1997) Treatment of late life depression: A response to the NIH consensus conference. *Behavior Therapy*, **28**, 3–21.

Zeiss, A.M., Lewinsohn, P.M., Rohde, P. & Seeley, J.R. (1996) Relationship of physical disease and functional impairment to depression in older people. *Psychology and Aging*, **11**, 572–581.

Zeiss, A. & Steffen, A. (1996a) Treatment issues with elderly clients. *Cognitive and Behavioral Practice*, **3**, 371–389.

Zeiss, A. & Steffen, A. (1996b) Behavioral and cognitive-behavioral treatments: An overview of social learning. In S.H. Zarit & B.G. Knight (Eds), *A Guide to Psychotherapy and Aging: Effective Clinical Interventions in a Life-Stage Context*. Washington, DC: American Psychological Association.

Zesiewicz, T.A., Gold, M., Chari, G. & Hauser, R.A. (1999) Current Issues in depression in Parkinson's Disease. *American Journal of Geriatric Psychiatry*, **7**, 110–118.

Zigmond, A.S. & Snaith, R.P. (1983) The hospital anxiety and depression scale. *Acta Psychiatrica Scandinavica*, **67**, 361–370.

FURTHER READING

Barber, J.P. & Crits-Christoph, P. (1993) Recent advances in the evaluation of psychodynamic formulations. *Journal of Consulting and Clinical Psychology*, **61**, 574–585.

Beck, J.G., Stanley, M.A. & Zebb, B.J. (1996) Characteristics of generalized anxiety disorders in older adults: A descriptive study. *Behaviour Research and Therapy*, **34**, 225–234.

Blazer, D.G., Hughes, D.C. & George, L.K. (1987) The epidemiology of depression in an elderly community population. *The Gerontologist*, **27**, 281–287.

Borkovec, T.D. (1988) Comments on 'Worry as a phenomenon relevant to the elderly'. *Behavior Therapy*, **19**, 381–383.

Bruce, M.L. (1999) The association between depression and disability. *American Journal of Geriatric Psychiatry*, **7**, 8–11.

Bruce, T.J., Spiegel, D.A. & Hegel, M.T. (1999) Cognitive-behavioral therapy helps prevent relapse and recurrence of panic disorder following alprazolam discontinuation: A long-term follow-up of the Peoria and Dartmouth studies. *Journal of Consulting and Clinical Psychology*, **67**, 151–156.

Cohen, J. (1992) A power primer. *Psychological Bulletin*, **112**, 155–159.

Copeland, J.R.M., Gurland, B.J., Dewey, M.E., Kelleher, M.J. & Smith, A.M.R. (1987) Distribution of dementia, depression, and neurosis in elderly men and women in an urban community: Assessed using the GMS-AGECAT package. *International Journal of Geriatric Psychiatry*, **2**, 177–184.

Craik, F.I.M. & Salthouse, T.A. (Eds) (2000) *The Handbook of Aging* (2nd edn).

Crits-Christoph, P. & Connolly, M.B. (1995) Progress on case formulation (Commentary) *Archives of General Psychiatry*, **52**, 639–641.

Crits-Christoph, P., Cooper, P. & Luborsky, L. (1988) The accuracy of therapists' interpretations and the outcome of dynamic psychotherapy. *Journal of Consulting and Clinical Psychology*, **56**, 490–495.

Dooneief, G., Mirabello, E., Bell, K., Marder, K., Stern, Y. & Mayeux, R. (1992) An estimate of the incidence of depression in idiopathic Parkinson's disease. *Archives of Neurology*, **49**, 305–307.

Evans, S.R. (1995) Physical treatments. In J. Lindsay (Ed.), *Neurotic Disorders in the Elderly*. Oxford, UK: Oxford University Press.

Falk, B., Hersen, M. & van Hasselt, V.B. (1994) Assessment of post-traumatic stress disorder in older adults: A critical review. *Clinical Psychology Review*, **14**, 383–415.

Gardner, D. (1996) Outcome research in cognitive therapy in late-life depression. *PSIGE Newsletter*, 56.

Grosscup, S.J. & Lewinsohn, P.M. (1980) Unpleasant and pleasant events and mood. *Journal of Clinical Psychology*, **36**, 252–259.

Hamilton, M. (1967) Development of a rating scale for primary depressive illness. *British Journal of Social and Clinical Psychology*, **6**, 278–296.

Hartz, G.W. & Splain, D.M. (1997) *Psychosocial Intervention in Long-Term Care: An Advanced Guide*. Binghamton, NY: The Haworth Press, Inc.

Havighurst, R.J. (1961) Successful aging. *The Gerontologist*, **1**, 8–13.

Hayslip, B., Schneider, L.J. & Bryant, K. (1989) Older women's perception of female counselors: The influence of therapist age and problem intimacy. *The Gerontologist*, **29**, 239–244.

Heeren, T.J., Derksen, B.F. & Bryant, K. (1989) Treatment, outcome and predictors of response in elderly depressed in-patients. *British Journal of Psychiatry*, **170**, 436–440.

Henderson, A.S. (1994) Does ageing protect against depression? *Social Psychiatry and Psychiatric Epidemiology*, **29**, 657–666.

Horowitz, M.J. (1997) *Formulation as a basis for planning psychotherapy treatment*. Washington, DC: American Psychiatric Press.

Hunter, J.E. & Schmidt, F.L. (1990) *Methods of Meta-analyses: Correcting Error and Bias in Research Findings*. London, UK: Sage Publications.

Jarvik, L.F., Mintz, J., Gerner, R. & Steuer, J. (1997) Cognitive therapy for depression in the elderly. *International Journal of Geriatric Psychiatry*, **12**, 131–132.

Kaelber, C.T., Moul, D.E. & Farmer, M.E. (1995) Epidemiology of depression. In E.E. Beckham & W.R. Leber (Eds), *Handbook of Depression* (2nd edn). New York: Guilford Press.

Katz, I.R. & Alexopoulos, G. (1996) Introduction: The diagnosis and treatment of late-life depression. *American Journal of Geriatric Psychiatry*, **4** (Suppl.), S1–S2.

Katz, I.R. & Streim, J.E. (1994) America's other drug problem. *Provider*, **20**, 70–72.

Knauper, B. & Wittchen, H.U. (1994) Diagnosing major depression in the elderly: Evidence for response bias in standardized clinical interviews? *Journal of Psychiatric Research*, **28**, 147–164.

Laidlaw, K. (1997) Psychological approaches to the management of depression in older people. *Newsletter of the Psychologist Special Interest Group in Elderly People (PSIGE)*, **59**, 9–13.

Laidlaw, K., Davidson, K.M. & Arbuthnot, C. (1998) GP referrals to clinical psychology and treatment for depression: A pilot study. *Newsletter of the Psychologist Special Interest Group in Elderly People (PSIGE)*, **67**, 6–8.

McDonald, A. (1986) Do general practitioners 'miss' depression in elderly patients? *British Medical Journal*, **292**, 1365–1367.

Miranda, J. & Persons., J.B. (1988) Dysfunctional attitudes are mood-state dependent. *Journal of Abnormal Psychology*, **97**, 76–79.

Muran, J.C., Samstag, L.J., Segal, Z.V. & Winston, A. (1998) Interpersonal scenarios: An idiographic measure of self-schemas. *Psychotherapy Research*, **8**, 321–333.

Nezu, A.M., Nezu, C.M., Friedman, S.H. & Haynes, S.N. (1997) Case formulation in behavior therapy: Problem solving and functional analytic strategies. In T.D. Eells (Ed.), *Handbook of Psychotherapy Case Formulation*. New York: Guilford Press.

Norris, F.N. & Murrell, S.A. (1987) Older adult family stress and adaptation before and after bereavement. *Journal of Gerontology: Psychological Sciences*, **42**, 609–616.

O'Brien, N., Albert, S., Neil, M., Muller, C. & Butler, R.N. (2001) *When does 'Old Age' begin? Change in American attitudes over 25 years.* Paper presented at the 54th Annual Gerontological Society of America Conference, Chicago.

Orrell, M., Collins, E., Shergill, S. & Katona, C. (1995) Management of depression in the elderly by general practitioners: Use of antidepressants. *Family Practice*, **12**, 5–11.

Padesky, C.A. (1998) *Protocols and personalities: The therapist in cognitive therapy.* Paper presented at the European Association of Behavioural and Cognitive Therapies, Cork, Ireland.

Padesky, C.A. & Greenberger, D. (1995) *Clinician's Guide to Mind over Mood*. New York: Guilford Press.

Persons, J.B. (1992) The patient with multiple problems. In A. Freeman & F.M. Datillo (Eds), *Comprehensive Casebook of Cognitive Therapy*. New York: Plenum Press.

Persons, J.B. & Tompkins, M.A. (1992) Cognitive-behavioral case formulation. In T.D. Eells (Ed.), *Handbook of Psychotherapy Case Formulation*. New York: Guilford Press.

Persons, J.B., Mooney, K.A. & Padesky, C.A. (1995) Inter-rater reliability of cognitive-behavioral case formulations. *Cognitive Therapy and Research*, **19**, 21–34.

Reynolds, C.F., Frank, E., Dew, M.A., Houck, P.R., Miller, M.D. & Mazumdar, S. (1999a) Treatment of 70+ year olds with recurrent major depression: Excellent short-term but brittle long term response. *American Journal of Geriatric Psychiatry*, **7**, 64–69.

Reynolds, C.F., Frank, E., Perel, J.M., Imber, S.D., Cornes, C.M., Miller, M.D. et al. (1999b) Nortriptyline and interpersonal psychotherapy as maintenance therapies for recurrent major depression: A randomized controlled trial in patients older than 59 years. *Journal of the American Medical Association*, **281**, 39–45.

Riskind, J.H., Beck, A.T. & Steer, R.A. (1985) Cognitive-behavioral therapy in geriatric depression: Comment on Steuer et al. *Journal of Consulting and Clinical Psychology*, **53**, 944–945.

Robinson, R.G., Bolduc, P.L. & Price, T.R. (1983) A two year longitudinal study of post-stroke mood disorders: Findings during the initial evaluation. *Stroke*, **14**, 736–741.

Ryynanen, O.P. (1993) Psychotropic medication and quality of life in the elderly. *Nordic Journal of Psychiatry*, **47** (Suppl. 28), 67–72.

Scheife, R.T., Schumock, G.T., Burstein, A., Gottwald, M.D. & Luer, M.S. (2000) Impact of Parkinson's disease and its pharmacologic treatment on quality of life and economic outcomes. *American Journal of Health System Pharmacy*, **57**, 953–962.

Spielberger, C.D., Gorsuch, R.R. & Luchene, R.E. (1970) *State-Trait Anxiety Inventory*. Palo Alto, CA: Consulting Psychologists Press.

Weiss, D.M. (1995) Serotonin syndrome in Parkinson disease. *Journal of the American Board of Family Practice*, **8**, 400–402.

Wisocki, P. (1994) *The experience of worry among the elderly*. Chichester: John Wiley & Sons.

Wood, R.T. & Roth, A. (1996) Effectiveness of psychological interventions with older people. In A. Roth & P. Fonagy (Eds), *What Works for Whom? A Critical Review of Psychotherapy Research*. New York: Guilford Press.

Woodruff-Pak, D.S. (1997) *The Neuropsychology of Aging*. Oxford, UK: Blackwell Publishers.

Zarit, S. & Zarit, J. (1998) *Mental Disorders in Older Adults: Fundamentals of Assessment and Treatment*. New York: Guilford Press.

AUTHOR INDEX

SUBJECT INDEX

54カ2L∞ SS88